ABSOLUTE BEGINNER'S GUIDE

Microsoft®
Windows Vista™

Shelley O'Hara
Ron Mansfield

D1122134

800 East 96th Street,
Indianapolis, Indiana 46240 USA

Absolute Beginner's Guide to Microsoft® Windows Vista™

Copyright © 2007 by Que Publishing

All rights reserved. No part of this book shall be reproduced, stored in a retrieval system, or transmitted by any means, electronic, mechanical, photocopying, recording, or otherwise, without written permission from the publisher. No patent liability is assumed with respect to the use of the information contained herein. Although every precaution has been taken in the preparation of this book, the publisher and author assume no responsibility for errors or omissions. Nor is any liability assumed for damages resulting from the use of the information contained herein.

International Standard Book Number: 0-7897-3576-8

Library of Congress Cataloging-in-Publication Data

O'Hara, Shelley.
  Absolute beginner's guide to Microsoft Windows Vista / Shelley O'Hara, Ron Mansfield.
    p. cm.
  Includes index.
  ISBN 0-7897-3576-8   1. Microsoft Windows (Computer file) 2. Operating systems (Computers)   I. Mansfield, Ron. II. Title.
  QA76.76.O63O34387 2007
  005.4'46--dc22   2006038674
Printed in the United States of America
First Printing: December 2006
10 09 08 07   4 3 2 1

Trademarks

All terms mentioned in this book that are known to be trademarks or service marks have been appropriately capitalized. Que Publishing cannot attest to the accuracy of this information. Use of a term in this book should not be regarded as affecting the validity of any trademark or service mark.

Windows Vista™ is a trademark of Microsoft Corporation.

Warning and Disclaimer

Every effort has been made to make this book as complete and as accurate as possible, but no warranty or fitness is implied. The information provided is on an "as is" basis. The authors and the publisher shall have neither liability nor responsibility to any person or entity with respect to any loss or damages arising from the information contained in this book.

Bulk Sales

Que Publishing offers excellent discounts on this book when ordered in quantity for bulk purchases or special sales. For more information, please contact

U.S. Corporate and Government Sales
1-800-382-3419
corpsales@pearsontechgroup.com

For sales outside of the U.S., please contact

International Sales
international@pearsoned.com

This Book Is Safari Enabled

The Safari® Enabled icon on the cover of your favorite technology book means the book is available through Safari Bookshelf. When you buy this book, you get free access to the online edition for 45 days.

Safari Bookshelf is an electronic reference library that lets you easily search thousands of technical books, find code samples, download chapters, and access technical information whenever and wherever you need it.

To gain 45-day Safari Enabled access to this book:

- Go to http://www.quepublishing.com/safarienabled
- Complete the brief registration form
- Enter the coupon code H2H5-A2LI-EP1C-XRIU-VKPX

If you have difficulty registering on Safari Bookshelf or accessing the online edition, please email customer-service@safaribooksonline.com.

Associate Publisher
Greg Wiegand

Acquisitions Editor
Michelle Newcomb

Development Editor
Todd Brakke

Managing Editor
Gina Kanouse

Production
codeMantra

Technical Editor
Mark Reddin

Publishing Coordinator
Cindy Teeters

Interior Designer
Anne Jones

Cover Designer
Dan Armstrong

Contents at a Glance

Table of Contents

About the Authors

Shelley O'Hara is the author of more than 120 books, including the best-selling *Easy Windows XP* and other top-selling titles. She has authored books on subject matters from the philosopher Nietzsche to how to buy and sell a house to a children's book for the iPod. Her main focus is teaching beginning users how to use technology, including Windows. She has a B.A. in English from the University of South Carolina and an M.A. in English from the University of Maryland.

Ron Mansfield is a best-selling author with more than 30 books under his belt including *eBay to the Max and Launching a Successful eBay Store*, published by Que. He is also an eBay and computer consultant and instructor.

Dedication

To St. Jude, patron saint of those in despair, in thanksgiving for many, many answered prayers. – Shelley O'Hara

Dedicated to beginning computer users everywhere. – Ron Mansfield

Acknowledgments

After writing a couple books, the acknowledgements can become boring—thanks, thanks, and more thanks. But (the Scarlett O'Hara in me says) y'all know how hard you worked. Without the complete team, this book wouldn't be as good, as polished, as helpful to the reader as it is. I'm not sure I'll ever get across completely how each person contributes to the final product, this book. For this thank you list, I'll start with Todd Brakke, Developmental Editor, because he was with me from the beginning, offering excellent comments on the content and organization; in the middle, reviewing the text and providing insightful suggestions; and through the end, helping out enormously during crunch-time. Next? My co-author. Without Ron Mansfield pitching in and working on some of the most difficult chapters in this book, I'd probably be gluing macaroni onto paper plates at some Writing Nervous Breakdown Center. His knowledge and his goal of helping beginners shine in his work. Finally, my appreciation to Kelly Maish, Production Editor; Liz Lamoreux, Copy Editor; Cindy Teeters, Publishing Coordinator; Michelle Newcomb, Acquisitions Editor; Mark Reddin, Technical Editor; all the design and layout staff; and, of course, Greg Wiegand, Associate Publisher.

— Shelley O'Hara

Hats off to Shelley O'Hara, the "real" author of this book and the architect of its style, organization, and flow. Thanks for letting me pitch in, Shelley. The team at Que worked their usual magic, as Shelley has already told you. Thanks gang!

— Ron Mansfield

We Want to Hear from You!

As the reader of this book, *you* are our most important critic and commentator. We value your opinion and want to know what we're doing right, what we could do better, what areas you'd like to see us publish in, and any other words of wisdom you're willing to pass our way.

As an associate publisher for Que Publishing, I welcome your comments. You can email or write me directly to let me know what you did or didn't like about this book—as well as what we can do to make our books better.

Please note that I cannot help you with technical problems related to the topic of this book. We do have a User Services group, however, where I will forward specific technical questions related to the book.

When you write, please be sure to include this book's title and author as well as your name, email address, and phone number. I will carefully review your comments and share them with the author and editors who worked on the book.

Email: feedback@quepublishing.com

Mail: Greg Wiegand

Associate Publisher
Que Publishing
800 East 96th Street
Indianapolis, IN 46240 USA

Reader Services

Visit our website and register this book at www.quepublishing.com/register for convenient access to any updates, downloads, or errata that might be available for this book.

Introduction

If you are new to Windows Vista or to Windows in general, this is the book for you. In easy-to-understand language and with step-by-step explanations, this book examines all the key tasks for using Windows Vista.

Windows is an operating system. You don't need to know the hows and whys of an operating system. You just need to know there is one, and that the operating system is like the behind-the-scenes manager who takes care of all the basic computing tasks, such as saving your work, printing a document, starting a program, and so on.

Therefore, you need only to learn how to perform these basic actions once. That is, after you learn how to print, you follow the same basic steps to print in all Windows programs. After you learn how to start a program, you can start any program. After you learn how to move or resize a window, you can perform this action for any window.

You'll find that learning how to use Windows is the same thing as learning how to use your computer.

Some Key Changes in Windows Vista

Introduced in 2007, Windows Vista includes a major overhaul to the interface from the desktop to the content windows (called Explorers). The programmers have attempted to make the interface easier to use, more consistent, and more intuitive.

Finding files has also been a big priority with this version. Starting with the Instant Search feature included on the Start menu and throughout Vista's Explorers, and including special Search Folders, Windows seeks to make finding documents and all kinds of information (music, movies, email messages, and so on) easier.

Security has also been enhanced and emphasized. Not to scare you off, but as computers become more popular the dangers and the need for caution have become more important. You need to protect against viruses, someone getting your personal information (called phishing), someone installing a program on your computer without your permission, someone spying and tracking what websites you visit, and more. Windows Vista includes features to address each of these security concerns; it also offers updates so that new threats are taken care of as soon as possible.

In addition to design changes and security upgrades, you find other fun and useful features built-in to Windows, including the Windows Photo Gallery, an updated Media Center, a partnership for online music purchases with MTV (called Urge), and more.

If you are entirely new to Windows, you don't have to worry about these changes. If you are upgrading, you'll find it easy to see and work with the many changes and upgrades.

Some Key Terms

To use Windows, you need to know the basic terminology used for common actions:

- *Point*—Move the mouse on the desk to move the pointer onscreen. The tip of the arrow should be on the item to which you are pointing. To open a menu or an icon, you point to the item you want.

- *Click*—Press and release the left mouse button once. You use click to select commands and toolbar buttons and perform other Windows tasks.

- *Double-click*—Press and release the left mouse button twice in rapid succession. Double-clicking opens an icon. (See the next section for exceptions or changes to double-clicking.)

- *Right-click*—Press and release the right mouse button once. You often right-click to display a shortcut menu.

- *Drag*—Hold down the mouse button and drag the pointer across the screen. Release the mouse button. Dragging is most often used for selecting text.

Some Things to Keep in Mind

You can personalize many features of Windows so that it is set up the way you like to work. That's one of the benefits of Windows. For consistency, though, this book makes some assumptions about how you use your computer. When working through steps and especially when viewing the figures in this book, keep in mind the following distinctions:

- Windows provides many ways to perform the same action. For instance, for commands, you can select a command from a menu, use a shortcut key, use a command bar button, or use a shortcut menu. This book covers one main method (the most common for that particular task) and also mentions other methods, usually in a tip.

- Your particular Windows setup might not look identical to the one used in the figures in this book. For instance, if you use a desktop image, you see that. (The figures in this book use a plain background.) Don't let these differences distract you; Windows might look different, but it works the same way.

> **caution**
>
> Some computer displays will not display Vista's new Aero interface; this interface gives Windows a transparent or glass-like look. If your computer doesn't support Aero, you'll see the same screens and dialog boxes only they will look slightly different from the images captured for his book. Virtually all of Vista's features still function in the same way (with the exception of Flip3D and live thumbnail previews), so don't worry!

■ Your computer setup is most likely different than the one used in the book. Therefore, you see different programs listed on your Start menu, different fonts in your Font list, different folders and documents, and so on. Again, don't be distracted by the differences.

The Basic Structure of This Book

This book is divided into six parts, each centered on a certain theme. The book builds on the skills you need, starting with the basics and then moving to more complex topics or lesser used features, such as accessibility. You can read the book straight-through, look up topics when you have a question, or browse through the contents, reading information that intrigues you.

This section provides a quick breakdown of the parts.

Part I, "The Basics," explains all the key tasks for using your computer. If you read only this section, you have enough skill knowledge to perform most basic computer tasks. This part covers understanding the Windows desktop and starting programs (Chapter 1), saving and print your work (Chapter 2), managing files (Chapter 3), and viewing and finding files (Chapter 4).

Part II, "Communication," includes six chapters, each devoted to a particular Windows communication feature, including getting set up for communication (Chapter 5), sending and receiving email (Chapter 6), browsing and searching the Internet (Chapter 7), ensuring security and privacy (Chapter 8), sending and receiving faxes (Chapter 9), and setting up Windows Vista on a home network (Chapter 10).

Part III, "Digital Media," centers on the various ways you can use Windows as an entertainment medium, including playing music and videos and working with photographs and movies.

Part IV, "Customizing Your Computer," explores the many changes you can make to how Windows operates. As you become more proficient, you'll find that you might want to change certain Windows elements, such as adding a desktop image (covered in Chapter 13 with other desktop customizing options), adding new programs (Chapter 14), customizing email and Internet (Chapter 15), and setting up Windows for multiple users (Chapter 16).

Although you don't need to know the ins and outs of computer maintenance (the topic of Part V) as a beginner, you'll find that you do need a reference and guide for the various maintenance tasks. Some tasks are especially key, such as securing your PC and your data (Chapter 17). Other tasks you use less often, but might want to refer to. Topics in this part including improving performance (Chapter 18), upgrading your computer (Chapter 19), and upgrading Windows (Chapter 20).

The final part, Part VI, "Windows Special Features," examines what the part's name implies: Special features for special situations. This part includes chapters on the many Windows accessory programs (Chapter 21) and accessibility options for those with special needs (Chapter 22).

Enjoy your learning journey!

Conventions Used in This Book

There are cautions, tips, and notes throughout this book.

caution

A *caution* will tell you to beware of a potentially dangerous act or situation. In some cases, ignoring a caution might cause you significant problems—so pay particular attention to them!

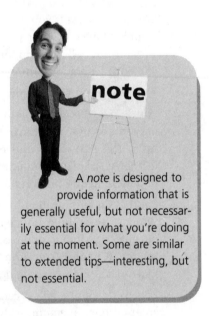

note

A *note* is designed to provide information that is generally useful, but not necessarily essential for what you're doing at the moment. Some are similar to extended tips—interesting, but not essential.

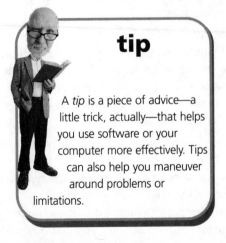

tip

A *tip* is a piece of advice—a little trick, actually—that helps you use software or your computer more effectively. Tips can also help you maneuver around problems or limitations.

PART 1

THE BASICS

1

GETTING STARTED WITH WINDOWS VISTA

Checking Out the Desktop

The Windows desktop is where all your work starts and ends. Becoming familiar with the tools and features you can access from the desktop is the backbone of using a computer. Without these skills, you aren't able to do much. But with these skills, you are able to start programs, work with files, check the status of any activities such as printing, and more. Luckily all these skills are easy to learn and practice.

The desktop is what you see when you first start your computer and Windows Vista. The desktop provides access to all the programs and files on your computer (see Figure 1.1). Here's a quick overview of what you see:

FIGURE 1.1
The Windows Vista desktop, by default, is uncluttered.

Recycle Bin   Desktop

Start button

Quick Launch toolbar   Taskbar   Notification area

- The desktop is the background area. Think of this area as your computer "desk." You can place handy tools on the desktop.

- You can place additional icons on the desktop so that you have fast access to commonly used programs and folders. For instance, suppose that you use Microsoft Word, a word processing program, often. You can add a program shortcut icon to the desktop so that you can quickly start the program from the desktop rather than a command. Your computer might come with some shortcut icons already added to your desktop. For more information on adding desktop icons, see Chapter 14, "Setting Up Programs."

tip

You can change the appearance of the desktop by selecting a different set of colors or using a picture for the background. See Chapter 13, "Customizing Windows Vista," for more information.

■ The Start button is located in the lower-left corner and is used to display the Start menu. You learn more about this button in "Displaying the Start Menu" and "Starting a Program" later in this chapter.

■ Next to the Start button you see the Quick Launch toolbar. You can use this toolbar to launch frequently used applications, such as Internet Explorer.

■ The taskbar displays a button for any open windows or programs. For instance, if you are working in a Paint document, you see a taskbar for the program (see Figure 1.2). You'll also see taskbar buttons when you have Explorers (windows that display contents such as files or folders) open. By showing open windows and applications, the taskbar provides not only information about what's currently going on, but also provides a quick and simple way to switch among open windows.

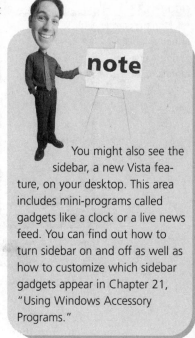

note

You might also see the sidebar, a new Vista feature, on your desktop. This area includes mini-programs called gadgets like a clock or a live news feed. You can find out how to turn sidebar on and off as well as how to customize which sidebar gadgets appear in Chapter 21, "Using Windows Accessory Programs."

FIGURE 1.2
The taskbar gives you a view of what you are currently working on.

Running program

■ The notification area includes status icons for current tasks. For instance, if you are printing, you see a printer icon. If you are connected to the Internet, you see a connection icon. For more on the notification area, see the section "Viewing the Notification Area" later in this chapter.

Displaying the Start Menu

The Start menu provides a list of common programs and folder windows and buttons. As its name implies, the Start menu is, of course, where you start! You can start programs or open common folders, such as Documents or Pictures, from this menu.

To display the Start menu, click the Start button. The menu is displayed (see Figure 1.3). From this menu, you can do any of the following:

FIGURE 1.3

Clicking the Start button reveals various commands.

■ **Start a program.** At the top of the menu, you see the programs you use for the Internet and email. You can click the appropriate program icon to start the program. Beneath the Internet and email programs is a list of several programs that you use most frequently. You can click any of these programs to start them. For other programs not listed on this menu, select the All Programs command menu. See "Starting a Program" later in this chapter.

■ Under the left pane of the Start menu, you see the Instant Search box. This is a new feature in Windows Vista and provides fast access to search for files, programs, music, pictures, and other items on your computer.

■ **Access commonly used folders.** On the right side of the Start menu, you see a list of folders. You can click any of these folders—Documents, Pictures, Music, Games, Computer—to open that folder. Chapter 3, "Managing Files," examines more on working with folders.

■ **Select a command.** In addition to programs and folders, Windows Vista lists commands, such as Control Panel, Connect to, Help and Support, Default Programs, and Search, on the Start menu. You learn more about the purpose of these commands in later chapters in this book.

tip

You can turn off the "last used program" feature. Also, you can customize this list so that only your favorite programs appear as opposed to the last ones used.

See Chapter 14 for more information.

■ Turn off or log off the computer. At the bottom of the right pane, you see icons. You can use these icons to log off, restart, shut down, switch users, and perform other similar tasks.

Working with Desktop Icons

You can include the icons you want, in the placement you want, on your desktop. This is like arranging your physical desk, putting the papers, pens, and other tools you need where you can find and easily access them. Likewise, you can add icons to your desktop for programs, files, folders, printers, and other hardware. Adding new icons, naming these icons, and deleting the icons are examined in Chapter 14.

caution

If your computer freezes or if you make changes to key system features, you might need to restart. Click the down arrow next to the Lock icon and then select Restart. See "Restarting and Shutting Down the Computer" later in this chapter.

When you have icons on the desktop, you can move them around so that they are positioned as you please. The simplest way to arrange the icons is to drag an icon to a new location. Follow these steps:

1. Position the mouse pointer over the icon.

2. Press and hold down the left mouse button and drag the icon to the location you want. The combination of press, hold, and drag is commonly referred to as simply "drag." That is, drag means to press and hold the mouse button while you move the mouse on the desktop.

3. When the icon is in the place you want, release the mouse button. The icon is moved to its new location.

In addition to moving the icons yourself, you can have Windows automatically align and arrange the icons on the desktop. To do so, follow these steps:

1. Right-click a blank area of the desktop.

2. Click Sort By from the shortcut menu that appears and then select an order. You can arrange the icons by name, size, type, or modification date (see Figure 1.4).

   Or

   Click View, Auto Arrange. Windows Vista moves icons to the upper-left corner, spacing them equally down and then in a second column (to the right of the first column of icons) if needed.

   Or

   Click View, Align to Grid. When this command is checked, Windows Vista keeps icons aligned to an underlying grid that spaces the icons automatically.

To turn off this feature (if you want to place them closer together, for instance), uncheck the command.

FIGURE 1.4

From the desktop shortcut menu, you can select arrangements for the icon.

Right-click desktop to open menu

Viewing the Taskbar

The taskbar, as mentioned, contains buttons for all open windows and programs. The taskbar, then, gives you an idea of what you have running and which program or window is active (where you can work).

The taskbar also enables you to switch among these open windows. To display a particular program or window, click the button in the taskbar. For instance, suppose that you have windows open for the WordPad and Windows Photo Gallery. To switch to the Windows Photo Gallery, click its button. That window becomes the active window. If your display supports the Aero interface, you can hover the mouse pointer over a taskbar button to show a thumbnail preview of the window, as shown in Figure 1.5.

tip

To save space, Windows sometimes stacks similar windows and displays one button. You can click the arrow on the button to display all of the open windows. Then click the window you want to open.

FIGURE 1.5

FIGURE 1.5

You can use the taskbar to view and change among open windows.

Thumbnail preview

Viewing the Notification Area

The notification area is part of the taskbar and displays the current time and status icons (see Figure 1.6). For instance, Windows Vista includes a notification icon for automatic updates. You see icons for Internet and network connection information, as well as an icon for adjusting the volume. You might also see icons for hardware components, such as a scanner.

tip

You can move the taskbar to another location and also change its appearance. See Chapter 13 for more information.

FIGURE 1.6

The notification area displays icons highlighting anything going on with your system.

Periodically, a notification message pops up from the system tray alerting you to events or suggesting actions. For instance, when a print job is successfully printed, you see a printer icon and then a message noting that the print job is complete. To close a message, click its close button. Or you might see a reminder about updating a program, such as your virus program or Windows itself. You can click the message itself to find out more information.

tip

You can hover the mouse pointer over the time to display the current date. Or resize the taskbar (by dragging its edge) so that it displays two rows of buttons, and the full date will be displayed.

Also, Windows Vista can collapse the notification area to hide icons especially when there are a lot. To expand the area, click the left-pointing arrow next to the icons. The area automatically returns to the original view after a few seconds. You can also immediately hide some icons by clicking the now right-pointing icon.

Working with Windows

In Windows, everything is displayed in a window, a rectangular box on the screen that contains a running program. For instance, file and folder content are displayed in a window called an Explorer. Applications are also displayed in a window.

Part of mastering Vista is learning to manipulate the windows so that you can see and work with the area you want. For instance, you might want to move windows so that you can see more than one. You might want to maximize a window so that it fills the entire desktop area. You use the window controls and other window parts (title bar and border) to manipulate the window. This section covers common window tasks.

Opening and Closing Windows

To open a program window, start the program (as covered later in this chapter). To open an Explorer, click Start and then click the folder name (such as Documents or Pictures). Figure 1.7 shows the Documents Explorer.

FIGURE 1.7

All windows include common controls for working with that window.

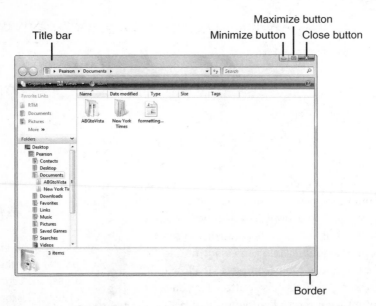

Maximize button

Minimize button | Close button

Title bar

Border

When a window is open, you see the controls for the window in the upper-right corner (from left to right: Minimize, Maximize, and Close). For example, to close a window, click its Close button as shown in Figure 1.7.

The window closes and disappears from the taskbar and desktop. If you close a program window, you also exit the program. (See "Exiting a Program" later in this chapter.)

Changing the Size of Windows

In addition to opening and closing, you can change the size of the windows. Windows Vista uses special terms to describe the various sizes of a window: maximized, minimized, and restored. The changes you can make to the size of a window are covered here.

Maximizing a Window

A maximized window fills the entire desktop and does not have borders (see Figure 1.8). You commonly maximize program windows when you want to have the maximum display area for the work. To maximize a window so that it fills the entire screen, click its Maximize button.

When you maximize a window, the Maximize button changes to a Restore button, which you can use to return the window to its original size.

FIGURE 1.8

Maximize a window when you want to make it as big as possible.

Restore button

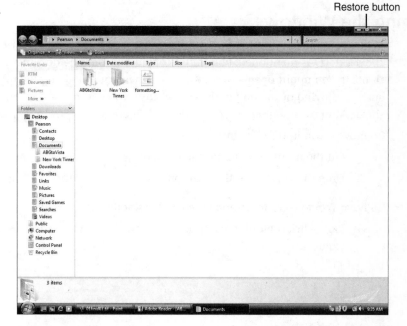

Minimizing a Window

A minimized window is hidden from view (not closed) and is represented with a taskbar button (refer to Figure 1.2). To minimize a window (shrink it to a taskbar button), click its Minimize button. You can redisplay the window by clicking its button on the taskbar. You often minimize a window when you need handy access to it but don't want to use desktop space for the display of that window.

Restoring a Window

When a window is open and not maximized, Windows uses the term "restore." Basically, you restore the window to its original size. To restore a maximized window, click the Restore button (refer to Figure 1.7). Use this size when you want to display more than one window on the desktop. For instance, if you are copying data from one program to another, you can view both windows and move between them. When a window is this size, it has borders so that you can resize it manually. You can also use the title bar to move the window (see "Arranging the Windows" later in this chapter).

Resizing a Window

When a window is restored, you can change its size. To resize a window, put the mouse pointer on a border (the pointer icon changes to show directional arrows indicating in which directions you can resize the window) and then drag the border to resize the window. Remember that you can only resize restored windows. You cannot resize a maximized window.

Arranging the Windows

When you have more than one window open, you might need to arrange them on the desktop. As mentioned, you might copy data from one document or program to another. You might open several windows when you are doing file maintenance, such as copying or moving a file. In any case, you can move the windows around the desktop by dragging, or you can have Windows Vista arrange the windows.

To move a window, follow these steps:

1. Put the mouse pointer on the title bar.

2. Drag the window to the location you want. The window is moved.

To have Windows Vista arrange the windows, follow these steps:

1. Right-click a blank area of the taskbar to display the shortcut menu (see Figure 1.9).

FIGURE 1.9
Use one of these commands to arrange the windows on your desktop.

2. Click one of the following commands for arranging the windows:

Click Cascade Windows to arrange the windows in a waterfall style, layered on top of each other from the upper-left corner down.

Click Show Windows Stacked to make all the windows the same size and place them vertically next to each other (see Figure 1.10).

Click Show Windows Side by Side to make all the windows the same size but place them horizontally next to each other.

FIGURE 1.10

You can stack open windows.

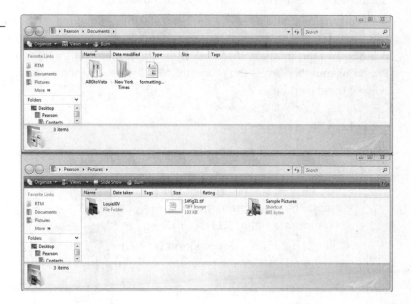

Click Show the Desktop to minimize all open windows. If you redisplay the taskbar shortcut menu, you can select Show Open Windows to redisplay the windows.

Starting a Program

Most of your time on the computer is spent working in some type of program—a word processing program to type letters, a spreadsheet program to create budgets, a database to keep track of contacts, and so on. Therefore, one of the most important skills to learn is how to start a program.

Because different people prefer different ways of working, Windows Vista provides many options for starting programs. What's the best way? The way *you* like. Pick the one that is easiest for you.

tip

You can undo the arrangement and revert to the original placement by right-clicking the taskbar and then selecting the Undo command. The name of the command varies depending on the arrangement. For instance, if you have tiled the windows, the command is Undo Show Side by Side.

When you install a new Windows program, that program's installation procedure sets up a program icon and sometimes a program folder if the program includes several components. For example, a scanning program might include a program for executing the scan and a program for working with and saving the scanned document. These are listed within the Start menu.

The Start menu provides two methods for starting a program. Windows tracks and lists programs you use most often; therefore, you can select a program from the left pane of the Start menu if it is listed. If the program is not listed, you can display All Programs and then select the program from the longer menu. This section covers both of these methods.

Starting a Listed Program

Follow these steps to start a recently used program:

1. Click the Start button. The left pane displays the most commonly used programs (see Figure 1.11).

2. Click the program. That program is started, and you see the program window.

> **tip**
>
> You can change how many programs are listed and also clear the list. See Chapter 13 for more information.

FIGURE 1.11

If you see your program listed, select it from the short list on the Start menu.

Listing All Programs

Follow these steps to view and select from a list of all programs:

1. Click Start and then click All Programs. You see a list of all the program icons and program folders (see Figure 1.12).

FIGURE 1.12

You can access all installed programs by clicking the All Programs button on the Start menu.

2. If necessary, click the program folder (looks like a folder). When you click the program folder, you see the program icons within that folder.

3. Click the program icon to start the program. The program opens in its own window, and a taskbar button for the program appears in the taskbar. Figure 1.13 shows Paint, a program included with Windows Vista.

FIGURE 1.13

The program is opened in its own program window.

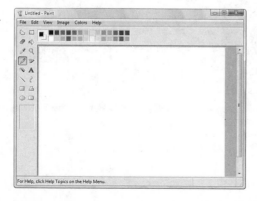

Starting a Program from a Shortcut Icon

In addition to the Start menu, you can also start programs from shortcut icons. Some programs automatically create shortcut icons, placing them on the desktop. You can also add shortcut icons to programs yourself, as covered in Chapter 14, "Setting Up Programs."

Figure 1.14 shows a shortcut icon for Windows Mail, a shortcut icon to a folder named EZWinFigs, and another to a program called Capture. Notice the little arrow on the icon; this indicates that the icon is a shortcut to that program.

note

You also see the Recycle Bin which, by default, is always included on the desktop. This icon holds files and folders you have deleted. You learn more about deleting and undeleting files in Chapter 3.

FIGURE 1.14

You can place shortcut icons to programs on your desktop and then double-click these icons to start the program.

Shortcut icon

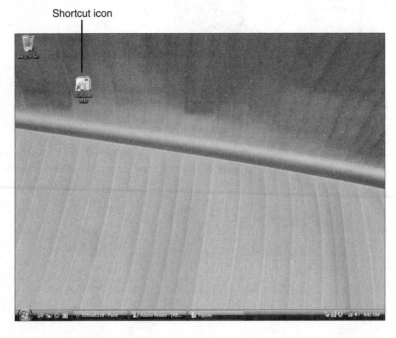

To start a program from a shortcut icon, double-click the shortcut icon on the desktop. The program starts and is displayed in its own window. A taskbar button appears for the program.

Switching Between Programs

You often work with more than one type of program at the same time. Windows Vista enables you to quickly switch from one program to another. For example, you might want to review sales figures in a worksheet while at the same time creating a sales report in a word processing program. Switching between programs enables you to view data from several sources and also to share data among programs.

As mentioned, when you start a program, a button for that program is displayed in the taskbar. To switch to another program, simply click the button for that program. That program becomes the active program.

You can also press Alt+Tab to scroll through open programs; this feature has been revamped in Windows Vista. You see the programs and thumbnails, if your display supports the Aero interface (see Figure 1.15).

caution

If the program doesn't start, you might not have double-clicked quickly enough. You must keep the mouse pointer in the same location and click twice. Sometimes beginners click, move, click the mouse, and this does not work. If you continue to have problems with clicking, change the mouse speed. See Chapter 13 for more information.

FIGURE 1.15

You can use Alt+Tab to switch among open programs as well as the taskbar.

Untitled - Paint

tip

If your computer supports the Aero user interface, you can also use Windows Flip 3D. Press the Windows key+Tab or click the Switch Between Windows button on the Quick Launch taskbar. You see a cascading angled view of all open applications and you can flip between them using your mouse's scroll wheel.

Working in a Program

When the program is started, you see the program window. A great thing about Windows Vista is that all program windows share similar features (see Figure 1.16). Learning to use one program helps you master key skills for almost all other programs. For example, most programs include a menu bar that works the same in all programs. This section covers some basic skills for working in programs.

tip

As you become more proficient, you might experiment with other ways of starting a program. See Chapter 14 to explore other methods.

FIGURE 1.16
Get familiar with the basic program window features.

Title bar   Menu bar   Toolbars

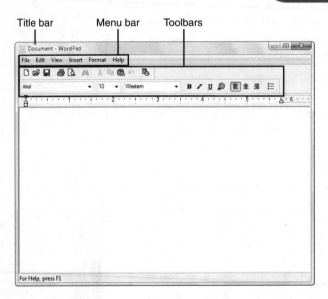

Selecting Commands

The top line of the program window is called the *title bar* and includes the name of the document (or a generic name if the document has not been saved) and the program name.

Below the title bar, you see the menu bar. You use this to select commands. For instance, open the File menu and select the Save command to save a document. To use a menu, follow these steps:

1. Click the menu name. The menu drops down and displays a list of commands.

2. Click the command. Depending on the command you select, one of the following happens:

    The command is executed. For instance, if you select File, Exit, the program is closed.

You see a submenu. Any commands followed by an arrow display a submenu. Click the command in this menu to execute the selected command.

You see a dialog box prompting you for additional information about how to execute the command. For example, if you select File, Print, you see the Print dialog box. Select options and confirm the command (see Figure 1.17). For printing, for instance, select which printer to use and the number of copies to print and then click Print.

FIGURE 1.17
Get familiar with the basic program window features.

You'll find that the menus work the same in most programs, and also many programs include the same commands. For example, you can commonly find a File, Save command for saving documents and a File, Print for printing documents (both covered in Chapter 2, "Saving and Printing Your Work"). The Edit menu usually has commands for cutting text (Cut), copying text (Copy), and pasting cut or copied text (Paste). The Help menu provides access to online help; you can use the commands in this menu to look up help topics for the program.

tip

Many commands have a keyboard shortcut. Instead of selecting the command, you can press the keyboard shortcut. For instance, the shortcut for printing is Ctrl+P (press and hold the Ctrl key and then press the P key). These shortcuts are listed next to the command name on the menu.

Using Toolbars or Ribbons

In addition to using the menus and keyboard shortcuts, you can also use toolbar buttons to select commands (refer to Figure 1.16). In the newest version of Microsoft Office, Office 2007, this feature has been revamped and renamed to "Ribbon." Ribbons function in the same way as a toolbar, but they're organized into a series of tabs (see Figure 1.18). Most Windows programs include toolbar(s), which are displayed right under the menu bar. The buttons vary depending on the program, but most of them are similar.

FIGURE 1.18

Ribbons are a new kind of toolbar found in Microsoft Office 2007.

Each tab represents an individual ribbon

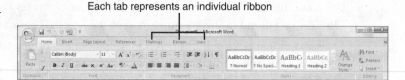

The following list gives you some insight on how to work with toolbars:

- Toolbar or ribbon buttons are shortcuts to commands. You can click the button instead of selecting the command.

- If you aren't sure what a toolbar or ribbon button does, hover the mouse pointer over it. A ScreenTip (the button name) should appear that explains its function.

- Some programs have more than one tool-bar. Usually the standard toolbar includes buttons for common commands (Save, Open, New, and so on). For example the formatting toolbar (refer to Figure 1.16) includes buttons that let you quickly make formatting changes, such as making text bold, changing the font, and so on. In Word 2007, those same commands are found on the Home tab.

- If you see a down arrow next to a command, you can click this arrow to display a drop-down list of choices. Then click the option you want to select.

- If you don't use the toolbar and want more room for the document to be displayed, turn off the toolbar. (You cannot turn off ribbons in Office 2007.) You can also select to display more than one toolbar in some programs. Look for a View, Toolbar command.

note

Programs might also include other onscreen ele-ments to help you work in the program. For instance, in WordPad you see a ruler that helps you set tabs and indents. In Paint (a draw-ing program) you have a toolbox with the various drawing tools. Check out these features because they can save you time and effort.

tip

Right-click the taskbar and then click Properties. Click the Toolbars tab. Any tool-bars that are checked are displayed. The command is a toggle: Select the com-mand to uncheck and hide the toolbar. To display the toolbar, select it again so that there is a check next to it.

Exiting a Program

When you finish working in a program, close it to free system memory. (Your system memory is the working area of the computer where data and programs are stored temporarily while you are working within the program and on a document.) Too many open programs can tax your system's memory and slow the computer's processes.

First, save your work; saving is the topic of the next chapter. After your work is saved, you can use one of several methods to close a program:

caution

If you have not saved changes to the document and you close that program, you are prompted to save. To save the document, click Yes. To close the document without saving, click No. (Do this if you don't need the document or want to abandon any changes you made.) To return to the document without exiting the program, click Cancel.

- Click File and then click the Exit command. The program is closed.
- Click the Close button for the program window.
- Press Alt+F4.

Dealing with Stuck Programs

Sometimes programs get stuck and won't close. (It's just something that happens when dealing with a complex piece of equipment like a computer, although this should happen far less in Vista than in previous versions of Windows.) If a program won't respond to any of your commands, follow the suggestions in this section to see whether you can close the program without losing your work.

Try each solution in the order listed so that you look for easy solutions first before moving on to more drastic steps (such as restarting or turning the computer off and then back on, the topic of the next section).

- If you think a program is not responding, make sure that it is not busy with another task. Is the disk light active? Can you hear the drives moving? (Though many newer drives are so quiet you'll rarely, if ever, hear them spinning.) Does the keyboard respond? If the computer is active, you might just have to wait a few seconds to get the program to respond.
- Make sure that the program is the active window. It is an easy mistake to have more than one window displayed and *think* you are working in one window (but it's not responding), but actually another program or window is active. Click in the program window or use the taskbar to switch to the program.

■ Make sure that the menu bar is not active. If you press Alt, the menus are activated. If you try to type, nothing happens (or a menu opens). Press Esc a few times to make sure that you are actually in the working area (not in the menu bar).

If these solutions don't work you'll need to take a more authoritative stance in dealing with the stuck program.

Closing a Program from the Taskbar

If the computer is not busy and you still can't get a program to respond, try closing it from the taskbar. Follow these steps:

1. Right-click the taskbar button for the program. You see a shortcut menu for that window (see Figure 1.19).

FIGURE 1.19
Use the taskbar button to try to close a program.

2. Select the Close command. The program might be closed. If it's not closed, Windows Vista displays an error message saying that the program is not responding.

3. Click End Now to force the program to shut down. (Be patient. Clicking End Now doesn't guarantee that the program closes immediately. Give it a minute or two.)

Closing a Program from the Task Manager

If the taskbar method doesn't work (or if you are not sure what's running on your computer), you can display the Task Manager. The Task Manager displays all the open programs (and any behind-the-scenes Windows programs that are running). From the Task Manager, you can close a program. This method usually works.

Follow these steps:

1. Right-click a blank area of the taskbar.

2. Select Task Manager. The Windows Task Manager appears (see Figure 1.20), listing all the programs that are running. (Make sure the Applications tab is selected.)

3. Select the program you want to close.

4. Click End Task.

FIGURE 1.20

The Task Manager displays what programs are running.

5. The program is either closed or still stuck. If the program is "stuck," you see a message that the program is not responding. Click End Now to close down the stuck program.

Logging Off and Shutting Down Your Computer

When you're done using your computer Vista provides several ways to finish off your computing experience. You can simply log off your PC, put it into sleep mode, or shut it down completely. As you have probably guessed, putting your system to sleep or shutting it down, also logs you off.

Vista provides three buttons on the Start menu that give you access to all of its shut down related features. There's the power button, lock button, and Options menu that appears if you click the arrow next to the lock button (see Figure 1.21).

FIGURE 1.21

You can use these commands to restart and shut down your computer.

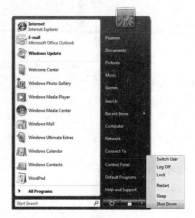

Putting Your Computer to Sleep

Vista's preferred way to shut down your system isn't to shut it down at all. Instead, clicking the Start menu's power button puts your system into a "sleep" state in which all information (open programs and documents, and so on) is saved to both system memory and your computer's hard drive. When that is done (it takes only a couple seconds), Vista goes into an ultra-low power mode. Your system will look like it's shut off, but when you activate it by pressing a key on your keyboard, it pops back to life far more quickly than when starting up cold. When coming out of sleep mode, Vista also restores any open programs and documents from when you put it to sleep.

Shutting Your Computer Off

If you prefer that your system be fully shut down when you're done with your work or play, open the menu shown in Figure 1.21 and select Shut Down. If you've used previous versions of Windows, this option works just like shutting off your computer in those older versions. That is, Windows closes all open programs, logs you out, and shuts your computer completely off. This process takes longer than putting a system to sleep and it takes longer to power up your system (from your PC's power button) than it does to wake a computer up from sleep mode.

tip

If, for whatever reason, you just need to restart your computer, select the Restart option from the menu shown in Figure 1.21.

Logging Off

Finally, if you don't want to shut your PC down or put it to sleep but you are done using the system, you have two options. You can lock the system down by clicking the Start menu's Lock icon. In lock-down mode Vista leaves all open programs and documents open and sends you to a secure screen that requires you to log back on using your password (if you have one) or as another user before you can do anything with the computer. This mode is useful if you want to securely leave your system unattended for a few minutes without closing all your open programs and documents.

tip

You can learn more about using the Log Off and Switch User commands in Chapter 16, "Setting Up Windows Vista for Multiple Users."

The more common method of exiting your user account without shutting down your system is to use the Log Off option found in the menu shown in Figure 1.21. This option closes any open programs or documents and returns you to the main Vista logon screen.

The Absolute Minimum

This chapter gives you a good basic framework for learning to work with Windows Vista. You learned the basics of working with the desktop, manipulating windows (which display content), and starting and exiting programs. In summary, keep these points in mind:

- The desktop is your starting place. Any programs you run or windows you open are displayed on the desktop.

- The Start menu is what it says—your starting place! Use this menu to start programs, open folders, access commands, such as Help and Support, log off, and turn off and restart.

- To see what programs and windows are open, check the taskbar. Also, to review any system notifications or information, check the notification area, the far-right corner of the taskbar.

- Content is displayed in an Explorer. For example, when you want to view the contents of a drive or folder or start a program, you open an Explorer. Programs are opened in a window. Every Explorer or program window has controls so that you can place it and resize it in a way that is most convenient for the task at hand.

- You can start a program using the Start menu or a shortcut icon.

- In a program, you can use the menu bar to select commands. Click the menu name to display the menu and then click the command you want. You might be prompted to select additional options for the command in a dialog box. Make your selections and click the command button (usually OK).

- When you are finished working in a program, save your work (covered in the next chapter) and then exit the program. You can exit using the File, Exit command or by clicking the program window's Close button.

- Use the Start menu's power button to quickly put your computer into an ultra-low power Sleep state. All open programs and documents are saved to your computer's memory and to the hard drive for safe keeping.

2

Saving and Printing Your Work

Saving a Document

The most important computer skill you can learn is saving your work. Whether you are creating a budget, typing a resume, or entering checks in a checkbook program, saving your work is key. This chapter covers the basics of saving a document, opening a saved document, creating a new document, printing a document, and more. Similar to the previous chapter, the skills you learn in this chapter are skills you can use throughout your computing experience. That's one of the great things about Windows Vista: Basic skills, such as saving, opening, or printing a document, work the same way in most Windows programs.

When you work in most programs, you save your work as a type of document—a word processing file, such as a memo, a worksheet file, such as a budget, a database file, such as a list of clients, and so on. One of the most important things you should remember about using a computer is that you need to save your work and save often.

When you save your work, the program saves the file in an appropriate file format or type, and this type is indicated with an extension. For instance, if you save a document created in Word, that program saves the file as a .DOC file. Excel saves your spreadsheets (formally known as *worksheets* and *workbooks*) as .XLS files. By default Vista does not display file extensions for known file types. However, the Details pane at the bottom of any Explorer window will tell you what type of file is selected.

> ## caution
>
> Don't wait until you finish a document before you save it. If something happens, such as the power goes off or the computer gets stuck, you lose all your work if you have not saved. Instead save periodically as you create and edit the document.

The first time you save a file, you must assign that file a name and location. You can include up to 255 characters for the name, including spaces. Sometimes the program suggests a name, but it's better to replace the suggested name with a more descriptive name that you can remember.

For the location, you can select any of the drives and folders on your computer. The dialog box for saving a document has tools for navigating to and selecting another drive or folder for the file.

Follow these steps to save a document:

1. Create the document in the program. Here you see a WordPad document. You can start WordPad by clicking Start, All Programs, Accessories, and then WordPad.

   To learn more about WordPad, see, "Using WordPad" in Chapter 21, "Using Windows Accessory Programs."

2. Click File and then click the Save As command. You see the Save As dialog box (see Figure 2.1).

FIGURE 2.1

Dialog box for saving in WordPad. The dialog box options can vary from program to program.

Address bar   Instant Search box

3. Type a name—for example, **Stacey Letter**, or something you can readily relate to as discussed previously.

4. Select the location for the file:

   To save the document in another folder, click any of the listed files in the address bar. Or click the down arrow next to the address bar and select any listed folder.

   Or

   Click the Browse Folders button (see Figure 2.2). From here you click any of the folders in the Navigation pane. Or double-click any of the listed folders.

FIGURE 2.2
For more options for saving files, click the Browse Folders button.

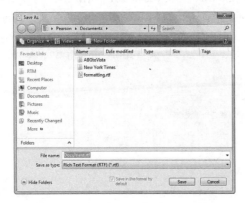

5. Click Save. The document is saved, and the title bar displays the name of the document.

Keeping Files Organized

Windows Vista sets up several folders for specific types of files, such as Documents, Pictures, and Music. It's easier to use this structure because you can easily access these folders from the Start menu and Explorers, but you aren't forced to do so. To keep files organized, folders are created (by Windows, a program, or you) and like files are stored together.

Note that you don't want to lump all your documents into that one main folder.

Therefore, create folders (sometimes called *subfolders*) within your main folders and place your work in one of these folders. For example, within Documents, you might have folders for reports, worksheets, memos, and so on. Or you might create folders for each project. (As an example, I create a new folder for each book that I write.)

tip

For more information on navigating among the folders on your system, see Chapter 3, "Managing Files."

Creating a New Folder

You can set up folders before you save your document and then navigate to them when you're ready to save. You also can create a new folder on-the-fly—that is, when you are saving the document. To create a new folder on-the-fly, follow these steps:

1. With a Save As dialog box open (as described in the "Saving a Document" section), click the Browse Folders button, if necessary (see Figure 2.3).

2. Click Organize and then New Folder. A new folder is added with the default name selected so that you can type a more descriptive name.

FIGURE 2.3

You can create a new folder when you save a docu- ment.

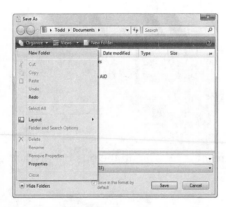

3. Type the new folder name and press Enter. The folder is added.

4. Open the new folder (double-click it) and then follow the steps for saving (type a filename and click Save). The document is saved to this new folder.

tip

You can also create folders from an Explorer in Windows Vista as covered in Chapter 3.

Tips for Saving a Document

Because saving is critical, most programs provide many shortcuts and safeguards for saving. Review the following list of tips for saving:

- The first time you save a document, you see the Save As dialog box even if you do not select the Save As command. This dialog box is displayed automatically to remind you to type a filename and select a location for the file.

- After you've saved and named a file, you can click File and select Save to resave that file to the same location with the same name. When you save again, the disk file is updated to include any changes or additions you made to the file.

- Instead of the Save command, you can also use the toolbar shortcut (look for a Save button) or a keyboard shortcut (most often Ctrl+S).

- If you close a document or exit a program without saving, that program prompts you to save (see Figure 2.4). You can click Cancel to return to the document, click No to close the document without saving, or click Yes to save the document. If you have saved previously, the program saves the document with the same filename and in the same location. If you have not yet saved, you see the Save As dialog box for entering a name and location.

FIGURE 2.4

Most programs remind you to save if you close the document or exit the program without saving.

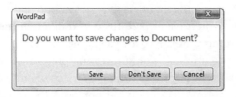

- Just because the program reminds you to save doesn't mean that you should rely on this reminder. Get in the habit of saving before you exit. It is easy to whiz past the reminder prompt and possibly lose your work.

- Some programs save your work automatically. For instance, a database is saved each time you add a new record. You do not have to select a particular command to save the data. The same is also true of check-writing programs, such as Quicken or Microsoft Money. Again, be careful and think "save" first and then check out any automatic save features.

Saving Backup Copies

You often want to have more than one copy of a document. For instance, you might save a backup copy to another drive or disk. You also might use one document to create a new, similar document. You learn more about backing up files in Chapter 17, "Safeguarding Your Work." You can also use the File, Save As command to create a duplicate document.

For instance, you might have a cover letter that you want to reuse and need to change the address or other information. Instead of retyping the letter, you can open the original letter, save it with a different name (and therefore create a new document), and then edit and resave this copy. To use the Save As command to create a new document, follow these steps:

1. Click File and then click the Save As command. You see the Save As dialog box (refer to Figure 2.1).

2. Type a new name.

3. Select a different location for the file if you want to store the new file in another location.

4. Click Save.

A new document is created and saved. This document remains open so that you can continue working. The original document remains on the original drive or disk, intact or unchanged.

Saving in a Different File Format

Another common saving task is to save a document in a different format. Sometimes you share your work with someone who doesn't have the same version of a particular program that you have or perhaps uses a different program entirely. Because sharing data is common, most programs enable you to select from several basic file formats. For instance, in most word processing programs, you can save a document in a plain vanilla format (as a text file), as a document with some formatting changes (rich text format—RTF), as other popular program file types, or as previous versions of the same program.

To save a document in a different file format, follow these steps:

1. Click File and then click the Save As command. You see the Save As dialog box (refer to Figure 2.1).

2. Type a new name, if necessary.

3. Select a different location for the file, if needed.

4. Display the Save as type drop-down list (see Figure 2.5).

5. Click Save.

A new document is created and saved using the filename, location, and type you selected. This document remains open so that you can continue working. The original document remains on disk, unchanged.

FIGURE 2.5

You can select
different file for-
mats in which to
save a document.

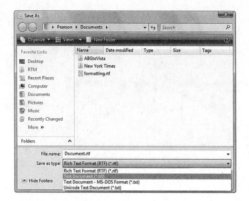

Closing a Document

When you finish working with a document, close it to free up system resources.
Most programs, with the exception of WordPad and Paint, include a Close com-
mand and a Close button for the document window. To close the document, select
File, Close or click the Close button for the document window. In WordPad,
Notepad, and Paint, you must open another document, create a new document, or
exit the program to close the document.

Note that closing a document is not the same as exiting the program. To close the
document and exit the program, select File, Exit or click the Close button for the
program window.

Opening a Document

When you save a document, the information
is saved in a file at the location (folder and
drive) you select. When you want to work on
that file again—to make changes, to print the
file, and so on—you open the file.

Follow these steps to open a document:

1. Start the program you used to create
   the file.

2. Click File and then click the Open command. You see the Open dialog box
   (see Figure 2.6). If you see the file you
   want to open, skip to step 4.

tip

In addition to the File,
Open command, look for
shortcuts for opening files.
You can click the Open button in the toolbar or use the
keyboard shortcut (usually
Ctrl+O). Some programs
also list the last few files that were
opened at the bottom of the File
menu. You can click File and then
click the filename listed on the
menu to open that document.

FIGURE 2.6

Use the Open dialog box to display and then open the document you want to work with.

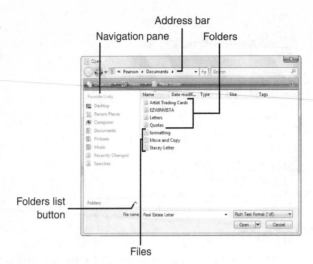

3. If necessary, change to the location where the file was stored by doing any of the following:

    Double-click the folder that contains the file. For instance, in Figure 2.6, double-click the Letters folder icon to view files within that folder.

    To display another drive or folder, click any of the folders listed in the address bar. Or click the down arrow next to the address bar and select a folder from this list.

    Click any of the folders in the Navigation pane. For instance, to open the Documents folder, click the Documents link in the Navigation pane.

4. When you see the file you want to open, double-click its name to open the file.

    For example, in Figure 2.6, you can double-click the Stacey Letter file to open that document. The document is displayed onscreen.

> **tip**
>
> If you can't find the file you want, it might be because you did not save it where you thought you did. Try looking in a different drive or folder. Or make sure that you are not just looking for a specific file type (like looking for just TXT files). If you still can't find it, try searching for the file. For more information about searching for files, see Chapter 4, "Viewing and Finding Files."

Creating a New Document

When you start most programs, a blank document is displayed. If you want to create another new document, you don't have to exit and restart. You can create another new blank document at any time from within the program.

In addition to a blank document, many programs enable you to select a template on which to base the new document. A *template* is a predesigned document that can include text and formatting. To get a head start on content or formatting, you can select a template for the new document—if the program has a template that matches your needs.

To create a new document, follow these steps:

1. In the program, click File and then click the New command.

2. If you see a New dialog box, click the type of document you want to create and then click the OK button. For instance, in WordPad, you can select from several document types (see Figure 2.7). When you click OK, a new document is displayed. You can use any of the program tools to create and save this new document.

tip

In addition to the File, New command, look for a New icon in the toolbar or a shortcut key (usually Ctrl+N).

FIGURE 2.7

If the program includes templates, you are prompted to select the template or document type from the New dialog box.

After the blank document is displayed, you can start entering data. Entering data in most programs is pretty straightforward. For example, in a word processing program, you just start typing. In a worksheet, you select the *cell* (intersection of a row and column) and type the entry. Instructions for more complex programs—for example, a database program—might require more upfront work. For exact instructions on how to use a program to create a document, check the program's documentation.

Printing a Document

Often when you create a document, you print the end results. (You might also print and proofread as you create, edit, and format the document.) Like saving and opening, printing is a common task, and most programs follow the same basic procedure for printing.

To print a document, follow these steps:

1. Click File and then click the Print command. As a shortcut, look for a Print button in the program's toolbar or use the shortcut key combination (usually Ctrl+P). You see the Print dialog box shown in Figure 2.8.

2. Make any changes to the print options. Most programs enable you to select a printer, select what is printed (for instance, a particular page range), and select the number of copies to print. Note that the available options vary from program to program. Setting print preferences is covered later in this chapter.

3. Click the Print button. The document is printed.

note

You most often set up a printer when you first purchase a new computer or a new printer. If your printer is not set up on your computer, you must complete this action first before printing. Setting up a printer is covered in Chapter 19, "Upgrading Your Computer."

tip

Most programs enable you to preview a document to check the margins, heads, graphics placement, and so on before you print. Previewing can save time and paper because you can make any needed adjustments before you print. Click File and select the Print Preview command. After you finish viewing the preview, click the Close button.

FIGURE 2.8

The Print dialog box for WordPad.

Viewing and Canceling Print Jobs

When you are printing a document, you might need to stop or cancel a print job. To do so, you start by displaying the print queue, which lists the documents that have been sent to a printer and shows how far along the printing is. Using the print queue, you can pause, restart, or cancel print jobs. For instance, you might need to pause a print job to change paper. You can cancel a print job that you started by mistake.

Follow these steps to make changes to a print job in progress:

1. Click the Start button and then click Control Panel.

2. Under Hardware and Sound, click Printer. You see a list of all the installed printers and faxes (see Figure 2.9).

3. Click the printer you used for the print job.

4. Click See what's printing to display the print queue (see Figure 2.10).

5. Select the print job you want to change.

note

If the print queue window is empty, either the print job never made it to the queue or the printer already processed it. Short print jobs are printed quickly, so you might not have time to stop the job.

FIGURE 2.9

You can view the installed printers when you want to view the print queue.

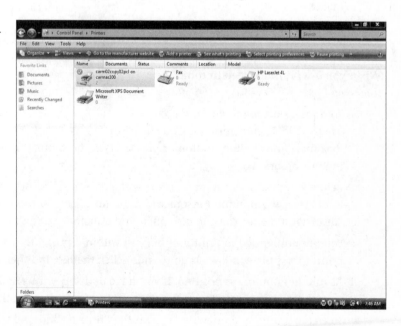

FIGURE 2.10

You can view
print queue and
make any
changes.

6. Do any of the following:

   To cancel all print jobs, click Printer and
   then click the Cancel All Documents
   command. Click Yes to confirm the
   cancellation.

   To pause printing, click Printer and then
   click Pause Printing. To restart after
   pausing, click Printer and then click
   Pause Printing again.

   To cancel, pause, resume, or restart a
   particular print job, click the print job
   in the list. Then click Document and
   select the appropriate command
   (Pause, Resume, Restart, or Cancel).

7. Click the Close button to close the
   queue.

Printing Tips

When you are printing, keep in mind the
following tips:

- To print a document within a program,
  use the File, Print command. You can also
  look for a Print toolbar button or press Ctrl+P (the shortcut key for printing
  in most programs).

- Before you print in a program, preview the document. Most programs have a
  Print Preview command (or something similar). Look for this command in the
  File or View menu. You can also often find a toolbar button for Print Preview.

- You are not limited to printing from just within a program. You can also
  print from a file window. To do so, right-click the file and then click Print.

- As another option for printing, if you have added a printer shortcut icon to
  your desktop, you can drag a file to this printer icon to print the document.

- To create a printer shortcut icon, open the Printers window and then drag
  the icon from the printer window to your desktop. Windows Vista creates a
  shortcut printer icon.

caution

If you don't see the
option See what's print-
ing in the command bar,
it's because you have not
selected the printer. Be
sure to select the printer first.

tip

You can also double-click
the printer icon in the
notification area to open
the print queue.

Changing Printing Preferences

Printing preferences are settings, such as the order pages are printed (beginning to end of document or end to beginning), orientation (portrait or landscape), and paper source. If you always print a certain way, you can change these settings.

Changing the printer's preferences changes them for all documents you print on this printer. If you want to change settings for just one document, change the setting in that document instead.

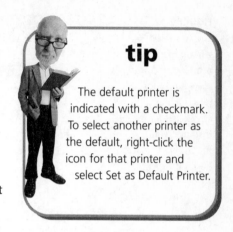

tip

The default printer is indicated with a checkmark. To select another printer as the default, right-click the icon for that printer and select Set as Default Printer.

To change the printing preferences for all print jobs, follow these steps:

1. Click Start and then click Control Panel.

2. In the Control Panel window, click the Printer link under the Hardware and Sound heading. You see all of the printers installed on your computer (refer to Figure 2.9). Your printer list will look different from what's shown here; you'll see the printers you have installed on your system.

3. Right-click the printer you want to customize and select Printing Preferences to open the dialog box shown in Figure 2.11.

4. On the Layout tab, shown in Figure 2.11, select a default orientation and a default page order.

5. Click the Paper/Quality tab. Select a default paper source from the drop-down list (see Figure 2.12).

6. Click OK.

FIGURE 2.11

Printers have different preferences corresponding to their unique features. Your printer's preferences will be different than these.

FIGURE 2.12

You can select what paper the printer uses. For special print jobs, such as envelopes, for instance, you might select Manual Paper Feed.

THE ABSOLUTE MINIMUM

This chapter covers the main skills you need to save, open, close, and print documents. In summary, keep these points in mind:

- You should save and save often the work that you create. The first time you save, you enter a filename and select a location for the document.

- You can save a copy of a document or save a document in a different file format as needed.

- When you want to work on a document that you have previously saved, use the File, Open command.

- When you are finished working in a document, close the document. If you are finished with that program, close the document and exit the program.

- To create a new document, use the File, New command.

- Printing works the same in most programs: Select File and then select Print. The Print dialog box enables you to make selections, such as what to print and which printer to use.

- You can view the print queue to modify any print jobs in progress. For instance, you can cancel a print job you didn't intend, or if you need to change paper, you can pause a print job.

- If you want to make changes to how the printer operates, you can change the printer preferences.

3

Managing Files

As you work with a computer creating more and more documents, you need to find a way to keep this information organized. Without a good organizational method, all your files are lumped together in one place. This is the equivalent of shoving all your files into one filing cabinet.

Keeping your files organized provides many benefits. First, you can more easily find the folder or file you want. Second, you can keep your disk running in good shape by periodically weeding out old files. Third, with a good setup, backing up files is easier. (Chapter 17, "Safeguarding Your Work," covers backing up files.)

Good file management does not take much time and involves just a few key ideas. This chapter covers these ideas and explains the important tasks for working with files.

Displaying Your Computer's Contents

Windows Vista includes many tools for file management, and the most commonly used tools are Explorers. Explorers are windows that display the contents of the folders on your computer. Vista comes with several preset folders that you'll find useful: Documents, Pictures, Music, and Computer, for instance. Explorers display the contents of that particular folder, and they contain tools to work with the contents and navigate to other folders on your computer.

To open an Explorer, click Start and then click the Explorer you want to open. For instance, click Computer to see the various drives connected to your PC (see Figure 3.1).

FIGURE 3.1

When you want to work with the drives on your computer, open Computer.

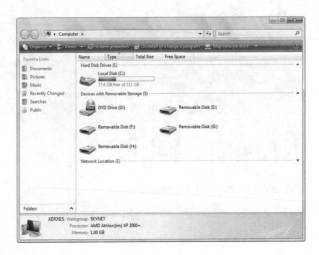

To open a folder that contains your user files (and other folders versus your drives), click Start and then click Documents (see Figure 3.2).

FIGURE 3.2

When you want to work with the folders or files on your computer, open a content-based folder like Documents.

Folders   Files

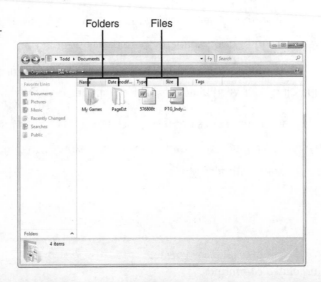

To help you keep your documents organized, Windows sets up several special folders in addition to your primary Documents folder. These include Pictures, Music, and the new Games Explorer. You can view the contents of any of these folders by clicking Start and then clicking the folder you want to open.

Understanding Files and Folders

Folders, at heart, are containers. They can hold files and other folders (sometimes called subfolders). In Vista, folders actually look like file folders. Files are work you have created and saved, such as a word processing document, spreadsheet, database, presentation, music track, programs, and so on. Files are indicated by an icon, but these icons vary depending on the type of file (refer to Figure 3.2).

Understanding an Explorer Window

When you open a folder or drive, you see the contents in an Explorer window. Windows Vista has made the features in this window consistent to make it easier for users to figure out how to use the features in the windows. Learning the various elements in an Explorer window can help you better learn how to navigate among folders and keep your folders and files organized.

Elements you can expect to find in an Explorer include the following (see Figure 3.3):

- The list pane displays the contents of the window.

- Because folders can be nested within other folders, the address bar shows you the path of how the folders are nested.

- The command bar lists the commands for working with the contents of this window. These commands vary depending on the type of window. For instance, if you are working in the Music folder, you see music-related commands. If you are working with pictures in the Pictures folder or the Windows Photo Gallery, you see picture-related commands.

tip

Next to the address bar, you see the Instant Search bar; you can use this text box to type a word or phrase to find a file, program, or folder. See "Using Instant Search," in Chapter 4, "Viewing and Finding Files," for more information.

note

Note that by default the menu bar does not appear in Explorer windows. You can turn them on by clicking Organize, Layout, Menu Bar. The rest of the figures in this chapter show the menu bar displayed because those users who are used to having easy access to the menu bar might prefer to keep it available. After activating the menu bar through an Explorer's Organize menu, it will remain on until you turn it off by following the same steps. However, if you just want temporary access to the menu bar you can also press the Alt key to display it.

FIGURE 3.3

An Explorer pro-
vides tools to
navigate among
the contents of
your computer
and work with
the contents of
that particular
folder.

Menu bar (disabled by default)

Address bar

Command bar

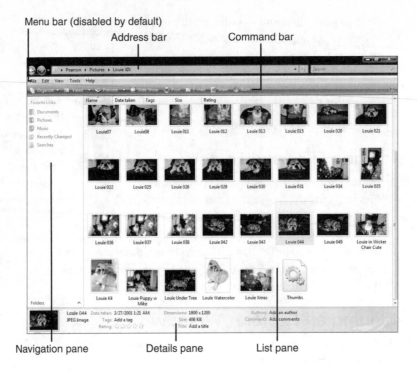

Navigation pane   Details pane   List pane

- The Navigation pane contains commonly accessed folders. Just click a folder to select it.

- The Details pane displays information about the selected item. If no item is selected, you see only the number of items in this window.

- As mentioned at the start of this section, the menu bar does not appear by default but is a tool that most beginners find useful.

tip

You can display a hierarchi-
cal list of all the folders on
your system in the Navigation
pane. To do so, click the arrow
next to Folders in the
Navigation pane. This is similar to the Windows Explorer
in previous Windows editions.

Navigating Folders

Part of using a computer is learning to navigate among the various folders on your system. You might need to find a document; to do so, you need to open the folder that contains that document. You might want to create new folders; you need to open the folder in which you want to place this new folder. Windows Vista provides several ways to navigate among the folders and drives on your computer.

To change to a different folder, use any of these methods:

- In the address bar, click any of the listed folders to view that folder. Or, you can click the down arrows next to any of the folders to see a list of all of the folders it contains (see Figure 3.4). Microsoft refers to this new way of navigating folders as breadcrumbing.

- Click the down arrow next to the address bar to display a list of folders you have previously viewed. You can click any folder in that list to go to that folder.

- If you have gone from one folder to the next, you can click the Back and Forward buttons to move back to a previous folder or forward (if you have gone back).

- To go to a folder in the Navigation pane, double-click the folder name. You see the contents of that folder.

FIGURE 3.4

Use the address bar to back up to a previous folder in the folder path or to display a list of previously visited folders.

Back button
Forward button
Click a folder to navigate to it
Click arrow to see a list of subfolders for that folder
Click to see a list of previously viewed folders

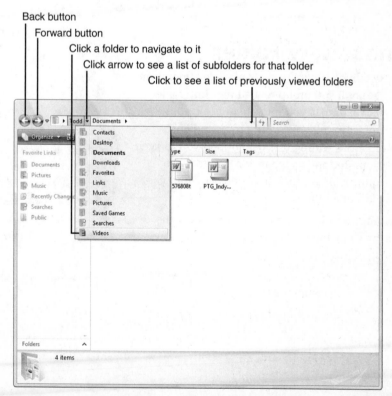

■ To view and navigate using the Folders list, click the up arrow next to Folders. Folders contained within other folders are indented under the containing folder so that you can see how they folders are nested. Then click any of the folders to display its contents (see Figure 3.5). To hide the Folders list, click the down arrow.

FIGURE 3.5

You can display the Folders list in the Navigation pane and use it to open and move to other folders.

Click to open or close folder list in Navigation pane

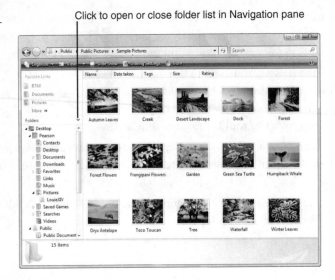

Creating a New Folder

Finding, saving, and opening documents are easier if you group related files into folders. For example, you might want to create a folder for all your word processing documents. Creating a folder enables you to keep your documents separated from the program's files so that you can easily find your document files.

You can create a folder within any of the existing folders on your computer. Follow these steps:

1. Open the folder in which you want to create the new folder.

2. Click Organize and then New Folder (see Figure 3.6).

tip

Windows Vista includes several shortcuts to the Documents folder. Therefore, you might want to set up all your document folders within this one key system folder.

FIGURE 3.6

You can create
additional fold-
ers to store your
files.

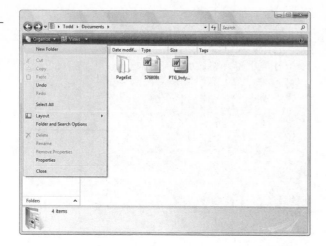

3. The new folder appears in the window, and the name is highlighted. Type
    a new name and press Enter. The folder is added.

Displaying and Selecting Files

When you want to perform some file- or folder-related task, you start by selecting
that file or folder. You can select a single file or multiple files. For instance, if you
wanted to delete a group of files, you could select the ones to delete and then give
the command to delete them.

For any task, the first step is to open the drive and folder where the file is stored.
After you display the files you want to work with, you then select the file or files by
doing any of the following:

- To select a single file, click it.

- To select several files next to each other, click the first file of the group that
  you want to select, and then hold down the Shift key and click the last file.
  The first and last files and all files in
  between are selected. Figure 3.7 shows
  multiple files selected.

- To select several files that are not next
  to each other, hold down the Ctrl key
  and click each file you want to select.

- To select all files, click the Organize
  menu and then click the Select
  All command. Or press Ctrl+A.

- To deselect a file, click outside the file
  list.

tip

When you select a single
file, you can view details
about the file in the Details
pane. This is a new feature in
Windows Vista's Explorers.

FIGURE 3.7

Note that when several files are selected, Windows Vista displays the number of items selected and the approximate size of all the selected files in the Details pane.

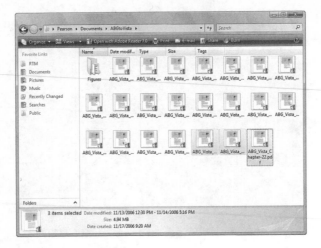

Deleting and Undeleting Files and Folders

Eventually, your computer will become loaded down with files you no longer need, and you might find that you have a hard time organizing and storing them all. You can delete any files you no longer need. You can also delete entire folders. When you delete a folder, the folder and all its contents are moved to the Recycle Bin.

Windows Vista doesn't really delete a file or folder, at least not initially; instead, it moves it to the Recycle Bin. While a file or folder resides in the Recycle Bin, if needed, you can still retrieve it. This common task is also covered in this section.

tip

You can have Windows clean up files as part of your maintenance routine. See Chapter 18, "Improving Your Computer's Performance" for information on using the Disk Cleanup wizard.

Deleting a File or Folder

Follow these steps to delete a file or folder:

1. Right-click the file you want to delete and then click Delete.
2. Confirm the deletion by clicking Yes (see Figure 3.8). The file is deleted and no longer appears in the file list. (The file is actually moved to the Recycle Bin, which you can retrieve; this task is covered next.)

tip

You can also press the Delete key to delete selected files or folders.

FIGURE 3.8

Before deleting, Windows Vista prompts you for confirmation.

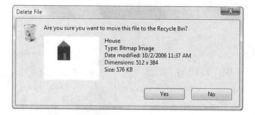

Undeleting a File from the Recycle Bin

Sometimes you delete a file or folder by mistake. If you make a mistake, you can retrieve the file or folder from the Recycle Bin (as long as the Recycle Bin has not been emptied) and return the file or folder to its original location. Usually Murphy's Law goes into effect: The minute you delete an old file is a minute before you determine you need it. Don't fret, though, you can undelete a file.

To undelete a file or folder, follow these steps:

1. Double-click the Recycle Bin icon on your desktop. You see the contents of the Recycle Bin, including any folders, icons, or files you have deleted.

2. Right-click the file you want to undelete and click Restore (see Figure 3.9). The file is restored to its original location. You can also select multiple files and then click Restore all items.

3. Click the Close button to close the Recycle Bin.

FIGURE 3.9

Use the Restore command to undelete a file from the Recycle Bin.

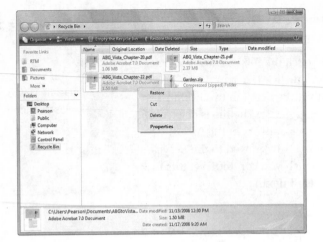

Emptying the Recycle Bin

The contents of the Recycle Bin take up disk space, so periodically you should empty it. You can permanently delete the contents by emptying the Recycle Bin. Be sure that it doesn't contain any items you need. Follow these steps:

1. Double-click the Recycle Bin icon.

2. Check the contents of the Recycle Bin and undelete any files or folders you need.

3. Click the Empty Recycle Bin in the command bar.

4. Click Yes to confirm that you want to permanently delete all these items (see Figure 3.10).

> **tip**
>
> You can change how the Recycle Bin operates, setting a maximum size and selecting to just delete files without placing them in the Recycle Bin. (I don't recommend this, especially for beginners.) To customize the Recycle Bin, right-click its icon and select Properties. Make any changes and click OK.

FIGURE 3.10

To make sure you do want to permanently delete these files, you are prompted to confirm this action.

Click to empty Recycle Bin

Deleted files and folders

If you are sure the Recycle Bin doesn't contain anything you need, you can also right-click the Recycle Bin icon and then select the Empty Recycle Bin command from the shortcut menu. (It's usually best to open and check the contents of the Recycle Bin before emptying it.)

Renaming a File or Folder

If you did not use a descriptive name when you saved the file, if you misspelled the file name, or if the current name doesn't accurately describe the file contents, you can rename it. You can also rename folders you created, selecting a more descriptive name as needed. You can rename only a single item at a time.

Follow these steps:

1. Right-click the file or folder you want to rename.

2. Click Rename. The current name is highlighted (see Figure 3.11).

3. Type the new name and press Enter. The file or folder is renamed.

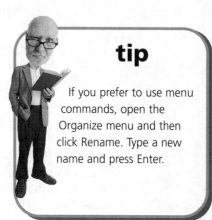

tip

If you prefer to use menu commands, open the Organize menu and then click Rename. Type a new name and press Enter.

FIGURE 3.11

Type a new name for the highlighted file.

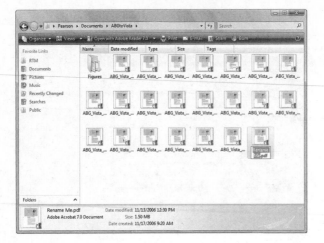

Moving Folders and Files

As you create more and more documents, you might need to do some rearranging. For example, say you have several documents all within one folder, and you decide it makes sense to create subfolders to further organize and categorize the files. You can create a new folder and then move files (or folders) to this new folder.

To move a file or folder, follow these steps:

1. Right-click the file you want to move and click Cut.

2. Navigate the folder where you want to move the file.

3. Right-click a blank area of the file list and click Paste.

4. The file is pasted to the new location.

If you make a mistake, you can undo the move by right-clicking a blank area of the file window and then clicking Undo Move. (Or press the shortcut key Ctrl+Z.)

tip

As an alternative, you can display the Folders list, select the files to move, and then drag them to the folder or drive.

Copying Folders and Files

In addition to moving folders and files, you can also copy files or folders. You might want to keep an extra copy of files or folders. Rather than use a backup program (covered in Chapter 17), many users simply copy files or folders to create a backup copy. As another example, you might copy files to a floppy disk or a CD, for instance, to share with others or to bring home from your office.

Windows Vista provides several methods for copying files and folders. If you want to copy folders to other folders, consider using the Copy command. If you want to copy files or folders to another drive, consider using the Send To command, both covered in this section.

Copying with the Copy Command

To copy a file or folder, follow these steps:

1. Right-click the file(s) you want to copy and click Copy.

2. Navigate to the folder where you want to place the copy.

3. Right-click a blank area of the window and click Paste.

4. The file is copied to the new location.

Copying Files to a CD or DVD

Virtually all new and recent computers include a writable CD or DVD drive. Because these drives can hold lots of information (DVDs hold over six times as much data as a CD), it makes a good medium for making a copy of files you want to save. Copying files to a CD or DVD is often called "burning." To burn to one of these optical disc drives you need a disc of the appropriate type. Disc types you're likely to encounter include:

- CD-R (a recordable disc that you can only write data to once)

- CD-RW (a rewritable disc that you can erase and burn again)

- DVD-R and DVD+R

- DVD-RW and DVD+RW

If you have a read-only (ROM) CD or DVD, you can read only information from the drive; you cannot record information.

caution

Because reading files from an optical drive is slower, don't use this as a primary storage device. However, use it for big files you want to keep. It's a great way to make a backup copy of important files. Also, note that some audio discs created on CD-RW drives can't be read in some conventional CD players. The same is true of recordable DVDs and conventional set-top DVD players.

tip

You can use this same process to copy a file to a floppy disk or any of the folders or drives listed on the Send To menu.

To copy files or folders to a disc, follow these steps:

1. Select the file(s) or folder you want to copy.

2. Right-click the selected item(s), select Send To, and then select your CD or DVD drive from the submenu.

3. When prompted, type a title for this disc and then click Next. The files are copied to the media.

tip

Drives can often read and write at different speeds. If you find that your discs are not burning properly, you can display the Recording speed drop-down list and select a slower speed to try and overcome the problem.

THE ABSOLUTE MINIMUM

This chapter provides the basics of file management, including the following concepts:

- You have at least one hard drive on your system, and this is the C: drive. You might have additional drives, lettered consecutively.

- To view the drives, folders, and files on your computer, open the Computer icon. You can then navigate and open any of the drives and folders on your system.

- You can open the preset folders that Windows creates including the Documents, Pictures, and Music folders.

- To keep your files organized, you can create folders. You can create new folders as needed.

- When you want to perform an action on a file (such as delete it), you select it. You can select a single file, multiple files, or all files within a window.

- Delete files you no longer need. If you delete a file by accident or find that you really do need it, you can undo the deletion by retrieving the item from the Recycle Bin.

- If you did not use a descriptive name for a file or a folder, you can rename it.

- If you need to change the location where a file or folder is stored, you can move the file(s) or folder.

- You can copy your folders or files to keep an extra copy, or to move a copy of a file(s) or folder to another location.

4

VIEWING AND FINDING FILES

Even if you are fairly organized with your files, you can still easily misplace a file or forget where a file is stored. Windows Vista provides methods for viewing and sorting files to help you locate a particular file. In addition, Windows Vista has greatly enhanced its search capabilities. First, you can use the new Instant Search text box that appears on the Start menu and in Explorers to search for a file, program, or music, and you can search based on the filename, its content, or other criteria. Second, if you frequently perform the same search, you can save this search in a special Search folder. You can then run this search anytime you want to view this same group of files. This chapter covers these options for viewing, sorting, and finding files.

Viewing and Sorting Files

It is pretty common to save a file and then not be able to find it again. Either you didn't save it to the location you thought, or you cannot remember in which folder you saved it. Sometimes you don't remember the exact filename. One way to find files is to change how they are displayed in the folder window. You can view the contents of a window in a variety of ways. You can also sort the contents so that files are listed in alphabetical order, by date, or by type. As another option, group similar files together (by name, type, and so on). All these viewing and sorting options are covered in this section.

Changing the View

You have several choices for how the contents of a window are viewed: thumbnails, tiles, icons, list, and details. Changing the view can help you better locate the item you want. Each view has its advantages. For instance, if you want to see more of a window's contents at one time, you can change the view to List. Figure 4.1 shows files in List view.

FIGURE 4.1

List view is the bare bones—a simple compact list of the filenames.

Another simple view is Icon view, which displays the filename and icon (see Figure 4.2). In Windows Vista, you can select the size of the icons. If you have trouble viewing the screen, you might choose a bigger size icon. If you want to see as many icons as possible, you might choose a smaller icon size.

As another alternative, you can add a little more information by changing to Tiles. In this view, you see the file icon, plus the document type and size (see Figure 4.3).

tip

When you want to select a group of files, List view is the best view in which to work.

FIGURE 4.2

In Icon view, the filename and icon are displayed.

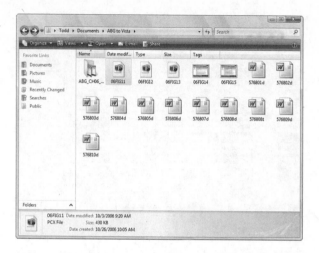

FIGURE 4.3

Use Tiles to view the filename, file type, and file size.

Do you still want more information? Change to Details view to see the size, name, type, and modification data. Figure 4.4 shows Details view. Use this view if you want to find out, for instance, the date a file was last accessed.

Another helpful way to view a summary of a file's details is to select it in the Explorer window and view its properties in the Details pane. You can also right-click the file and click select Properties to view its complete details.

FIGURE 4.4

If you want
detailed file
information,
change to Details
view.

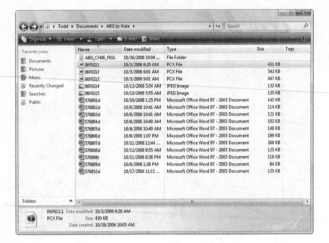

FIGURE 4.4

If you want
detailed file
information,
change to Details
view.

To change to a different view, follow these steps:

1. In the window you want to change, click
   the View button on the Command bar (see
   Figure 4.5).

2. Select the view by dragging the slider bar
   to the view you want. The window displays
   the contents in that view.

FIGURE 4.5

You can see the
current view
selection and
select another
view from the
View menu.

note

If you see a faint gray
highlighting in one of the
columns, this means the contents
have been sorted on that field. The
field name also has an arrow next
to it. You learn more about sorting
in later sections in this chapter.

Sorting Files

In addition to changing the view, you can also sort the contents of a folder window, so that you can more easily find the folders and files you want. Windows enables you to arrange the contents of a window by name, type, date, and size. Your sorting is visible in all views, but the change is most apparent in Details view because this view includes columns for size, date, and type.

Follow these steps to sort files:

1. Open the window you want to sort.

2. Click the column headings that appear above the files. The files are sorted based on that column in ascending order (see Figure 4.6). If you click the heading again, the list is sorted in descending order.

> **caution**
>
> You can also use the menu bar to select commands. If the menu bar is not displayed, click Organize in the command bar and then click Layout. Check Menu Bar. You can also access the same commands by right-clicking a blank area of the window to display the shortcut menu and select the command from that menu.

FIGURE 4.6

You can sort files in ascending or descending order.

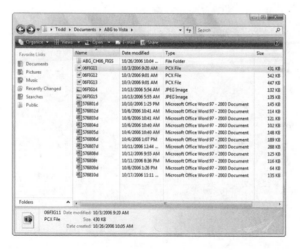

When working in an Explorer window using the Details view, you have different options for arranging the icons. You can arrange by name, type, total size, or free space. You can also display additional fields on which you can sort. Just right-click the header bar, click More, and select the fields you want displayed.

Grouping Files

As another option, you can group similar files together. You can group by name, by type, and other options. Grouping enables you to work with a select group of files or folders more easily.

Follow these steps to group files:

1. Right-click a blank area of the window and then click Group By and select the grouping option you want. You can select Name, Date modified, Type, Size, Tags, or others if you click More.

2. Select a grouping option. The contents are grouped as selected. In Figure 4.7 you can see both that the files are now grouped by their file type and the menu used to view them that way. Notice that there is a group for file folders, JPEG images, and Microsoft Word documents.

3. To undo the groups, right-click a blank part of the window and select Sort By. Then select a new sort order.

note

Grouping does not work in List view. Change to one of the other views (Thumbnails, Tiles, Icons, or Details) if you want to group a window's contents.

FIGURE 4.7

You can group files together to make similar files easier to work with.

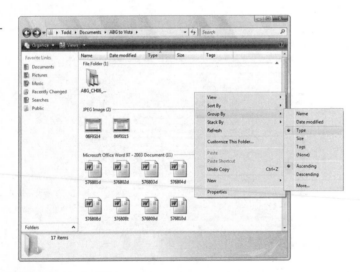

Choosing File Details

In addition to the file details in Details view, you can select to display other file information such as author or the date the file was created. These details are especially helpful for picture and music files; you can display the date a picture was taken or the artist for a song. You can also hide other file details.

To choose the file details that are displayed, follow these steps:

1. Right-click one of the column headings in an Explorer window and click More. You see the Choose Details dialog box (see Figure 4.8).

FIGURE 4.8

You can select to display other file information.

2. Check (Show) any details you want displayed. Uncheck (Hide) any details you don't want included. You can scroll through the list to select from several different file detail options.

3. Use the Move Up and Move Down buttons to change the order in which selected fields appear.

4. Click OK. The file list is updated to include the details you selected.

Choosing Window Layout

The redesigned Explorer window in Vista has a flexible layout with its various panes. You can choose which panes are displayed when you open an Explorer by customizing the window to contain only the panes you find most useful. You might use the new Reading pane, which displays the contents of a document. Or you may turn off a pane if you want more room to display the actual contents of the window.

Follow these steps to make a change:

1. Click the Organize menu and then click Layout.

2. Click the item you want to hide or display (see Figure 4.9).

3. There are four options you can select here, the Menu Bar, Details Pane, Preview Pane, and Navigation Pane. By default, most views show only the Details and Navigation panes. When you select one of these options that item is then either displayed or hidden. In Figure 4.10 you can see what an Explorer window looks like with each of these items enabled.

FIGURE 4.9

You can choose which panes appear in an Explorer.

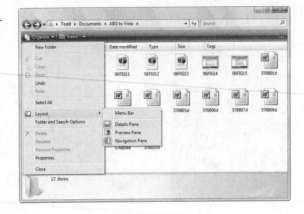

FIGURE 4.10

You can turn on or off panes such as the Preview pane shown here.

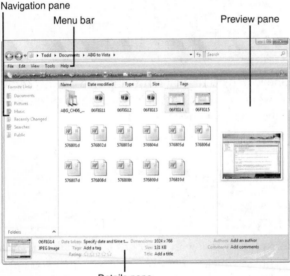

Customizing Folder Icons

In addition to viewing, sorting, and grouping, you can customize the appearance of your folders. You can change the folder icon itself.

Follow these steps:

1. Right-click the folder you want to customize and click Properties. You see the General tab of that folder's properties dialog box.

tip

To go back to the original icon, follow the same steps. In the dialog box with all the icons, click the Restore Defaults button and click OK.

2. Click the Customize tab (see Figure 4.11).

3. Click the Change Icon button; you see the various icons from which you can choose (see Figure 4.12).

4. Select the icon and click OK.

FIGURE 4.11

Use the options in this tab to change the icons used for folders.

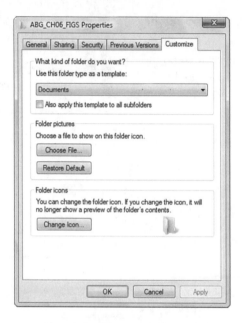

FIGURE 4.12

Use the options in this tab to change the icons used for folders.

Using Instant Search

It is easy to misplace a file. Perhaps you saved it in a different folder than you thought. Perhaps you named the file something different. If you have saved a document but cannot locate it by browsing through your folders, search for it. New with Windows Vista is Instant Search, and all of the Explorer windows and the Start menu include a search box; you can use this search box to search for files by a variety of criteria including name, content, file tags, and so on.

1. In an Explorer window, click in the search text box.

2. Type an identifying word within the file to search for.

3. Windows displays any matching files (see Figure 4.13). You can double-click the file to open it or perform any other file-related tasks.

FIGURE 4.13

Use Instant Search to search by filename, folder name, content, or tag.

Click to save your search   Search word

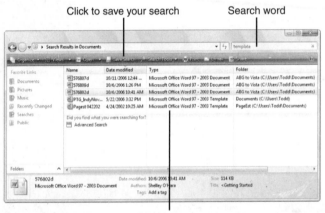

Search results

Using Search Folders

If you frequently search for a file or set of files, you can save the search. That way you can quickly locate the file or group of files without having to perform a search each time. For instance, you might work with a group of files relating to a project, and these files might be saved in various folders throughout your computer. You can quickly gather them together in one window by searching for the common element (for instance, a name or tag). You can then run this search at any time when you want to view or work with this same set of files.

Saving Searches

To save a search, follow these steps:

1. Perform the search that you want to save as described in the previous section.

2. In the command bar, click the Save Search button.

3. Type a name for this search and click Save (see Figure 4.14). The search is saved in your Searches folder, which appears in the Navigation pane. See the next section for how to open this folder to view (and use this saved search).

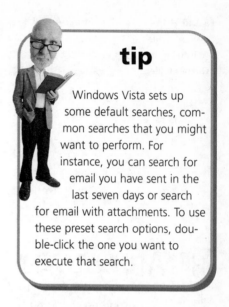

tip

Windows Vista sets up some default searches, common searches that you might want to perform. For instance, you can search for email you have sent in the last seven days or search for email with attachments. To use these preset search options, double-click the one you want to execute that search.

FIGURE 4.14

You can save frequently used searches to the new Searches folder.

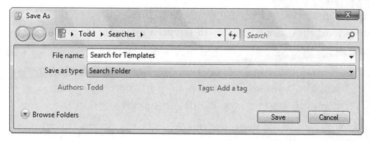

Running Saved Searches

When you want to view the files you've set up and saved as a search option, use the Searches folder; this folder is listed in the Navigation pane. Follow these steps:

1. In the Navigation pane, click the Searches folder. You see any searches you have saved and some of the default searches that Windows Vista has created (see Figure 4.15).

2. Double-click the search you want to perform.

3. You see the results of that search. You can open or perform any file- or folder-related tasks on the matches.

FIGURE 4.15

Saved searches are listed in the Searches folder.

Double-click a saved search to open it

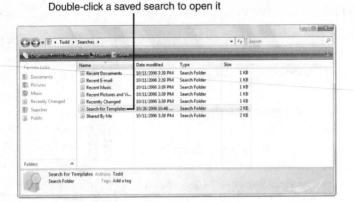

THE ABSOLUTE MINIMUM

Luckily, Windows Vista has several old and new ways to help you locate a file, including changing how the contents are displayed, sorting files, grouping files, and finally searching for files using new search features added to Windows Vista. For finding lost files, use the following guidelines:

- The view of a file window can help you find a particular file. For instance, if you are looking for a picture, use Thumbnail to view a small image of the picture. If you are looking for a particular type of file, use Details view. You can even select which file details are included in the view.

- To change the view, use the Views button in the file window's toolbar and then slide the slider bar to the view you want.

- You can sort files by name, type, size, or modification date. To do so, click the column heading.

- Another handy feature for working with files of the same type (or other grouping) is to sort and then group the files. For instance, you can group all worksheet files together, all word processing documents together, and so on.

- You can also search for a file, and Windows Vista provides many search options. You can use the Instant Search feature that is accessible from the Start menu and all Explorers.

- If you frequently work with a group of files, you can set up a search that groups them. You can then save this search in the Searches folder and run the search when you want to view those files.

PART

COMMUNICATION

5

GETTING WIRED FOR COMMUNICATION

Getting the Right Equipment

To gain basic Internet access your computer needs certain hardware and software components. These are already installed on most contemporary computers. You also need a connection to the Internet via an Internet Services Provider, (often abbreviated to ISP). At a minimum, here's what's required:

- A modem
- An Internet service provider
- A connection to that provider (phone line, cable, and so on)
- A program for browsing the Internet (such as Internet Explorer)
- A program for handling mail (such as Windows Mail)

This section describes each of these items.

What's an Internet Service Provider?

An Internet service provider acts as an intermediary between you and the Internet. You connect with them; they connect you to the Internet. Typically, they also provide email and website hosting services and more. Examples of ISPs include Earthlink, AOL, and Comcast, just to name a few.

Selecting a Connection Type

Many users still connect to the Internet by dialing up their service provider over a plain old phone line, but it is becoming increasingly popular to hook up through a cable provider or by using a special high speed phone connection such as DSL or Fiber Optics connections (also called FiOS).

These faster connections are called broadband because they deliver information so much more quickly than dial-up alternatives. Think of dial-up as a soda straw and broadband as a fire hose, and you have a pretty good sense of the difference between the two experiences.

With so many of Vista's features being Internet savvy and data intensive, (automatic updates, downloading music, gaming, and so on), broadband is almost essential now. Moreover, as websites become fancier and more graphic-laden, dial-up connections seem painfully slow sometimes. Broadband costs more but provides a faster connection and a much more satisfying experience. Common broadband connection types include:

- Cable—You can connect to the Internet through the same company that provides your cable television. Usually, the cable company sells or rents you the cable modem, runs the cable line if you don't have one already; and optionally sets up and tests your computer(s) for you. You pay a monthly fee for the service, and perhaps something for the installation.

- DSL—These high-speed phone lines provide faster connections than dial-up but require a special modem and demand a higher service fee. (They are, however, generally slower and less expensive than cable Internet service.) DSL providers use your regular old phone line, but they use

caution

Broadband connections usually operate 24/7 (24 hours a day, 7 days a week), and you don't actually need to manually connect to the Internet as you do with a dial-up. However, being online 100% of the time also means you're a bigger target for hackers. To protect your computer, you need to turn on a safety device called a *firewall*. Fortunately, Vista does come with an effective one. You should also make a point of purchasing antivirus software that keeps itself up to date. You can find more on these topics in Chapter 8, "Ensuring Security and Privacy."

it in such a way that it doesn't prevent you from making or receiving calls despite having an always-on Internet connection. The only catch is that you need to be within a specific distance of the phone company's facility to have a useful DSL connection. Check with your phone company for details.

- Wireless connections—One of the most popular new methods of getting connected is through a wireless connection. For example, folks who use their laptops to browse the Internet at Starbucks use Wi-Fi ISP connections. The choices of wireless connections continue to grow and now include such exotic options as microwave and satellite for remote users. Chapter 10, "Setting Up Windows Vista on a Home Network," covers wireless options in more detail.

- T1 or other business grade connections— Businesses, apartment complexes, and hotels, among others, often use blazing fast lines purchased or leased from specialty carriers. As a beginner you might have heard of these, but you won't need or probably even benefit from having one at home or in a small office.

> **tip**
>
> If you have more than one computer in your home or small office it's easy to share one broadband connection among all your computers. Some cable and DSL modems have built-in features to facilitate this. If not you'll need a device called a router to manage your home network's Internet connection. Note that many routers also have built-in firewall functionality that can help hide your computer from Internet predators.
>
> Plan ahead if you have, or will have more than one computer. Also be sure your ISP lets you share the connection this way. You can learn more about these topics in Chapter 10.

Finding an Internet Service Provider

An Internet service provider (ISP) enables you to connect to the Internet for web surfing, email, and other tasks. Most ISPs let you connect using dial-up, cable, or DSL, but not all. If you need to use a dial-up modem, for example, check with the ISP to see if they support dial-up first, and if there is a local number to eliminate long distance charges.

In addition to providing online Internet browsing, your ISP also serves as your email service provider. When someone sends you an email message, it goes to your provider's mail server, which is a host computer dedicated to receiving and storing your email until you can download it to your own computer. When you get connected, you can then *download* or transfer any messages from your ISP's email server to your computer.

Microsoft and computer vendors often provide links and even free trials for popular Internet providers such as America Online (AOL) and Microsoft Network (MSN). Some providers are nationwide; some are local. Picking a local provider does not limit your connection to local sites; it just means that the company that provides the service is local.

If you do not already have a provider or you are thinking of upgrading or changing your provider, do some research first. Here are some suggested questions to ask:

tip

A great site for finding ISP options is The List at `www.thelist.com`.

- Does the company provide service for your type of connection? That is, if you want to use a cable connection, can that company provide cable hookups in your neighborhood? (Today, most providers of cable TV service also provide Internet service.)

- What is the cost? Expect a monthly fee around $10 for basic dial-up service, $20 for standard DSL, and up to $50 or more for cable or other high-speed access. Fees also vary from one area of the country to another.

- Are they running, or are they about to run a discount promotion? Some ISPs offer six-months or more at reduced rates or even several months for free. Some provide free installation, free modems, and other incentives. Always ask before you commit!

- Can you save money with "package deals"? Some cable companies discount your TV cable service fees if you add their ISP services, and so on. Phone companies often bundle cell phone, landline, DSL offerings, and so on. Again, take the time to ask and compare. While you are at it, check into the possibility of Voice over IP (VoIP) telephone services, which are sometimes low cost alternatives to traditional phone services.

- Does the service operate month-to-month or does it require you to sign up for a long-term commitment. If it's the latter, how long is the commitment and what will it cost to get out early? Is there a trial period?

- What other services are available? As you become more proficient, you might want to expand your Internet skills. If you think that down the road you might want to create your own website, see whether your provider has web hosting services. If so, what is the fee? Also, if more than one person uses your computer, make sure your ISP provides you with multiple email addresses, at least one for each person. Most ISPs provide you with multiple email addresses at no extra charge.

- What is the top connection speed? Speed is measured in bits per second (bps) or kilobytes per second (Kbps). Regular dial-up modems max out at about a speed of 56,000 bps or 56Kbps. Cable and DSL lines are much, much faster. DSL lines and cable connections include speeds ranging from 128K to 768K, but cable Internet service often can reach speeds even higher than that. Unless you will be sending large files out to the Internet (videos, and so on), you are more concerned with the download speed than the upload speed. Check out the various speeds for providers in your area. A great website for reviewing broadband speeds is BroadbandReports.com.

About Modems

A *modem* is a device used with a telephone line or cable wiring and your computer. The modem enables your computer to connect to and communicate with other computers via the phone line or a cable line. Examples of modems include *dial-up modems*, *DSL modems*, and *cable modems*. Your modem needs to be compatible with your service provider and, of course, your computer.

When using a dial-up connection you need to own your own modem. Some desktop PCs, and most laptops, come with a built-in dial-up modem connection. However, if you intend to use dial-up service you'll need to buy a modem for your PC before you sign up.

To use a cable connection, you need a cable modem (see Figure 5.1). You can purchase one, or sometimes the cable company gives or rents you one when you subscribe. If you purchase your own cable modem, be certain it's on the cable company's approved list (most are).

FIGURE 5.1

A typical cable modem. It connects between your computer(s) and your cable company's connection.

DSL connections require a compatible DSL modem (see Figure 5.2). Again you can purchase or rent one of these from your phone company or go "off the reservation" looking for your own.

You plug your computer into the modem and then the modem into the phone line or cable. Then you can connect to your Internet provider, which enables you to access email and browse the Web.

FIGURE 5.2

A typical DSL modem. It connects between your computer(s) and your DSL-ready phone line. This one can connect to your computers wirelessly if the computer supports Wi-Fi.

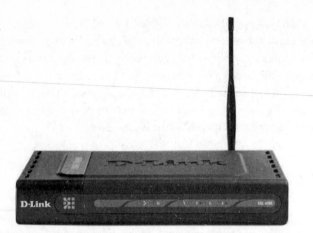

Increasingly cable and DSL modems are being designed to connect multiple computers to each other and the Internet. The process is called *routing*, which was traditionally handled by another, separate device, called a router, which looks similar to the modems shown here. Routing simply means the device can move information between multiple networked computers and the Internet simultaneously. Most new modems these days have built-in router functionality in them so that you don't have to have a separate modem and router.

If your modem has router features you can plug all of your computers into the modem's multiple ports. Some modems, like the one in Figure 5.2 act as wireless access points and also let you share your Internet connection without running wires if you have computers that support Wi-Fi. You learn more about networking and Wi-Fi in Chapter 10. If you have a separate modem and router, your router connects to the modem and your PC(s) connects to the router.

note

Some service providers require the installation of special software on your computer to make a secure connection. This is particularly true for DSL providers. As a beginner it's often wise to pay to have the phone company install and test this software. At a minimum be sure there's free installation tech support available.

Selecting Browser and Email Programs

In addition to the service provider and hardware equipment, you also need programs for browsing the Internet and for sending and receiving mail. Windows Vista includes a mail program called Windows Mail (see Figure 5.3). This program suits the needs of most users (see Chapter 6, "Sending and Receiving Email").

FIGURE 5.3

You can check
your email with
Vista's new
Windows Mail.

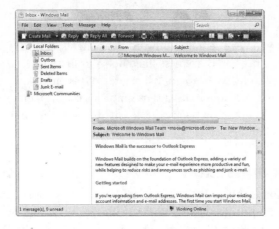

You might prefer a different mail program. For instance, your company might use a
different mail program for interoffice email. Or you might prefer a full-featured mail
program. For instance, if you use Microsoft Office, you can use Outlook, a personal
information manager program that includes mail, calendar, and contact features. You
might also find it convenient to use your web browser instead of a dedicated program
to wrangle your email, if you use web-based email services like Microsoft's HotMail,
Yahoo! Mail, or GMail (from Google).

Windows Vista also includes a browser program called Internet Explorer 7 (see
Figure 5.4). Browsing the Internet is covered in Chapter 7, "Browsing the Internet."
Figure 5.4 shows Internet Explorer.

FIGURE 5.4

The most popu-
lar Internet
browser pro-
gram is Internet
Explorer,
included with
Windows Vista.

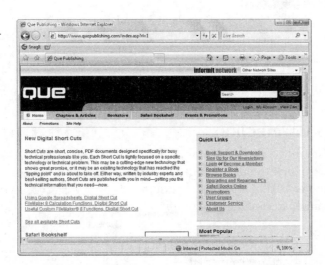

Getting Connected

To summarize so far, you need certain hardware components, software, and a provider to access the Internet. After you have these lined up, your first task is to set up Windows for your new connection. You only have to do this once. After that, starting your email program or going to a website is as simple as clicking an icon. However, the first time you start the program, you need to enter some technical information about your connection and provider.

Making a Broadband Connection

If you have an existing cable or DSL modem and you plug your computer into it, there is a good chance that Vista will automatically do everything necessary to get you connected to the Internet. (Yet another good reason to spring for broadband. No more dialing and waiting.)

You can confirm a successful connection either by opening a browser and attempting to surf the net, or by hovering your mouse pointer over the network connection status icon (the two little computer screens in the notification area of Vista's taskbar, shown in Figure 5.5). You learn more about this in Chapter 10.

FIGURE 5.5
Vista will attempt to connect to available wired and wireless Internet services automatically. The status bar shows the good or bad news.

Currently connected to:
Network
Access: Local and Internet
2:32 PM

Making a Dial-Up Connection

Windows Vista provides a New consolidated connectivity explorer that is explained in more detail in Chapter 10. But for now, let's just look at what's required to configure a dial-up connection.

Follow these steps to start the New Connect to a Network explorer and get connected:

1. Click the Start button and then click Connect To to open the Connect to a Network window shown in Figure 5.6.

caution

The other chapters in this part of the book assume that you have set up your Internet connection and email account. Because the process varies from provider to provider, this book cannot list the exact steps. If you have problems, try Windows help or call your ISP's technical support line.

FIGURE 5.6

The Connect to
a network
explorer.

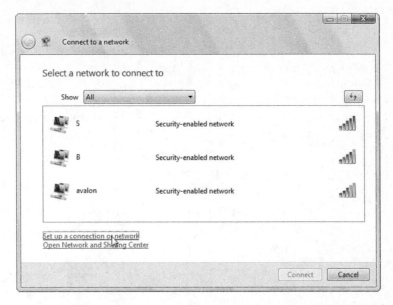

FIGURE 5.6

The Connect to
a network
explorer.

2. Although this window is designed to show all available network connections
   (you might not have any), skip over those and click the Set up a connection
   or network link and then Set up a dial-up connection as shown in Figure 5.7.
   Click Next.

FIGURE 5.7

Set up a dial-up
connection and
then click Next.

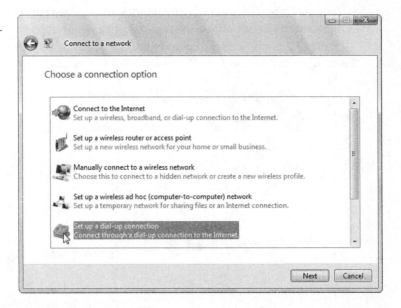

3. Enter the phone number, user name, and password given to you by your
   service provider in the resulting dialog box shown in Figure 5.8.

FIGURE 5.8

Enter the phone number user name, password, and then name the connection something easy to remember (Earthlink, in this example).

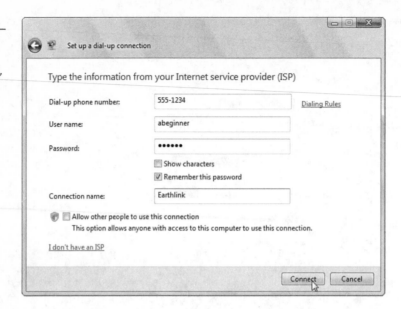

The Dialing rules link shown here lets you set such options as "dial 9 first." It also lets you specify your local area code, and so on. Also, because sharing a dial-up connection is painfully slow, I don't recommend enabling the Allow Other People to Use This Connection check box.

4. When you have completed all your entries, make sure your modem is properly connected, click the Connect button, and watch what happens. You should see a series of progress screens similar to the one in Figure 5.9 and eventually connect. If the connection fails, Vista even helps you troubleshoot. Cool or what?

FIGURE 5.9

Watching the connection progress.

When using a dial-up connection and not actively working online, you should exit your mail and browser program and log off. To do this, click the Close button for the program window.

You should be prompted to log off the connection if you have a dial-up connection. Select Yes or Disconnect. If you are not prompted, right-click the connection icon in the Notification area and select Disconnect.

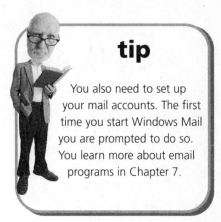

tip

You also need to set up your mail accounts. The first time you start Windows Mail you are prompted to do so. You learn more about email programs in Chapter 7.

The Absolute Minimum

This chapter explains what you need to access the Internet for mail, Web browsing, or both. In particular, this chapter covered these key points:

- To get connected, you need a modem, an Internet service provider, a connection (usually a phone line or cable line), and software for email and web browsing. You can use two programs included with Windows Vista for email and browsing: Windows Mail and Internet Explorer.

- To set up a new connection, use Windows Vista's New Set up a connection or network feature, completing each of the required steps by entering specific information about your provider and connection.

- After you have set up your Internet account, you can log on to the Internet and check and send email and browse the Internet. If using dial-up, you can close your email program or browser. Many programs prompt you to disconnect when you quit them, but you need not.

6

SENDING AND RECEIVING EMAIL

Electronic mail (or email) is a fast, convenient, and inexpensive way to stay connected. You can send a message to anyone with an email address, and it is sent immediately. You can send a message to a friend down the street or a colleague across the world! Recipients can then, at their convenience, respond to your message.

In addition to typing messages, you can send pictures or other documents. For instance, you might want to submit an expense report to your home office. Or you can send pictures of your new puppy to your family.

Windows Vista includes a mail program called Windows Mail. You can use this program to create new mail and handle mail you have received. This chapter covers the basics of sending and receiving email with Windows Mail.

Setting Up Your Email Account

Before you can use Windows Mail, you need to set up your Internet connection and email account information. Setting up an Internet connection is covered in Chapter 5, "Getting Wired for Communication." You also need to set up information about your particular email account.

Setting Up a Windows Mail Account

The first time you start Windows Mail you are prompted to set up your email account. To set up a new email account in Windows Mail follow these steps.

1. Open the Tools menu and select Accounts.

2. On the Internet Accounts dialog that appears, click the Add button.

3. From the Select Account Type dialog box, select E-mail Account and click Next.

4. Enter your name and click Next.

5. Enter your email address and click Next.

6. From here you are asked for some technical information about your account (see Figure 6.1), so be sure you have handy all the connection information from your Internet service provider (ISP), such as the incoming mail server name (called the POP3 or IMAPserver) and the outgoing mail server (called the SMTP server). Most providers use a POP3 server to handle your email. If you have problems or questions about this information, contact your Internet service provider. Click Next to continue.

7. Enter your email username and password. Typically you username is the part of your email address preceding the @ symbol. Again, if you run into trouble, you need to contact your ISP. Enter the requested information and click Next.

note

Despite its many advantages, email also opens the door for possible problems—viruses that come as file attachments, links that "phish" for personal information (such as your Social Security number), and spam (or junk mail). The security precautions for email are covered in Chapter 8, "Ensuring Security and Privacy."

note

An email server is a computer owned by your mail provider (usually your Internet service provider) that receives and holds onto your mail until you can download it to your computer.

FIGURE 6.1

You need to
enter the infor-
mation needed
to set up a
Windows Mail
account.

8. That's it. The next screen tells you that you've completed entering information for you email account. Click the Finish button to wrap it all up.

Setting Up a Web Mail Account

If you want to be able to check your email from any location and from any computer, you can use a web mail account using a web browser such as Internet Explorer. Web mail enables you to log on to the Internet from any site and access the mail. For instance, Microsoft's HotMail (www.hotmail.com) is a popular Web mail provider. Yahoo.com and Google also provide web email services.

To set up an account, go to the mail site and then follow the specific instructions for that site. Usually you set up an account with that provider, entering your personal information. Then you can set up a mail account. To check your email, you enter your user name and password.

> **tip**
>
> Most Internet service providers provide you with the ability to have more than one account. Most of the time you'll create an individual email for each person who has an account on your computer (consult your ISP to learn how to do this). But you might want to set up more than one email just for yourself. If you do this, you can set up multiple accounts in Windows Mail using the same steps outlined previously.

Checking Your Email

After your email account is set up, you can start Windows Mail and check your mail. Follow these steps:

1. Click Start and then click E-mail (Windows Mail).

2. If prompted, connect to your Internet service provider. If you have a dial-up connection—that is, you connect through a regular phone line—you are

most likely prompted to log on to your mail provider. If you have a different connection type, such as cable or DSL, you are not prompted.

Windows Mail starts and checks your email server for any messages. Messages are then downloaded to Windows Mail. The number of new messages appears in parentheses next to the Inbox in the Folders list. The Message Header pane lists all messages. Messages in bold have not been read. You can open and read any message in the Message Header pane (see Figure 6.2).

FIGURE 6.2

Start Windows Mail and then check your Inbox for new messages.

Folders list   Message Header pane

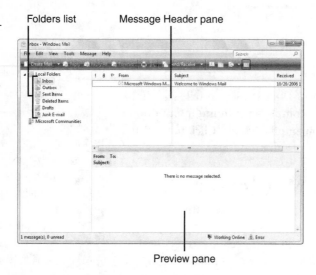

Preview pane

3. If necessary, in the Folders list of the Windows Mail window, select Inbox.

4. Double-click the message you want to read. The message you select is displayed in its own window (see Figure 6.3). You can display the previous or next message in the list by clicking the Previous and Next buttons in the message window. To close the message, click the Close button.

FIGURE 6.3

You can open and review any of the messages you receive.

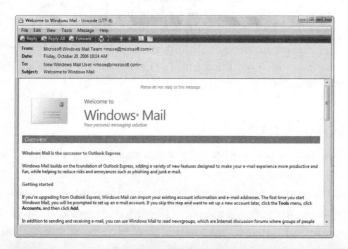

After you are done reading or sending messages (as I discuss in the next section), you can exit Windows Mail. If you have a dial-up account, you also need to be sure to log off from the Internet when you are done reading your mail (or doing any web browsing).

Sending Messages

In addition to reading messages you have received, you can also send your own messages. You have several options for creating new mail. You can reply to an existing message. For instance, suppose that your sister emails you some dates for the upcoming family reunion. You can reply to her message. Replying is convenient because you don't have to type the email address. Also, the text of the original message is included in the reply so that the recipient understands the context of the reply.

You aren't limited to just replies. You can create new messages and send them to anyone with an email address. For instance, you might send a message to a family member who lives out of town and keep in touch via email. Or you might email a company asking about a product or service.

As another option, you might forward a message you received to someone else. For instance, suppose that one of your co-workers sends you a funny joke. (You'll quickly get used to the many jokes and good luck chain letters that are swirling around the Internet.) You can pass it along to your father, the joke master of the family.

This section covers how to create and send email messages.

> **tip**
>
> If you share the same phone line for your Internet dial-up account and your regular phone, you can pick up your phone. If you can't dial out, you are most likely still connected to the Internet. That's why it's important to disconnect.

> **tip**
>
> Many web pages include email links. You can click this email link to send a message to someone at that site. Look for a link that says Contact Us; this is a fairly common item on web pages.

Responding to Email

You can easily respond to a message you've received. Windows Mail completes the address and subject lines for you and also includes the text of the original message; you can then type your response. You can reply to just the original sender or to the sender and any other recipients (anyone cc'd in the message). You can also forward the message to someone else.

To reply to a message you have received, follow these steps:

1. Display the message to which you want to reply.

2. Do any of the following:

   To reply to just the sender, click the Reply button.

   To reply to the sender and any other recipients, click Reply All.

   To forward the message to another recipient, click Forward. Then type the email address for that person or select it from your Contacts list.

   The address and subject lines are completed, and the text of the original message is appended to the bottom of the reply message (see Figure 6.4).

3. Type your message.

4. Click the Send button. The message is placed in your Outbox and then sent.

Depending on your email preferences, the message might be sent immediately or might be placed in the Outbox and sent when you click the Send/Receive button. Also, by default, Windows Mail saves a copy of all sent messages in the Sent Items folder. You can view this folder by clicking Sent Items in the Folders bar.

Creating New Mail

You aren't limited to replying to existing messages. You can send a message to anyone with an Internet email address. To do so, you must know that person's email address. You can type it or select it from your Windows Mail Contacts list. In addition to the address, you can type a subject and the message.

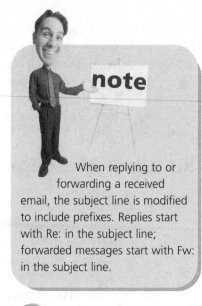

note

When replying to or forwarding a received email, the subject line is modified to include prefixes. Replies start with Re: in the subject line; forwarded messages start with Fw: in the subject line.

tip

The easiest way to reply to and create new messages is using the toolbar buttons. You can also use the commands located in the Message menu. These commands include create a new message, reply to sender, forward, and other options.

tip

You can customize your email setup. To change your email preferences, such as saving copies, use the Tools, Options command. See Chapter 15, "Customizing Email and Working with Contacts."

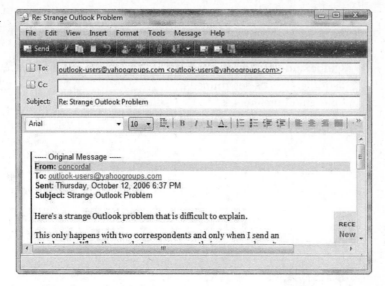

Follow these steps to create and send a new
email message:

1. In the Windows Mail window, click the
   Create Mail button. You see a blank
   email message.

2. Type the recipient's address.
   Addresses are in the format
   username@domainname.ext (for example,
   sohara@msm.com).

3. To send a carbon copy (cc) to another
   recipient, select the Cc field and type an
   address for that person.

4. Select the subject filed and type a subject title reflective of your email's content. (You can also wait until you've
   written the email to decide on an
   appropriate subject.)

5. Click the main body of the window
   and type your message (see
   Figure 6.5).

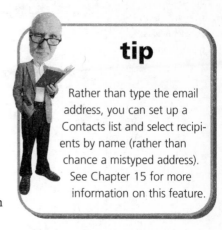

tip

Rather than type the email
address, you can set up a
Contacts list and select recipients by name (rather than
chance a mistyped address).
See Chapter 15 for more
information on this feature.

tip

You can also use the Tab
key on your keyboard to
move quickly from field to
field.

6. Click the Send button. Like replying to a message, the message is either sent immediately or placed in your Outbox and sent when you click Send/Receive, as determined by your email preferences.

caution

If you enter an incorrect address and the message is not delivered, you usually receive a Failure to Deliver notice. You can then check and correct the address and resend the message.

FIGURE 6.5

Create a new email message and then complete the To and Subject fields and type the message.

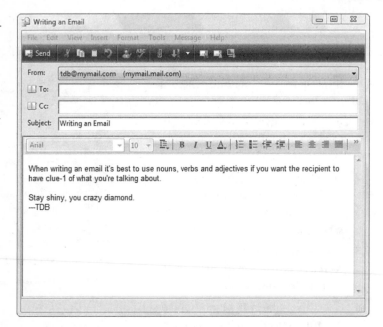

Sending New Messages

Depending on how Windows Mail is set up, your messages can be sent immediately when you click the Send button. Or they might be placed in your Outbox, waiting to be sent. You might save up all your messages and send them at once. Using the Outbox also enables you to compose messages offline (when you are not connected). You can then get connected and send the messages.

tip

If you've configured Windows Mail to use more than one email address, you can click the down arrow for the From field of an outgoing message to change the address you want to use to send the email.

Keep in mind these tips when sending messages:

- The Folders list displays the mail folders and information about the contents. For instance, if you have messages in your Outbox, the Outbox folder appears in bold, and the number of messages to be sent is listed in parentheses after the folder name. You can view these messages by clicking Outbox in the Folders list.

- You can hide the Folders list by clicking the Folder List button in the toolbar. You can also create new mail folders. See "Handling Messages" later in this chapter.

- If you have not yet sent a message, you can cancel it by opening the Outbox and deleting the message. (See "Deleting and Undeleting Messages" later in this chapter.) After you send a message, you cannot retrieve it.

- You can control what is included with a reply and a forward, whether copies of your sent messages are saved, and when messages are sent. To do so, click Tools and then Options. Use the tabs in the Options dialog box. For more information on mail options, see Chapter 15.

- If your messages are stored in the Outbox, you can click the Send/Receive button in Windows Mail to send the messages. To send messages with a dial-up account, you must be connected. If you are not connected, you are prompted to do so. Follow the logon procedure for your particular ISP. The messages are then sent.

> **caution**
>
> If you intend to send an email while you are angry or upset with the recipient, it's usually best to let the message sit for some time before sending. Wait overnight or at least a few hours. Then read your message and make any edits. Because you cannot convey tone of voice, facial expressions, or body language through typed comments, your message might not have the intent you wanted. Double-check any sensitive messages before sending them.

Handling Messages

After you've been using email to communicate with friends, colleagues, and family for a while, you'll find that it isn't long before your inbox quickly fills up with messages. To keep Windows Mail streamlined, get in the habit of handling messages and then deleting them or saving them, as needed. Delete old, unneeded messages. Move messages you want to save to a special folder. This section includes some of the options you have for dealing with messages, including deleting messages, moving or copying messages, printing, handling junk email, and more.

Deleting and Undeleting Messages

As part of keeping your Inbox uncluttered, you can delete messages. If you make a mistake, you can always undelete the message because it's not permanently deleted, but is only moved to the Deleted Items folder.

To delete a message, follow these steps:

1. Open the message or select the message you want to delete in the Windows Mail window.

2. Click the Delete button. The message is moved to the Deleted Items folder.

If needed, you can undelete a message. Follow these steps:

1. In the Folders list, click the Deleted Items folder from the Folders list. You see the messages that have been deleted.

2. Click the message you want to undelete.

3. Drag the message from the Message Header pane to one of the folders in the Folders list. For instance, drag the message from Deleted Items to Inbox. For more information, see "Moving and Copying Messages" later in this section.

To permanently delete a message, follow these steps:

1. Open the Deleted Items folder.

2. Select the message.

3. Click the Delete button or press the Delete key.

4. When prompted to confirm the deletion, click Yes; the message is permanently deleted.

> **tip**
>
> If you want to delete all messages in this folder, click Edit and then select Empty 'Deleted Items' Folder. Confirm the deletion by clicking Yes. Be sure that this is what you want to do. When deleted messages are deleted this way, you cannot retrieve them.

Printing Messages

On occasion, you might want to print a hard copy of a message. For instance, suppose that someone sends you directions to a party. You can print the directions and take them with you. You also might want to print and save a hard copy of messages with important information, such as an online order confirmation.

To print a message, follow these steps:

1. Select the message from the Windows Mail window or open the message.

2. Click the Print button. You see the Print dialog box (see Figure 6.6).

FIGURE 6.6

Select the printing options for the message.

3. Make any changes to the print options, such as the number of copies to print.

4. Click OK to print the message.

Creating New Mail Folders

If you think you need to keep some of your messages, consider creating a mail folder and storing the messages in that folder. Doing so keeps your Inbox uncluttered. You can just keep messages that you need to handle in the Inbox and either delete, print, or move other messages out of the Inbox folder to another folder.

For instance, suppose that you have several business messages that you need to keep. You can set up a folder for these messages and then move them from the Inbox (or other folder) to the business folder. As another example, you might want to keep copies of the funny jokes you receive. You can set up a joke folder and move joke messages to this folder. You can use Windows Mail to create a new folder and move or copy items to different folders.

tip

Windows Mail sets up several mail folders for you including Inbox, Outbox, Deleted Items, Sent Items, and Drafts. Some messages are automatically moved or saved to these folders. For instance, when you delete a message from your Inbox, it is simply moved to the Deleted Items folder. See Chapter 15 for more information on mail folder options.

To create a folder, follow these steps:

1. Click File, New, and then Folder. You see the Create Folder dialog box (see Figure 6.7).

2. Type the folder name.

3. Select Local Folders to place the folder on the same level as the default folders.

4. Click OK to add the folder.

tip

You can also nest mail folders within existing folders. For instance, you could create business and personal folders within the Inbox. To do so, click the Inbox for the first step or expand the Folders list in the dialog box by clicking the plus sign next to Local Folders and then clicking the folder you want.

FIGURE 6.7

Type the folder name here to create a new mail folder.

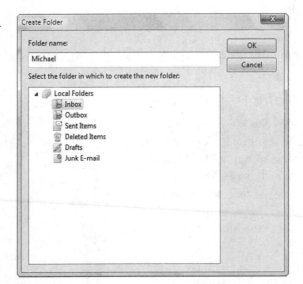

Moving or Copying Messages

You can move or copy messages to other folders. For instance, as covered in the preceding section, you can create mail folders and then move messages to these folders to keep them organized. You can also move or copy messages to the default folders.

To move or copy a message, follow these steps:

1. Select the message you want to copy or move from the Message Header pane. (You can't copy or move an open message.)

2. Click the Edit menu and then select Move to Folder or Copy to Folder. You see either the Move or Copy dialog box (see Figure 6.8). The dialog box is identical except for the name; both list the mail folders.

FIGURE 6.8

Select the folder to which you want to move or copy the selected message.

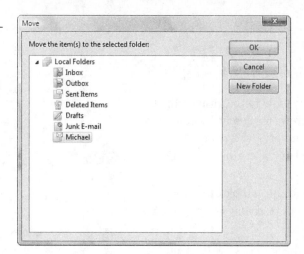

3. Select the folder you want and click OK. The message is moved or copied (depending on what command you selected).

Finding Messages

If you don't (and sometimes even when you do!) organize your messages, you might find it difficult to find a message you received. For instance, suppose that you placed an order for a product via the Internet and kept the order confirmation message. Because the product has not arrived, you want to review the confirmation. Rather then sift through the various folders and messages, you can just have Windows Mail search for it.

tip

You can also drag a message from the Message Header pane to the appropriate folder in the Folders list of the main Windows Mail window to move a message.

To help you find a message, Windows Mail includes a Find command. You can use this command to search for messages, matching the sender, the recipient, the subject, or a word or phrase in the content of the message. Follow these steps to search for a message:

1. Click the down arrow next to the Find button and click Message. You see the various options for searching. The Look in text box displays the current folder (see Figure 6.9).

2. To search for a message using the From, To, Subject, or Message fields, type an entry in these fields.

FIGURE 6.9

You can use this dialog box to search for a message based on a variety of criteria.

3. To select a date range, display the drop-down arrows for Received before and Received after. And from the calendar that appears, select the appropriate dates.

4. If the message you seek has an attachment or is flagged, check these check boxes.

5. To start the search, click the Find Now button.

tip

To search the subfolders within the selected folder, be sure Include subfolders is checked. You can also select another mail folder to search. Click the Browse button and then select the folder.

You see the results of the search (see Figure 6.10). You can double-click any message to open it.

FIGURE 6.10

You see a list of matching messages, which you can open as needed.

tip

You can also use Windows new Instant Search. Type what you want to find in the Search text box. You learn about using Instant Search in Chapter 4, "Viewing and Finding Files."

Sending and Handling Attachments

In addition to the text of a message, you can also attach a file. As mentioned, you might email an expense report to your home office. Or perhaps you have pictures you want to share with your family and friends. (You learn more about pictures in Chapter 12, "Working with Photographs.") This section covers how to attach and send files and how to handle files sent to your email address.

Attaching a File to a Message

If you want to share a file with someone else, you can attach it to an email message. Keep in mind that the recipient must have the appropriate software to open and work with that file. For instance, if you email an Excel worksheet to a co-worker, that person must have Excel (or a program that can open Excel files) to access the file.

To attach a file, follow these steps:

1. Create a new email message and click the Attach File to Message button in the email message window. (You can also click Insert, File Attachment.)

2. In the Explorer window, open the folder that contains the file you want to attach. (See Chapter 2, "Saving and Printing Your Work" for information on how to open a file or Chapter 3, "Managing Files," for help on navigating in an Explorer window.)

3. Select the file to attach and click Open (see Figure 6.11).

4. The file attachment is now listed in the Attach text field of the message (see Figure 6.12).

5. Click the Send button to send the message and file attachment.

FIGURE 6.11

Select the file you want to attach.

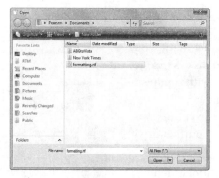

FIGURE 6.12

Your attachment
is listed in the
message header.

Attached file

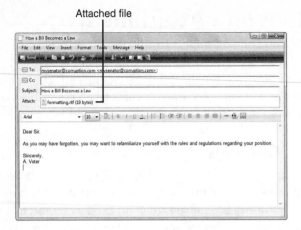

When sending attachments, keep a few pointers in mind:

- You can attach more than one file, but keep in mind that downloading attachments takes time. Also some ISPs have a limit to the size of file attachments. You can send files individually to get around the limit.

- If you need to send a large file or several files, create a compressed folder and then send the folder. This topic is covered in Chapter 3.

Opening a File Attachment

If someone sends you a file attachment, you can either open it or save it to disk. Messages with file attachments are indicated with a paper clip icon. Note that to open the attachment, you must have a program that can open and display that particular file type.

Follow these steps to open an attachment:

1. Double-click the message. The file attachment(s) is listed in the Attach text box (see Figure 6.13).

caution

One way computer viruses spread is through email attachments. Before you open any file—from strangers or people you know—scan the file for viruses. See Chapter 8 for more information on viruses and other email security issues.

tip

If you always want to open this file type, uncheck the Always ask before opening check box.

FIGURE 6.13

You can receive messages with attachments.

File attachment

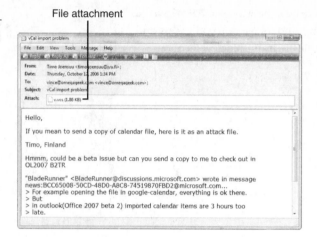

2. Double-click the attachment icon. You see the Mail Attachment dialog box (see Figure 6.14).

3. Click the Open button. The attachment is opened.

FIGURE 6.14

You are prompted to confirm opening the attachment.

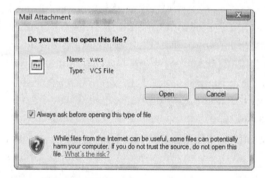

Saving a File Attachment

For some attachments, you might want to save the document to your computer. For instance, if someone emails you a document to revise, you can save it to your hard drive. Like saving other documents (covered in Chapter 2), you can specify the drive and folder in which to save the file.

Follow these steps to save a file attachment:

1. Right-click the file attachment and click the Save As command. You see the Save Attachment As dialog box.

   You are prompted to select a drive and folder in which to save the attachment.

2. Change to the drive and folder in which you want to save the attachment. You can navigate to other folders using the Browse Folders button. For more about opening files, see Chapter 2.

3. Click the Save button. The file is saved to the drive and folder. You can access and open this file from this new location.

tip

If the message contains multiple attachments, you can save them all. To do so, click the Save All command. In the dialog box that appears, click the Browse button and select the drive and folder for all the attachments. Select the folder from the folder list and click OK. Then click Save.

THE ABSOLUTE MINIMUM

This chapter covers the basics of using Windows Mail, the mail program included with Windows Vista. With this program (and an Internet provider), you can send and receive email messages from all over the world. Email is quick and free! Keep in mind the following key points about Windows Mail and email features:

- The first step to using Windows Mail is to set up a mail account. Use the information from your ISP to set up your mail account. The steps vary depending on the provider and type of provider (for instance, dial-up, cable, DSL).

- To check your mail, start Windows Mail. New mail messages are listed in your Inbox. You can open any messages by double-clicking them.

- You have several choices for creating new mail: you can respond to messages you received, you can forward messages, and you can create new messages. The fastest way to do so is using the toolbar buttons in the Windows Mail program window.

- Try to keep your Inbox uncluttered. You can do so by deleting messages you no longer need, setting up folders and moving messages that you want to save to these folders, and printing and saving hard copies if needed.

- If you cannot find a message you received by looking through the various mail folders, you can search for a message using the Edit, Find, Message command. You can search by sender, recipient, subject, or content.

- In addition to typing messages, you can also attach files to send, such as pictures. You can also receive email messages with attachments, which you can open or save to your computer.

7

BROWSING THE INTERNET

The Internet is a huge resource of information and entertainment. You can find sites with current news, financial data, online stores, music, computer articles and help information, and much more. You simply cannot sum up all the content that you can find on the Internet. You have to experience it yourself.

This chapter covers how to log on to the Internet and then navigate from site to site using several methods. You also learn how to search for a site, use shortcuts, and take advantage of some new Internet features, such as RSS (Real Simple Syndication).

Getting Started with Internet Explorer

To access the Internet, you need a program called a *web browser*. And luckily enough, Windows Vista includes Internet Explorer, a web browser. You can use Internet Explorer to go to and view web pages.

To start Internet Explorer, follow these steps:

1. Click Start and then click Internet.

2. If prompted, enter your username and password (some information might have been completed for you), and then click the Connect button. Usually only those with a dial-up access need to complete this step. If you have a cable or DSL connection, you are connected immediately.

Windows connects to your ISP and displays the Internet Explorer window. You see your start page, which by default is usually Microsoft's msn.com search page (see Figure 7.1).

tip

Before you can take advantage of all the benefits of the Internet, you must set up your Internet connection. The specifics of setting up depend on your type of connection and your provider. Therefore, follow the specific instructions you received from your Internet provider. You can learn more about getting connected in Chapter 5, "Getting Wired for Communication."

FIGURE 7.1

Take a look the various tools in the Internet Explorer browser window.

Back · Forward · Title bar · Browser tabs · Address bar · Toolbar · Web search box

Status bar

Understanding the Internet Explorer Window

Like most programs, the Internet Explorer window has a toolbar with various buttons to help you navigate from page to page. Before you start on your Internet journey, take a few minutes to look closely at the program window, including the following key items:

tip

You can select a different home page; this topic is covered later in this chapter.

- Title bar—Like other program windows, Internet Explorer displays a title bar at the top. This title bar lists the page title for the current page.

- Window controls—In the upper-right corner you see window control buttons for changing the size of the window. You can close the window (and exit Internet Explorer). You can minimize the window, as another option. For information on changing the size of the window, see Chapter 1, "Getting Started with Windows Vista."

caution

If you have problems connecting—the line is busy for a dial-up account, for example—try again. If you continue to have problems, check with your ISP.

- Toolbar—Underneath the title bar and menu bar, you see a row of buttons. Again, like many other programs, Internet Explorer includes a toolbar with buttons for frequently used commands. See the next section, "Using the Toolbar," for a description of each of the toolbar buttons.

- Address bar—The address bar lists the address of the current page. You can type another address to go to a particular site. Using the address bar is covered later in "Typing a Web Address."

- Search box—Use to search the Internet. See the section "Searching with Internet Explorer."

tip

When you are finished browsing the Internet, you should exit Internet Explorer and also log off your dial-up account. (If you have a broadband connection that is always connected, you do not need to log off.) To exit Internet Explorer, click its Close button.

- Page content—The main area displays the content of the page. Note that pages contain links that enable you to display another page or site. The section "Using Links to Navigate" examines how to use links.

▓ Window Tabs—New with Internet Explorer 7 is the capability to display more than one page at a time, each on its own separate tab. You can then switch among tabs to view various pages. See "Using Tabbed Viewing" later in this chapter for more information.

▓ Status bar—The status bar appears along the bottom of the program window. This displays link information. For instance, if you place your mouse pointer over a link (more on links later), you see the address of the linked page or site. If a page is secure, you see a Lock icon. (You can find out more on security in Chapter 8, "Ensuring Security and Privacy.") If Internet Explorer is busy downloading data for the page, you see the status of this activity in the status bar.

Using the Toolbar

The most common way to navigate from page to page is to use the toolbar buttons. To use most buttons, you simply click the button. Other buttons have a down arrow next to them. For these buttons, you can click the down arrow and then select your choice from the button menu. For instance, if you click the down arrow next to the Print button, you see commands for previewing and printing pages (see Figure 7.2).

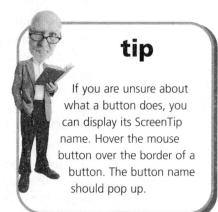

tip

If you are unsure about what a button does, you can display its ScreenTip name. Hover the mouse button over the border of a button. The button name should pop up.

Table 7.1 lists each of the buttons and provides a description of each one.

FIGURE 7.2
Some buttons have a drop-down menu for making a selection.

Table 7.1 Internet Explorer Buttons

Button	Name	Click To...
	Back	Go to the last page you visited.
	Forward	Go forward a page, after going back.
	Refresh Current Page	Redisplay the page, refreshing the data.
	Stop	Stop the display of a page.

Button	Name	Click To...
☆	Favorites Center	Display a list of Favorite sites. See "Adding Your Favorite Websites to the Favorites Center."
☆	Add to Favorites	Add the displayed page to your list of Favorite sites.
⊞	Quick Tabs	Display thumbnail versions of all the tabs.
▾	Tab list	Opens a list of all tabs that are currently open in Internet Explorer.
⌂ ▾	Home	Return to your home page
▾	Feeds	Use to subscribe to RSS feeds of live Internet information.
▾	Print	Print the current web page.
Page ▾	Page	Displays page options, such as opening a new window, sending a page, zooming the size of the window, and more.
Tools ▾	Tools	Displays commands for working offline, deleting your browsing history, display toolbars, and setting other Internet Options.

Using Tabbed Viewing

Often a page contains a lot of interesting links, and you'd like to look at several links versus one link at a time on one page, or you might want to display pages from two different sites. With new tabbed viewing, you can display the contents of other links on tabs. You can then switch from tab to tab.

To display a page on a tab, follow these steps:

1. To display a link on a tab, hold down the Ctrl key and click the link. It is added to a tab. You see a tab with the link you selected; click the tab to view the information.

2. Ctrl+click on any other links to display the pages associated with this link on a tab. You can open as many tabs as your memory allows (see Figure 7.3).

3. To switch to another tab, click that tab.

4. To close a tab, right-click the tab and click Close or click the tab's Close button (which appears when that tab is selected).

FIGURE 7.3

You can display tabs, each displaying a different site or page. Selecting a tab is as simple as clicking it.

Close tab button   Tabs

Navigating to a Site

You'll learn that there are several ways to find your way around the Internet. If you aren't sure where you want to go or what you are looking for, you can use links to browse. See a link of interest? Click it and then review the resulting page. If you know what site you want to visit, you can type its address. Both of these methods of navigating are covered here. You can also search for a site; this topic is covered later in this chapter.

Using Links to Navigate

Information on the Internet is easy to browse because documents contain links to other pages, documents, and sites. A *link* is a text or graphic reference to other sites. Links, also called *hyperlinks*, usually appear underlined and sometimes in a different color. Images can also be links.

Links are what makes the Internet so valuable; you can use the links to jump to related sites. For instance, if you see a link related to travel, you can click that link to view the travel page (shown in Figure 7.4 Yahoo's

tip

You can tell when text or an image is a link because when you point to it, the pointer changes to a hand with a pointing finger, and the address to that link appears in the status bar.

travel service). You might click other links on this page to navigate to other pages. Jumping from link to link is called different things: navigating, searching, surfing, and browsing. Using links is a simple way to become familiar with the wealth of information on the Internet.

FIGURE 7.4
When you click a link, you see the page or site associated with that link.

When you click a link, sometimes the link takes you to another section in the current page. Sometimes the link takes you to another page at the current website. Other times, clicking a link takes you to an entirely different site. Half the fun of browsing is exploring all types of topics and levels of information using links.

Remember that you can use the Back button to return to the previous page if you get too far off track. You can click the Back button as many times as needed to return several pages back. You can also click the down arrow next to the Back button and select the site from the list.

If you have gone back to a page, you can also move forward again to pages you have viewed. Use the Forward button to do so.

Finally, if you get lost or want to start over from the home page, you can click the Home button to go back to your start page (refer to Table 7.1).

Typing a Web Address

Browsing is a great way to explore the Internet, especially if you are not exactly sure what you are seeking. You can browse around to see what information or resources you can find. Think of browsing as flipping through the pages in a book to get a sense of its contents.

If you don't want to browse from link to link, you can go directly to a site. Typing a site's address is a quick way to get to that site. Keeping the book metaphor, typing an address is similar to looking up the page number in the index and then going directly to that page. When you know where you want to go—that is, when you know the site's address—you can use this method for accessing content on the Internet.

Every page on the Internet has an address (sometimes called a *URL* or *uniform resource locator*), and this address follows a certain naming method. For instance, the address to Que Publishing's website is `http://www.quepublishing.com`. The URL breaks down like this:

- The first part is the protocol (usually `http://`, *hypertext transfer protocol*) and indicates that the site is a graphical, multimedia page. This designation indicates a file site. You do not have to type that part (`http://`) of the address. Internet Explorer assumes that you want to go to an HTTP site.

- The next part of the address is the host name (usually www for web servers). When you type this part, you usually can leave off the www.

- The important part of the address is the domain name (which also includes the extension). The domain name is the name of the site and is usually the name or abbreviation of the company or individual. For instance, Que's domain name is quepublishing.

note

Another common protocol is `ftp://` (*file transfer protocol*). This type of site is commonly used for sharing files. Also, `https://` is the protocol used for secure sites, such as those that record your credit card number if you make a purchase online.

tip

Most website names are some form of the site or company name, so often you can simply guess. For instance, to go to the site of the NFL, type `www.nfl.com` (or just `nfl.com`). If the address is incorrect, you'll see a page explaining that the site is not available. You can try another version of the name or search for the site.

- The extension indicates the site type. Common extensions include .com, .net, .gov, .edu, or .mil (commercial, network resources, government, educational, or military, respectively).

- The address (or URL) might also include a path (a list of folders) to the document.

You can find website addresses in advertisements, newspaper or magazine articles, and other media sources.

To go to an address, follow these steps:

1. Click in the Address bar.

2. Type the address of the site you want to visit, and then press Enter. Internet Explorer displays the page for that address.

Searching with Internet Explorer

The Internet includes many different sites. Looking for the site you want by browsing can be like looking for the proverbial needle in the haystack. Instead, you can search for a topic and find all sites related to that topic.

You can use Internet Explorer's search tool, or you can visit and use the search features at several Internet search sites.

Searching from Your Home Page

Most popular home pages (such as Yahoo! and Microsoft's msn.com) include a search text box for you to search from this page. This provides fast access to searching without going to another site. In fact, by default Internet Explorer 7 sets your home page to the msn.com search engine. However, you can go to Yahoo!.com, Google.com or any one of the many search engines on the web.

To search for a site from msn.com, follow these steps:

1. Navigate to msn.com and, in the search box, type the topic.

2. Click the Search button; the name varies depending on your home page. You see the results of your search (see Figure 7.5).

FIGURE 7.5
When you see
the results of
your search, you
can click any of
the links to go to
that site.

Search text

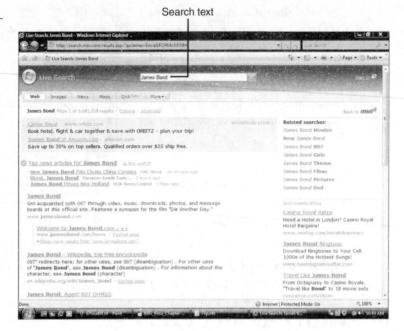

Using Other Search Sites

In addition to MSN's search tool, you can also
go to other sites dedicated to searching. New
search sites are popping up all the time, adding
to the several already established and popular
search sites. The search site is often called by
various names including *search tool*, *search
directory*, or *search engine*. Each search site uses
its own method for categorizing and cataloging
the sites. They also usually provide various
other research tools (such as access to maps or
email searches), and the options for searching
vary. However, the basics of using the services
remain the same.

Follow these steps to use another search site:

1. Go to the site by typing the address and
   pressing Enter.

2. Type the word or phrase you want to
   find. Be as specific as possible.

3. Click the Search button. (The name of
   the button varies.) You see the results of
   the search.

> **tip**
>
> Is one search engine better
> than another? Not defini-
> tively so. You'll find that you
> just prefer one site over
> another, usually when you
> get the most success on
> your searches from a site. I
> prefer, for instance, Google
> because the start page is stream-
> lined and doesn't include an over-
> whelming set of options.
>
> Also, try different search engines as
> the results you get from each vary.
> Something you couldn't find from
> one search site might pop up when
> you search using another site.

Some popular search sites include

- Google—www.google.com
- Ask— www.ask.com
- Alta Vista—www.altavista.com
- Lycos—www.lycos.com

Many sites also provide different categories to search. For instance, with Google, you can search for images, video, maps, news stories, and more. To do so, click the appropriate link from the starting page. Then enter a word or phrase and click the Search button to search. Figure 7.6 shows the results for searching for images of the Mona Lisa using Google. You can also search for news stories (by clicking the News link) or for usergroup postings (by clicking the Groups link).

FIGURE 7.6

You can search for an image using Google's Images page.

Different search sites include different options for searching, so follow the specific steps for using the features at your site of choice.

Changing Internet Explorer's Default Search Engine

You've no doubt noticed the search box in the upper-right corner of Internet Explorer. By default typing a search in this box performs a web search using msn.com. You can, however, change the default search engine. Just click the down arrow next to the Search button and select Find More Providers.

Clicking this option takes you to a Microsoft web page that lists more than a dozen different search engines, from general searches like Google to more specific engines, like if you wanted to find a product at Amazon.com. All you have to do is click one of the providers to add it to Internet Explorer's list of available search engines (see Figure 7.7).

To make a search engine you've added to Internet Explorer the default, open the Search box's drop-down list once again, but this time select Change Search Defaults. From the dialog box that appears you can pick the search engine you want to use as Internet Explorer's default.

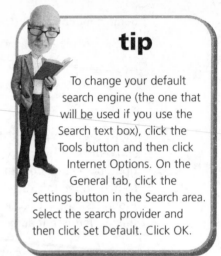

tip

To change your default search engine (the one that will be used if you use the Search text box), click the Tools button and then click Internet Options. On the General tab, click the Settings button in the Search area. Select the search provider and then click Set Default. Click OK.

FIGURE 7.7

Adding different web search engines to Internet Explorer's search box is a snap.

Click a search engine here...   Click to see a list of alternate search engines

...to add it here.

Working with Web Pages

Usually you go to a website and review the information. When doing so, you might want to email the link (or the page itself) to someone. For instance, you can email a book review to your mom. You might also print a page. For example, you might print an order form to order a product via the telephone or fax. You might find program updates or files you want to download from a site. For instance, you can download free fonts and use them on your computer. For long pages, you might have trouble finding the information you seek. In this case, you can search the web page for specific text. This section covers some of the basic tasks you can do with web pages and content.

Emailing Web Pages

Often in your web browsing, you come across sites that might be of interest to others. Internet Explorer makes it convenient to send a link to others. The link is attached and added to an email message; you simply add the address, subject, and any message.

Follow these steps to send a link via email:

1. Display the page you want to send.

2. Click the down arrow next to the Page button. You can select Send Page by E-mail or Send Link by E-mail. The page will include the page itself; recipients won't be able to access any links on the site. The link includes a link to the page; users can use this link to go to that page.

3. You see a mail window. Enter the recipient's address, type a subject, and click Send. This example shows sending a page (see Figure 7.8).

FIGURE 7.8
You can send a web page to someone in an email message.

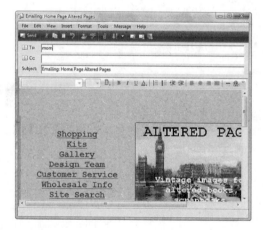

Printing Web Pages

In addition to emailing pages, you can also print a web page. For instance, suppose that you are doing research on Leonardo da Vinci and you find a site with a detailed bibliography. Rather than read this information onscreen, you want to print and review the information away from your computer. To do so, you can print the page(s).

tip

To preview how the page will look when printed, click the down arrow next to the Print button and then click Print Preview. Click the Close button to close the Preview window.

To print a web page, follow these steps:

1. Click the down arrow next to the Print button.

2. Make any changes to the print options (see Figure 7.9).

3. Click Print.

FIGURE 7.9
You can print a page selecting the printer and number of copies from this dialog box.

Entering Text

Another common way to work with web pages is to type information. For instance, if you order a product online, you need to type in your shipping and billing information. You fill out a form online by typing an entry and then moving to the next field. You can click in the field or press Tab to move from field to field. Usually the site indicates which information is optional and which is required; follow any specific instructions for entering information in the page directions.

Searching for Text on a Page

If you go to a site and you know it covers a particular topic but can't find it by eyeballing the page, you can search for a particular word or phrase. This is particularly useful for pages that are long and contain a lot of text.

To search for text on a page, follow these steps:

1. Display the page you want to search.

2. Press Ctrl+F or select Find on This Page from the drop-down list next to Internet Explorer's search box.

3. Type the word or phrase into the Find box and click Next. The first occurrence of that word or phrase is highlighted (see Figure 7.10). You can continue to search by clicking Next or click the Close button to close the Find dialog box.

FIGURE 7.10

You can search for text on a web page.

…and IE highlights it on the web page.

Enter search text here…

Downloading Files

Some sites provide programs, images, documents, or other file types for you to download. You can download programs to add to your computer—for instance, Adobe Reader, a popular program for sharing documents. Some companies provide add-ons to their programs or updates to their programs via the Web; you can download these add-ons or updates. You might also download documents, such as an Adobe Acrobat document (or PDF file), which you can open and read using Adobe Reader. If you have Microsoft Office, you can go online and access its clipart or design gallery and download templates, images, fonts, and so on.

The specifics for downloading a file depend on the site, but most commonly you click the link for the file and then are prompted to save or open the file. (Usually you save it, but you can open and run a document from a site also.) If you select to save the file, you next specify a drive and folder and then start the download process. Often a progress box shows the estimated amount of time needed to download the file as well as the time already lapsed.

Keep in mind that sharing files is one way to get a computer virus (and potentially put your documents and computer at risk). You should use a virus program to check any downloaded files, especially program files, before you run them. You can find out more about virus programs in Chapter 8.

Using Shortcuts for Web Browsing

To help you quickly get to sites, Internet Explorer provides several shortcuts including using the Favorites list, the History list, and setting your own home page. These shortcuts are the topic of this section.

Setting Your Home Page

You are not stuck with the home page set up by your Internet provider or by Microsoft. You can use any page as your home page. For instance, you might prefer to use a search site so that you start with tools for finding information. If you have your own website, you might want to make this your home page. You can select any site for your home page by following these steps:

1. Display the page you want to use as your home page.

2. Click the drop down next to Tools and then click Internet Options (see Figure 7.11).

3. Click the Use Current button. The current page is set as the home page.

4. Click OK. When you click the Home button on the Internet Explorer toolbar, the page you entered is displayed.

tip

To go back to the default page, follow the same steps, but click the Use Default button. The default used is msn.com. Rather than use the current page, you can also type the page you want to use into the home page field. In fact, you can enter multiple pages here (each on its own line) and when you open Internet Explorer each page listed will open in its own tab.

FIGURE 7.11

You can set the home page of your choice.

Adding Your Favorite Websites to the Favorites Center

If you find a site that you especially like, you might want a quick way to return to it without having to browse from link to link or have to remember the address. Fortunately, Internet Explorer enables you to build a list of favorite sites and to access those sites by clicking them in a list called your Favorites Center.

To add a site to your Favorites Center, follow these steps:

1. Go to the website that you want to add to your Favorites Center.

2. Click the Favorites Center button in toolbar and then click Add to Favorites (see Figure 7.12).

3. Type a name for the page or leave the default name (see Figure 7.13).

4. Click Add to save the page in your Favorites Center.

FIGURE 7.12

You can add a site to your Favorites Center and then quickly go to this site.

FIGURE 7.13

You can change the name (this is the name that appears in the list) and select a folder.

Going to a Favorite Site

After you have added a site to your Favorites Center, you can go to that site. Click the Favorites Center button on the toolbar. The Favorites Center is displayed in a window (see Figure 7.14). From there you need only click the site you want to visit. That site is displayed in your browser window, and the Favorites Center window is closed.

tip

You can add the site to a folder you have set up within the Favorites Center (covered in the next section, "Organizing Your Favorites Center"). To do so, display the Create in drop-down list and select the folder.

FIGURE 7.14

Use the Favorites Center to quickly go to your most visited sites.

Organizing Your Favorites Center

As you use the Internet and add more sites to your Favorites Center, the list might become too unwieldy to use, too difficult to find the site in the list. In that case, you can add folders and then group similar sites into folders. If you do use folders, when you want to go to a site, you have to open the folder and then select the favorite site you want to display.

tip

As another option for adding a favorite site, you can drag a site from an address bar to your Favorites list.

Follow these steps to add folders to your Favorites Center:

1. Click the Add to Favorites button on the toolbar.

2. Click Organize Favorites.

3. To create a new folder, click the New Folder button. The folder name is selected so that you can type a more descriptive name.

4. Type the folder name. The folder is added (see Figure 7.15).

FIGURE 7.15

You can add folders to keep your Favorites Center organized.

5. Click Close.

After the folder is added, you can place sites in folders when you add them to your Favorites Center. You can also move a site from the list to a folder. To do so, follow these steps:

1. Click the Add to Favorites button on the toolbar.

2. Click Organize Favorites.

3. Select the site you want to move and then click the Move button.

4. Select the folder to which you want to move the site and click OK (see Figure 7.16).

5. Click the Close button. The site is moved to the new folder.

FIGURE 7.16

You can move a site in your Favorites Center to another folder.

Using the History List

In addition to using the Favorites Center to store your Favorite websites, you can also the History list to go to a site. If you have recently visited a site that you liked but can't remember its address, you can view the History list, which lists the sites and pages you have visited in the last several weeks. From this list, you can find the site you want and click the link to go to that site.

Follow these steps to view and go to a site in the History list:

1. Click the Favorites Center button on the toolbar.

2. Click the History button. You see a schedule of dates from which you can select (see Figure 7.17).

3. Click the date heading to view the sites that you visited during that time period.

4. Click the site you visited; you see a list of pages visited at that site. Click the page to go to that page.

tip

To clear the History list, click the down arrow next to Tools and then click Delete Browsing History. Click the Delete history button. Click Yes to confirm the deletion.

tip

To sort the History list, click the down arrow next to the History button. Then click the sort order (by date, by site, by most visited, or by order visited today).

FIGURE 7.17
You can view a
list of recently
visited sites.

Using RSS Feeds

New with Internet Explorer 7 is the capability to subscribe to and download new feeds, often called RSS or Atom feeds. These are often useful for sites where the content is updated frequently such as news sites as well as blogs (user web logs). You can tell whether a site has feeds available because the Feeds button on Internet Explorer's toolbar turns bright orange (rather than dull gray).

To subscribe to a feed, follow these steps:

1. Go to the site to which you want to subscribe.

2. Click the Feeds button and select the type of feed. For instance, for CNN, you can subscribe to Top Stories or Recent Stories. Click the link to which you want to subscribe and you'll see a page for that feed (see Figure 7.18).

3. Click Subscribe to this feed. You are prompted to type a name and to select a folder for the feed from the Create in drop-down list (see Figure 7.19).

4. Click Subscribe.

tip

As another shortcut, you can click the down arrow at the far right of the address bar to display a list of sites you have gone to by typing the address. (Sites you have visited by clicking a link are not listed.) You can click any listed site to go to that site.

FIGURE 7.18

Subscribe to a feed by using the Feeds button and then clicking the link to which you want to subscribe.

FIGURE 7.19

Subscribe to a feed by using the Feeds button and then clicking the Subscribe to this Feed link.

Click this link to open the
Subscribe to this Feed dialog box

Name of the feed

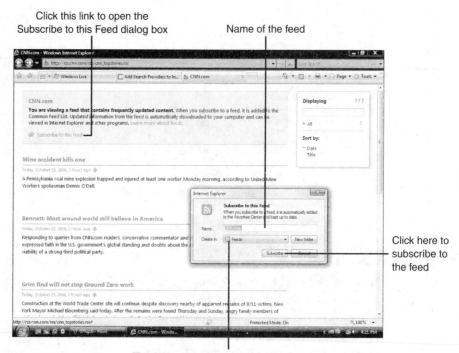

Click here to subscribe to the feed

The folder to which the feed will be stored

To access a feed to which you've subscribed, open the Favorites center and click the Feed button. Whenever one of the sites to which you've subscribed has updated content, the feed list will tell you so by noting the number of unread feeds next to its title in the Favorites Center.

tip

To delete (unsubscribe to) a feed, right-click it in the Feeds list in the Favorites Center and then click Delete. Click Yes to confirm the deletion.

The Absolute Minimum

This chapter examines the basics of using Internet Explorer, the web browser program included with Windows Vista. With this program (and an Internet provider), you can access the many resources of the Internet. Keep in mind the following key points:

- The first step to using Internet Explorer is to set up an Internet account. Use the information from your ISP to set up this account. The steps vary depending on the provider and type of provider.

- To start Internet Explorer, click Start and then Internet Explorer. The first page that is displayed is called your home page.

- New with Internet Explorer 7 is the ability to view several pages at once, each on its own tab. You can also subscribe to live feeds (RSS) for sites such as CNN where content changes often.

- You have two basic methods for displaying web pages: You can browse from page to page using links, or you can type the page address to go directly to a page.

- Use the toolbar buttons to navigate among pages. Click Back to go back a page, click Forward to go forward a page, and click Home to return to your starting page.

- You can print, email, and search web pages. You can also download items (images, program updates, fonts, and so on) from web pages.

- If you frequently visit a site, add it to your Favorites Center. You can then display this list and go to any of the sites by clicking its name. You can also organize the list into folders to keep similar sites together.

- You can display pages you have viewed on the current day as well as several weeks ago by using the History list.

- Internet Explorer enables you to subscribe to RSS feeds that automatically alert you when a website has updated content.

8

ENSURING SECURITY AND PRIVACY

Windows Security Center

Nothing is more annoying than having some outsider mess with or even destroy information on your computer. We also all want to preserve as much privacy as possible. Toward these ends Microsoft has added numerous security improvements and centralized most of them in the Windows Security Center, shown in Figure 8.1.

FIGURE 8.1

The new
Windows
Security Center
consolidates
many Vista
safety and pri-
vacy features.

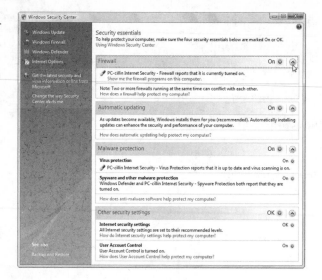

Perhaps the quickest way to reach the Security
Center is to type "Security Center" in the Start
Menu's Search box, and then click the Security
Center choice when it's displayed in the Start
menu. However, you can also reach it by
opening the Windows Control Panel from the
Start menu and selecting Security, Security
Center.

Most of the security settings and options have
been centralized in Vista's new Security Center
and you can easily check or change settings
from here. You learn more about specific settings in this chapter and elsewhere in the book.
Let's start with the Windows Defender feature.

tip

If, after you launch the
Security Center you see
"collapsed" headings without details, click on the circu-
lar buttons to the right of
each heading. This reveals
the details. Also, the links
visible in the expanded details provide feature-specific help.

Using Windows Defender

Windows Defender scans your computer looking for malicious software, including
spyware, (discussed in a moment) and reports its findings. Defender can be configured to run automatically on a schedule, or you can run it whenever you like.
Figure 8.2 shows a manually started scan in progress. To start a manual Defender
scan, follow these steps:

1. Open the Security Center as described in the previous section.
2. Click the Windows Defender link in the left area of the Security Center Explorer.
3. Click the Scan button in the resulting window. You see a scan progress screen similar to Figure 8.2.

With any luck it will report a clean bill of health.

FIGURE 8.2

A Windows Defender scan in progress.

If Defender reports a potential problem, suspicious program, or whatever, don't panic. Read the onscreen information carefully and realize that not everything that is suspicious is hostile. When in doubt, do some online research, contact the tech support folks associated with the program, and so on. Vista's online help can also be a useful resource.

Dealing with Spyware

Spyware programs are installed on your computer usually without your knowledge. They can track what websites you visit or other things you do on your computer and relay this information back to their sponsor. With this information, marketers and others track the sites you frequent. Many claim they use this information to provide customized advertising—advertising that is pertinent to your interest, but most people feel that this is a violation of their privacy, especially if they don't even know the program is running on their computer. Moreover, some spyware is truly malicious and can seriously invade your privacy or slow your computer to a crawl.

You should suspect that spyware has been installed if you notice new toolbars, links, or favorite links added to your web browser without your consent. If your browser's home page (the page you first see when starting Internet Explorer) changes without you changing it, spyware might be the culprit. This annoyance is often called *browser hijacking.* Dramatically slower overall computer performance can be an indicator of spyware as well.

Because Windows Defender is always on the watch for spyware, it can alert you when it senses an attempted spyware installation, and lets you disallow it.

If you join Microsoft's "SpyNet" (which you do by default when you install Vista), Defender also reports suspicious spyware findings back to Microsoft so that the company can evaluate the risks and perhaps update Windows to better resist them.

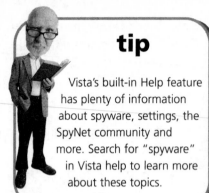

tip

Vista's built-in Help feature has plenty of information about spyware, settings, the SpyNet community and more. Search for "spyware" in Vista help to learn more about these topics.

Securing Your PC with Firewalls

Today, many home and small business users employ 24/7 broadband connections, creating more security risks than systems with dial-up access. Because broadband-connected computers are always attached to the Internet it is easier for attackers to locate them and this makes broadband users' computers tempting targets.

To protect your computer, you need a firewall. Firewalls are hardware or software features that sit between your computer and the Internet, attempting to hide, or at least isolate your computer from evildoers. Firewalls are designed to keep the bad guys, (and bad girls), from entering and co-opting your computer. Although it is essential that you employ a firewall (and Vista turns on its own by default), there are some things you should know.

Just One Firewall, Please

In addition to Vista's built-in *software* firewall, many antivirus programs also contain their own software firewalls. Some cable modems, routers, and DSL connections contain built-in *hardware* firewalls.

While an ideal system of protection involves using both a hardware firewall (typically a router provides this functionality) and a software firewall, running more than one software firewall simultaneously can cause considerable frustration. Most home and other "beginner" users should have one, and only one software firewall enabled, probably the one built-into Vista.

Some programs—particularly online games and advanced networking systems won't work properly if firewall settings interfere. For beginners, this probably means a troubleshooting call to tech support, so be sure you know which firewall(s) you have enabled, and how to reach them so that you and your helper can experiment with the firewall settings.

Turning Firewall Systems On and Off

Vista's firewall is automatically turned on at installation time, but if you install antivirus software *that* installer might have installed its own firewall as well, and perhaps disabled Vista's. To see which firewalls are installed on your computer and their status, visit the Security Center and click the "Show me the firewall programs on this computer" link. You see something similar to Figure 8.3 detailing your current configuration. You can enable and disable firewalls from this window.

FIGURE 8.3

This computer has two Firewalls. PC-cillin's firewall is on. Windows firewall is turned off.

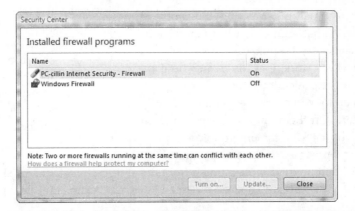

Checking Your Computer for Viruses

Computer viruses range from simple, mischievous programs that might display a stupid message to really dangerous ones that can wipe out all the data on your computer, or even on every computer connected to your network!

How does your PC get infected? Well, you can get a virus from any number of sources, including the Internet, email attachments, from malicious links on websites, and by opening a file that happens to be infected. Viruses can be passed via floppy disks, USB flash memory drives, and other removable media, such as a CD or DVD.

To protect yourself, you should purchase and use a virus scan program.

caution

You might think you are safe by scanning only programs, also called executable files. (Usually these files have the extension .exe and are called .exe files.) It's a common myth that you can only get a virus from this type of file. Not true. You can get viruses from documents with macros, as in an outbreak of Microsoft Word viruses that you can get simply from opening the infected document.

Using a Virus Protection Program

Amazingly, Windows Vista does not come with a built-in antivirus program. You need to purchase and maintain your own. Most new computers come with third-party antivirus programs already installed. Vista recognizes these, and reports their presence and status in the Security Center.

Popular antivirus programs include Norton's AntiVirus (visit www.symantec.com for more information), Trend Micro's PC-cillin, (www.trendmicro.com), and McAcfee VirusScan (visit www.mcafee.com for product information).

Antivirus programs each work differently. Most are started automatically when you turn on your computer, keeping an eye on it continuously as you work; they also scan your computer at scheduled intervals. You can also set them up to scan every file you open. Finally, you can start them and run them at any time by double-clicking the program icon for the antivirus program (it should appear in Vista's Notification area) or by selecting it from the Start menu. Figure 8.4 shows the disk and file virus-checking options for Trend Micro's PC-cillin Anti-Virus program.

> **caution**
>
> New computers frequently come with "trial versions" of antivirus software that need to be upgraded to the real thing after some short period of time. Make certain you have paid for and subscribed to automatic updates, then check to make sure updates are happening properly by visiting the Security Center as described in this chapter.

FIGURE 8.4

Different antivirus programs have different scanning options. This is PC-cillin's.

For instance, you can set up the program to scan all floppy disks inserted in your system and to scan files that are downloaded to your system, including email attachments. Check your particular antivirus program's manual or online help for information on setting virus options.

> **caution**
>
> You need to update your antivirus program periodically. New viruses are created all the time, so if you don't have the latest upgrade, you can get a virus even if you are checking for viruses. Turn on automatic updates!

Handling an Infected File

When your antivirus software detects viruses, the program usually offers you the option to repair the file if it can. In some cases infected files can be "cleaned" by your virus protection software; in others, the files have to be discarded. For really lethal viruses, you might have to reformat your hard disk and start over from scratch. In this case, you will be glad if you backed up your computer as described in Chapter 17, "Safeguarding Your Work."

> **tip**
>
> It's embarrassing, but when you do find out you have a virus, you should notify anyone with whom you've had email contact or anyone you otherwise might have unintentionally infected by exchanging files, and so on. (Many viruses can read your Contacts list and send everyone on the list an email containing a copy of itself.)

Ensuring Internet Security and Privacy

Although browsing the Internet presents many advantages, there are a few dangers as well. It's useful to know how to set Internet security levels for sites, change privacy controls, and use additional programs to prevent intrusions (harmful or simply annoying). This section discusses these security features.

Blocking Pop-Ups

Pop-ups are a blessing and a curse. Annoying pop-ups advertise things you don't want, or try to get you to click on potentially damaging links. Good pop-ups enable you to use online banking, instant messaging, and so on.

Internet Explorer lets you set different levels of pop-up blocking, and you can temporarily override blocks as necessary. Reach the settings by visiting the Tools list at the left of the Internet Explorer toolbar and choosing Pop-up Blocker Settings. You will see a dialog box similar to the one in Figure 8.5.

From the drop-down list near the bottom of the box in Figure 8.5 you can change the level of pop-up blocking from Low (enables pop-ups from secure sites) to Medium (stops most pop-ups) to High (disables them all). Medium is probably a good place to start. You can tweak later as you see the effects of these settings.

You can also specify sites for which you always want to see pop-ups, and you can specify what Vista should do when, pop-ups arrive—play a sound, and so on. The Pop-up Blocker FAQ link in this dialog box is worth a visit too.

FIGURE 8.5

Adding a site to
the approved
pop-up list.

Setting Privacy Options

Privacy is one of the key issues of debate about the Internet. A key part of the problem is browser "cookies," which are little files created on your hard disk when you visit websites. These can be real timesavers, remembering your logon info, for example, or distinct threats to your privacy.

How do you take advantage of all the Internet has to offer, while still retaining some privacy? To address this concern, the Vista version of Internet Explorer includes a Privacy settings tab used to set the level of the desired privacy options. Here you can specify sites to always trust, always block, and variations in between.

Follow these steps to select the level of privacy and check for pop-up blocking:

1. In Internet Explorer click the Tools drop-down list and click the Internet Options command.

2. Click the Privacy tab (see Figure 8.6).

3. Drag the lever to set the privacy at the level you want. As you change the level, Windows Vista displays an explanation of what that privacy setting means.

4. Make sure that the Turn on Pop-up Blocker check box is checked.

5. Click OK to close the Internet Options dialog box.

caution

If you set privacy on a high setting, you might have problems visiting or displaying information at some sites. If you do want to view the blocked pop-ups, simply hold down the Ctrl key while clicking in the blocked pop-up area to reveal the pop-up.

FIGURE 8.6

You can set the privacy level and make sure Pop-Up Blocker is on from this dialog box.

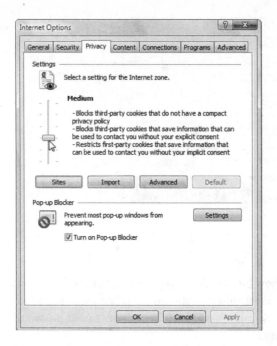

Internet Explorer Security Settings

If you have children, you might also use the Content Advisor on the Content tab of the Internet Options. You can also set up special security zones (trusted sites and restricted sites). You do this from the Security tab of the Internet Options dialog box, selecting the type of site (trusted or restricted), manually typing in the addresses of the sites in that category, and then adding them to the list. Learn more about how to protect your children online in Chapter 16, "Setting Up Windows Vista for Multiple Users."

Setting Email Filters

Junk email is everyone's bane. Each and every message in Figure 8.7 is junk. My Earthlink account is not about to be suspended, those messages seemingly from eBay are phishing tricks, not real messages from eBay or its legitimate members; the opera and US Airways offers—all bogus.

tip

If you are an online shopper, be sure to read that site's privacy statement before entering any information. Most reputable sites provide a link that specifically outlines their privacy rules. Also, watch out for check boxes for automatic alerts, new products, or joining mailing lists. Often these are checked (turned on), and if you don't make a change, you are placed on that mailing list and receive constant messages about "special" offers "just for you!"

The lesson: Be very careful about what you open and respond to even if you think you know the sender. Vista's new Windows mail program has some features to help you, but they are imperfect. Let's look.

FIGURE 8.7

A lot of legitimate looking email like this can be dangerous. Be careful.

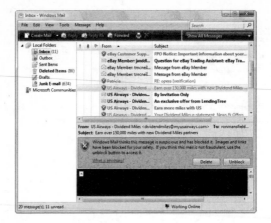

Phishing Filters

As you hopefully know by now phishing is the act of trying to trick you into revealing things about yourself that you shouldn't. When an email that asks you to enter your Social Security Number says "click here to reset your password," don't. It's almost certainly a trick.

Reach Vista's Windows Mail phishing filter settings by choosing Junk Mail Options... from the Tools menu, and clicking on the Phishing tab. You'll see something similar to Figure 8.8.

FIGURE 8.8

Set Phishing email handling options here.

Microsoft's latest Phishing filter (built into Internet Explorer 7) helps spot and shut down malicious websites three ways. As you browse, it consults a list stored on your computer containing a known bad address. It also looks at sites you visit to see if they have characteristics commonly used for Phishing, suspicious URLS, and so on. Finally, only with your permission, the tool will report suspected sites to Microsoft for further investigation, and possible inclusion in the banned list.

When your browser encounters a suspected site you will be advised, and given a chance to either avoid, or visit the site anyway.

To manually check a site:

1. Visit the website you wish to check, (but don't enter or click anything there).
2. Click the Tools button.
3. Click Phishing Filter.
4. Choose Check This Website.

Handling Junk Mail

As mentioned earlier, one way that computer viruses spread is through email attachments and deceptive links. Another downside to email is the amount of electronic junk mail (called *spam*) that you receive. You can easily get unwanted messages from people and companies. To handle this type of mail, you can block senders using features built into Vista's new Windows Mail program.

Blocking Senders

Windows Mail enables you to block certain senders' mail. If you receive an email from someone on your blocked list, it is placed in the Deleted Items folder, or optionally to a Junk mail folder. The message is boldface so that you can find and review the message. If it's not spam, you can undelete it. (Sometimes messages get tagged as junk mail by accident.)

To block a sender, follow these steps:

1. Right-click a message from that sender.
2. Choose Junk E-mail from the resulting drop-down list (see Figure 8.9).
3. Click Add sender to blocked senders list.

note

It's virtually impossible to get rid of all the unwanted mail. One thing you can do to keep spam at a minimum is to carefully check any information you agree to when you visit a site or purchase an item online. For instance, some sites include a check box (which is usually checked) that says in effect "go ahead and send me information about new services and products." After you are on one mailing list, your name pops up in many other lists. Uncheck any invitations for free newsletters or product information. Also, be careful when submitting personal information, such as your address.

If you want to unblock senders, you can remove them from your Blocked Senders List by going to the Junk E-mail or Deleted folder, selecting the message(s) that are not junk, and then click the Not junk button.

FIGURE 8.9

You can block certain senders from sending you email.

THE ABSOLUTE MINIMUM

Keeping your computer free of malicious files, emails, and such seems to get more challenging every year. Fortunately, Vista has added some new tools and improved some old ones in an effort to keep use safe and secure.

- Viruses are programs that can infect your computer and can wreak havoc. Use a virus protection program to scan files and email attachments for viruses and warn you of any viruses. Keep the software up to date.

- Use one (and usually only one) firewall.

- Experiment with antiphishing and pop-up controls to get the level of help that works best for you with a minimum of annoyance.

- Learn how to block nuisance email senders.

9

SENDING AND RECEIVING FAXES

In addition to communicating via email, you can also use Windows Vista to send and receive faxes. Windows Vista includes a preinstalled program, called *Windows Fax and Scan*. It organizes your incoming faxes and enables you to create and send new faxes from documents you create using programs, such as Microsoft Word, accounting software, and so on, or by scanning documents using your scanner if you have one.

To fax from Windows Vista, your computer needs a fax modem. (Most dial-up modems also function as a fax modem.) If you have a broadband connection (such as a cable or a DSL modem), you cannot use the broadband modem to send a fax.

To scan documents so that you can send them as faxes, include them as emails, and so on, you need a scanner connected to your computer.

This chapter covers the basics of sending and receiving faxes and scanning documents.

Setting Up Windows Fax and Scan

Before you can use your fax modem to send and receive faxes, you must set it up in Vista, entering information about your fax phone number and fax device.

Begin fax setup by opening the Fax and Scan explorer. Click Start, All Programs, Windows Fax and Scan or type **fax** in the Start Menu search box and choose Windows Fax and Scan from there.

- Choose Fax Settings from the Tools menu (see Figure 9.1). You might need to confirm your intentions, and possibly enter the Administrator password at this point.

> **caution**
>
> To send and receive faxes you need to plug your fax modem into a "plain old telephone" line, the kind we've used for decades. Many new residential Voice Over IP (VoIP) services from Vonage, Packet8, and such do not support fax traffic, or might require you to pay extra for optional fax support.

FIGURE 9.1

To use your fax, you need to set it up. Choose Fax Settings from the Tools menu.

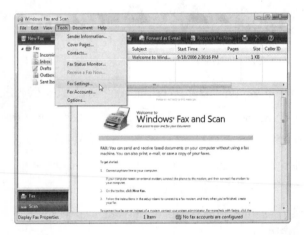

- Enable send and receive by checking their respective check boxes (see Figure 9.2).
- Finally, you can select to manually answer a fax call or to automatically answer the call after the number of rings you designate. Figure 9.2 shows where you make these choices.

> **tip**
>
> Be sure to check Enable Receive. A common problem is being unable to receive faxes, and this occurs if this option is not checked. (You can make this change later if you like.)

FIGURE 9.2

Set up your send
and receive
options here.

Before leaving the dialog box shown in Figure 9.2, click the More options...
button to reveal the dialog box shown in Figure 9.3.

FIGURE 9.3

You can choose
to print it on a
printer or store
incoming faxes
within a folder.

- Enter the TSID. (A TSID is an entry that identifies your fax when it sends a fax.)
  You can type your business name or fax number in this box.

- Enter your CSID. (CSID is a text line that identifies your fax machine when it
  receives a fax.)

■ Select how received faxes are handled (printed directly to a printer you specify or stored in a folder). If you choose to print the faxes on receipt, you can select the printer from the drop-down list. If you select to store the faxes in a folder (which you can then open and view the faxes in that folder), select this option and then select the folder to use. Figure 9.3 shows these options. You can enable both at the same time if you like.

■ Click OK to save your settings. You might need to give Vista permission to save fax files in the folder you specify. This completes the basic setup process.

Sending a Fax

After finishing the initial setup you can send and receive faxes. To help you create and send a fax, Windows Vista provides a Fax Send Wizard. This wizard leads you through the fax creation and sending steps, complete with a cover page if you choose.

Sending a Fax with the Fax Send Wizard

To send a fax using the wizard, follow these steps:

1. Open the Fax and Scan explorer.

2. Click the New Fax button. A fax window opens like the one in Figure 9.4.

FIGURE 9.4

Enter the fax number or choose one from your Contacts database.

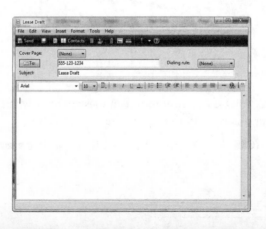

3. Enter the fax number of the recipient or choose a fax number from your Contacts database by clicking the To: button and choosing it from the resulting list.

4. If you want to use a different cover page template, display the template drop-down list and select the template you want.

5. Type a subject and the note you want to fax. The fax window acts like a simple word processor. You can change the font, sizes, styles, and so on. It's also possible to insert photos and other graphics using the Insert menu (see Figure 9.5).

6. Click Send and the fax goes out immediately. If the fax fails to go through, Vista makes multiple attempts, displaying a progress box explaining the status of undelivered faxes.

FIGURE 9.5

Type the contents for the fax in this dialog box, including the subject and note.

Scheduling a Fax

To schedule a fax, before clicking Send, choose Options from the New Fax Tools menu and specify the desired date and time as shown in Figure 9.6.

FIGURE 9.6

You can send the fax immediately or schedule it for delivery at another time.

Creating Cover Sheets

If you want to use a cover page choose one from the Cover Page drop-down list. Initially the choices are none, confidential, fyi, generic, and urgent. The first time you choose a cover page you are prompted to enter your sender information and make other cover page setup choices.

Faxing from a Program

You can also fax documents created in other Windows programs by "printing" to the fax. This method starts the Fax Send Wizard, which faxes all the pages in the document.

To fax a document from a program, follow these steps:

1. Open the document you want to fax. In this example, I've used WordPad (available in the Start menu's Accessories folder).

2. Click File and then click the Print command. You see the Print dialog box.

3. Select Fax as the "printer" and then click Print (see Figure 9.7).

4. This starts the Send Fax Wizard. Follow the same steps covered in the preceding section. That is, complete the recipient and other information for the fax, clicking Next to complete each step in the fax wizard. The document is then faxed to that recipient.

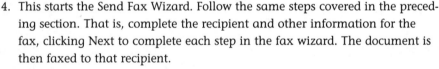

tip

You can also access and send a fax using the Control Panel by opening it, searching for "fax" in the Control Panel search box, and clicking the resulting "Send a fax" link.

FIGURE 9.7

To fax a document from within a program, print it, selecting Fax as the printer.

Faxing from a Scanner

If you have a scanner properly hooked up to your computer you can use it to capture images to send with the Windows Fax and Scan feature. These can be photos, drawings, contracts, 3D objects, or anything you can fit on your scanner's glass.

There are two general approaches to faxing scanned images. You can scan an image or group of images, prior to beginning to author a fax, then start your fax message and attached previously scanned images (and other images stored on your disk). Essentially, you just insert scanned images the same way you attach any other image from your disk.

A second approach is to begin a fax message before you do any scanning and scan from within the fax message window itself. Let's look at that option more closely.

To scan an image into a fax a document, follow these steps:

1. Start the Windows Fax and Scan Program.

2. Be sure the document you want to scan is on the scanner, then click the new Fax button.

3. When the New Fax window opens click the little scanner icon as shown in Figure 9.8.

4. When the New Fax window opens click the little scanner icon as shown in Figure 9.8.

5. The scanner will run and the scanned image will appear (be listed) as an attachment (see Figure 9.9).

6. When the New Fax window opens click the little scanner icon as shown in Figure 9.9. To see how the scanned image looks use the Preview command from the View menu, also shown in Figure 9.9.

FIGURE 9.8

Use the Windows Fax and Scan Explorer to scan images for faxes.

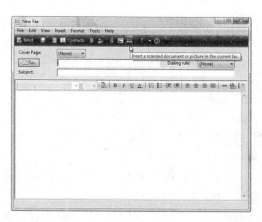

FIGURE 9.9

Scanned images show as attachments in Fax windows.

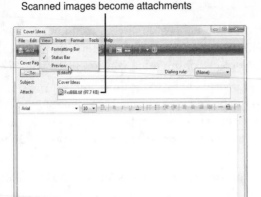

Scanned images become attachments

Receiving and Handling Faxes

Depending on what options you selected when you used the Fax Configuration Wizard to set up your fax modem, receiving faxes can vary. For instance, if you set up your fax to automatically answer a fax call, as long as your computer is powered up, all phone calls on the line are answered by the fax feature. This is fine if you don't also use the phone line for voice calls, in which case you might want to manually answer fax calls instead.

If you set up your fax to automatically answer your calls, the modem receives any incoming faxes and handles them according to the option you selected. If you opted to print the faxes on receipt, they are printed on the printer you selected. If you selected to store them in a folder, they are placed in that folder.

Opening Faxes

The Windows Fax and Scan Explorer lets you view, print, and organize both incoming and outgoing fax messages. Incoming faxes go to the Inbox. Clicking on the Inbox icon at the left of the Windows Fax and Scan window lets you preview faxes as shown in Figure 9.10.

- To open a fax you have received, click Inbox. You see a list of the faxes you have received. The fax list also includes identifying information about each fax including when the fax was received, the number of pages, and so on.

- To open a fax, double-click on it in the list.

- To print a fax, select it, right-click, and then choose print from the menu or select the fax and Print from the File menu.

- To delete a fax, select it and press the Delete key on your keyboard.

FIGURE 9.10

Use the Windows Fax and Scan Explorer to send, receive, and organize incoming and sent faxes.

Scanned images become attachments

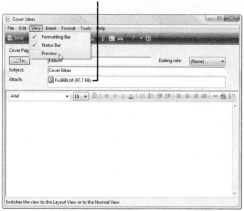

◼ To save a fax to another folder, click the Save As button. Select a folder, type a name, and select a file type. The default is .tif (a popular graphic file format). Click Save.

◼ To email a fax, click the Forward to email button. You see a New Message window with the fax attached. Complete the recipient, subject, and message and click Send. For more information on sending email messages, see Chapter 6, "Sending and Receiving Email."

The Absolute Minimum

This chapter covers the basics of using your computer to both send and receive faxes. Windows Vista includes the Windows Fax and Scan Explorer for these tasks. The important fax points to keep in mind include the following:

◼ Before you can use your computer to fax, you must set up the fax and connect your fax modem to a phone line. Do so using the Fax Configuration Wizard. This starts automatically the first time you open the Windows Fax and Scan Explorer.

◼ You can send simple faxes, typing a subject line and a note using the Send Fax Wizard. Or you can fax a document from within a program.

◼ You can set up Windows Fax and Scan Explorer to handle faxes the way you want. You can choose to answer a fax call manually or automatically. You can choose to print any received faxes or to store them in a fax folder.

◼ To view and work with received faxes, open the Windows Fax and Scan Explorer. You can then view, print, save, or delete any of the faxes.

10

SETTING UP WINDOWS VISTA ON A HOME NETWORK

Networking (interconnecting multiple computers so that they can share files, folders, printers, and other things) is quite common today, even in homes with only two computers. Besides making it easy to share files, networking your computers enables members of your household to enjoy multiplayer computer games, and it can let everyone share the same broadband Internet connection.

It used to be that setting up a network was a stupendous task, requiring expert assistance. The process is much easier now. This is partly because virtually all newly purchased computers arrive at your home or office network-ready, and because new network interconnection products have been streamlined for installation by beginners. Windows XP was also a large part of this entire process, and now Windows Vista has really made it possible for even the absolute beginner to get a small home network up and running in no time.

Although this chapter should not be confused with a comprehensive home networking reference title, it does introduce you to the basics of home networking and how to make it work in Windows Vista.

Home Networking Basics

If your household contains multiple Windows computers, you can easily interconnect them so that they can "see" each other and share resources. Setting up a home network involves three basic steps:

1. Planning your network.
2. Installing and configuring the appropriate network hardware on each computer on the network, if it's not already built-in.
3. Running the Windows Vista Network Setup Wizard.

This section provides a brief overview of steps 1 and 2. You also learn about using the wizard (step 3). Keep in mind that an in-depth discussion of networking is beyond the scope of this book, but you can find ample information in Vista's online help.

Planning Your Network

Computers can be interconnected over wires or wirelessly. It all depends on what your hardware supports and your needs. Many users employ a combination of both techniques. You first need to decide where your computers will be used. Will they be installed permanently in bedrooms, the family room, and home office? Do you want to roam around, perhaps sitting out by the pool while you surf the Internet on your laptop? Are you planning to use Vista's multimedia features near your television or stereo system? Do you have two or more floors in your building? Sketch a floor plan and decide where the networked devices are needed, both now and in the foreseeable future.

Installing and Configuring Network Hardware

To create a *wired* network you are best-served by computers with "Ethernet" network connections (sometimes referred to as 100Base-T or RJ45 ports). Virtually every computer new enough and powerful enough to run Vista already has one of these Ethernet connectors built in.

tip

New homes often come with built-in "Ethernet" wiring designed to network computers and other network-savvy peripherals. When purchasing a house look into this option, which can be quite affordable if added while the house is being built.

note

PCI refers to a slot-type interface used on most modern systems. You really don't need to know anything more about it than that. If you purchase a PCI-based network adapter, it comes with specific instructions to aid you in getting it installed.

The vast majority of Vista-capable notebook (laptop) computers have Ethernet jacks as well. Many portables also have built-in wireless adapters or can have them easily added.

Sometimes, particularly in older buildings, you might want to add wireless network adapters to "desktop" computers rather than run Ethernet wires in the attic or down the hall or through brick walls, and so on. Both internal (using a PCI card) and external wireless adapters (usually USB-based) are relatively inexpensive and easy to install. The internal cards, of course, require a bit more work: removing your system's case cover, locating an empty PCI slot, and inserting the card. Conversely, external adapters just need an available USB port into which you can plug them.

> **tip**
>
> Many broadband Internet Service Providers sell, rent, or give you a multipurpose modem/router/wireless device and install and test it for you! Installation fees are sometimes waived for promotional purposes, so it pays to bargain hunt, especially when signing up for new services. Having someone knowledgeable set up, test, and troubleshoot your network can be a big timesaver.

After your computers are set to support a network, you need some additional equipment to connect them. If you want to share an Internet connection you need a cable or DSL modem, and either a network *router* with a separate *switch*, or a combination router/switch. Confused? Fear not. There's an easier solution. Read on.

Alternately you can use an all-in-one device. These multifunction gadgets are generally the best way to go for a home network. Some broadband cable and DSL modems, for example, can enable all of your computers to share an Internet connection, *and* act as a router/switch to interconnect all your wired computers, so that they can share files and peripherals with each other, *and* provide wireless computer access around your house! Figure 10.1 shows an example of this.

> **caution**
>
> Wireless connections need to be secured. When first taken out of the box, wireless devices have most of their security turned off to simplify setup and troubleshooting. After you get your wireless network running, enable encryption and other features recommended by the hardware's vendor.

This one device acts as a cable or DSL modem, and then shares the Internet connection with all of the wired computers and any authorized wireless-equipped computers within its range. It also facilitates file sharing between wired and wireless computers. You can also share printers, scanners, and other peripherals with this one box. Is that slick, or what?

FIGURE 10.1
All-in-one
modem/wired/
wireless connec-
tivity devices are
ideal for home
and small
business users.

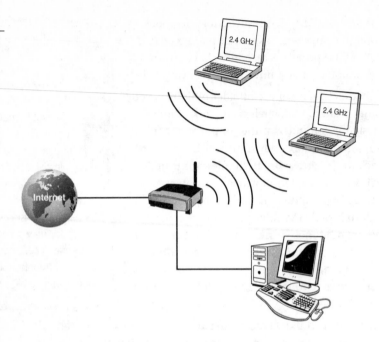

If you decide to set up a home network on your own, be certain that the products you
purchase are compatible with your Internet Service Provider. Read the instructions
carefully, and be prepared to spend some time on the phone with tech support if you
hit a snag.

Networking with Vista

After you install the necessary networking hardware, and perhaps run some cabling, connect
each computer to the network. If all of your hard-
wired computers are running Vista, simply plugging them into a nearby Ethernet jack should
connect them to the network and to the Internet.
Vista walks you through any necessary setup
steps. Read the screens carefully and be patient.

If your computers have wireless adapters, turning on the computers in the presence of your
household wireless device causes Vista to notice
that a wireless network is available and ask if
you want to connect to it. Again, Vista should walk
you through the process.

> **tip**
>
> You can also reach the
> Network and Sharing center
> by typing "Network and
> Sharing" in the Start menu's
> Search box then choosing the
> Center when it appears in
> the list.

Visiting the Network and Sharing Center shows you your network's configuration. You
can access the Network and Sharing Center by opening the Windows Control Panel
(click Start, Control Panel) and selecting Network and Internet, Network and Sharing

Center. Figure 10.2 shows a typical wireless network setup with a single laptop connected to the Internet over a wireless connection.

FIGURE 10.2

The Network and Sharing Center displays connection details.

Wireless Security Options

By now you have almost certainly heard horror stories about evil doers driving past peoples' houses and businesses "sniffing out" and then gaining unauthorized access to wireless connections that have not been properly secured. The risks should be obvious. If a stranger can access your computer(s), your data and privacy are at risk.

A myriad of wireless security options are available; and if a wireless access point has a particular security option enabled, any computer wanting to use that access point needs to have matching settings. This can be as frustrating for legitimate users as it is for hackers. The security settings you use with your laptop at Starbucks, for example, probably won't work

caution

Vista locates and displays any wireless network connection it finds, which might include your network, and the networks of nearby neighbors who have wireless connections. Although Vista offers you the opportunity to connect to your neighbors, which is possible if neighbors run unsecured networks, don't do it. This is as much of a security risk for you as for them. And it's an invasion of privacy. This is also why you should make sure your own network is secured using instructions provided with your wireless router.

with your home wireless access point or at the Marriott when you're on the road.

Vista helps you wrangle this by creating and remembering separate security settings for the various wireless access points your computer encounters. Whole books have been written about wireless security, and in reality, beginners are likely to need technical help now and then when first encountering a new wireless access point. Don't be embarrassed to ask for help. It's confusing.

The most common security roadblock you will encounter with wireless connectivity is *encryption*. This is a technology that scrambles your communications making them difficult if not impossible to intercept. The encryption method you will most likely encounter as a beginner is WEP (Wired Equivalency Privacy).

WEP employs "Keys" generated when the technician sets up the wireless access point. When attempting to use WEP protected access devices, you will need to know the type of encryption (64 or 128 bit) and a valid access key. You will need to get these from someone with responsibility for the access point.

> **caution**
>
> Public access points—at coffee shops, in airports, hotels, and so on, are notoriously insecure. This makes it easier for you to attach to them, but also makes them prime targets for hackers. If at all possible, avoid such things as online banking and sending confidential files or messages through public wireless access points. This also holds true for public places such as hotel rooms, convention centers or the airport VIP lounge where you plug into the Internet through your computer's Ethernet port.

Vista will ask you for it. Once you enter this information for a particular access point and successfully connect, Vista will remember it, and henceforth you will be able to connect without reentering the information unless, of course, the manager of the access point has changed the settings or generated new keys.

A second, more secure form of wireless security is called WPA (Wi-Fi Protected Access). WPA came along because WEP is, unfortunately, notoriously easy to circumvent. WPA comes in two forms, Personal and Enterprise. Obviously, most users should opt for the Personal configuration, which requires a set password for networked systems to access your network through our wireless access point. If you have a wireless access point, consult your documentation for setting up and configuring WPA.

Sharing Resources on a Network

As you should know by now, the primary purpose of a network is to make sharing documents and hardware components (such as a printer) easier. This section focuses on common networking tasks including sharing files, sharing printers, and setting up network security.

Enabling File Sharing

For our purposes Vista offers two kinds of file sharing—Private and Public. By default, Vista is configured so that Public file sharing, the easiest to use but least secure, is turned off.

To make folders available to other computers on your network, you must enable file sharing for those folders. To enable Public file sharing (the easiest type of sharing), follow these steps:

1. Open the network and Sharing Center as described in the previous section.

2. Click the down arrow next to the Public Folder Sharing option in the Sharing and Discovery section of the window (you might need to scroll down). You see something similar to Figure 10.3, but with *your* networked computers displayed, of course. The options shown here enable you to turn Public folder sharing on and off.

note

When sharing networked resources, (printers, files, folders, and so on) remember that if your computer is turned off, disconnected from the network, or enters Sleep or Hibernate mode other users on the network will not have access to your shared resources.

FIGURE 10.3

Open the network window and click the Network and Sharing Center button.

3. If you want to turn public sharing on, you have two options. You can allow network users only the ability to open files on this computer or you can allow them to do whatever they want to do with shared files on this computer. Obviously, the former is more secure than the latter, but many users do require the ability to access and change files on a networked computer. Select the option that works best for your needs.

4. Click the Apply button as shown in Figure 10.3.

5. You are now ready to share files and folders, and can close the Network and Sharing Center.

Sharing with Public Folders

Once you have enabled sharing any files you place in your Public folders can be seen by anyone with an account on your computer and by everyone else on your network. Copy or move whichever files you want to share to the Public folder or one of its subfolders, such as Public Documents or Public Music. The contents of your Public folder will be shared with anyone who has access to the Public folder.

You can't restrict access to individual files and folders within the Public. If users have access to the Public folder, they will have access to everything in it.

When you share files and folders this way others can open and view those files and folders just as if they were stored on their own computers. Any changes you allow them to make to a shared file or folder will change the file or folder on your computer.

For this reason you should be careful about what you put in your Public folder, and perhaps only place copies of important items there.

Sharing Any File or Folder

It is also possible to share files and folders not located in the Public folder. You can also define who gets to use the files, and what they can and cannot do with them. Here's an overview of the steps and options.

1. Locate the folder with the files you want to share.

2. Click the file(s) or folder(s) that you want to share, and then, on the toolbar, click Share.

3. In the resulting File Sharing dialog box either type the username of the person you want to share files with, and then click Add; or click the arrow to the right of the text box, click the person's username

tip

The Sharing Center shown in Figure 10.3 also contains a link you can use to see which items you are sharing. It's called, cleverly enough, "Show me all the files and folders I am sharing."

tip

If you don't see the name of the person you want to share files with in the list, click the arrow to the right of the text box, and then click Create a New User to create a new user account so that you can share files with the person using this account. The name of the person or group that you selected appears in the list of people you want to share files with.

in the list, and then click Add. If you want to share the folder with all users, select Everyone (All Users in This List).

4. Once you've added the users you want to share the folder with, click the Share button.

Browsing Shared Files

You can browse and use shared files on the network through the Network Explorer. It works just like File Explorer, except that it shows you files on the other network computers.

To view these files, follow these steps:

1. Click the Start button and choose Network. You see all available computers on your network (see Figure 10.4).

2. Double-click the icon or name of the computer of interest.

3. You see a list of shared folders for that computer similar to the one in Figure 10.5.

4. To open a folder or document, double-click it. If you have permission to do so, you can then perform the same actions on a file or folder that you can when working on your local PC's hard drive. You can edit, copy, print, and save as needed.

Sharing Printers

There are several different ways to share printers over a network. Some printers have their own Ethernet jacks and you can plug them right into your wired network for all the computers to use. Wireless printer "servers" are available as well. You plug your printer into one of these and any authorized wireless computer within range can print wirelessly.

note

Large organizations—corporations, hospitals, and so on, often break their networks up into "subgroups" called workgroups in Windows speak. Multiple workgroups complicate sharing, especially between groups. Beginners and small businesses should stick with the single, default Windows workgroup called "Workgroup." It's important to understand that all systems in your network share the same Workgroup name or Vista will not recognize them as part of your network. To change your workgroup name, open the Start menu, right-click Computer and select Properties. In the window that appears you can see your PC's computer name and workgroup. To change the workgroup name, click the Change Settings link and in the dialog box that appears, click the Change button.

FIGURE 10.4

See all the computers using your network here. Double-click to explore available shared resources.

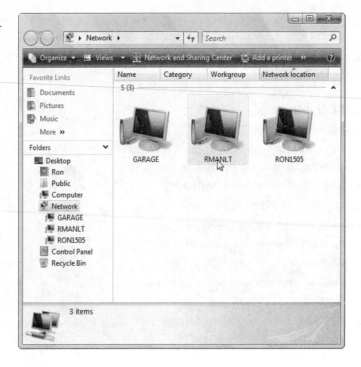

FIGURE 10.5

Open shared folders to access documents.

A third technique, quite common in home installations, is to plug a printer into one computer and then tell Vista that you want to share it with other computers on the network. Obviously, for this to work the computer "hosting" the shared printer must remain on for others to have access to the computer over the network. It must not enter sleep or hibernate mode either. To share a printer do the following:

1. Open the Control Panel from the Start menu.

2. Click the Printers link underneath the Hardware and Sound section of the Control Panel.

3. Right-click on the printer you want to share and select Sharing... (see Figure 10.6).

FIGURE 10.6

Computers on the network can share their printers with other users.

4. At this point, Vista walks you through the necessary steps to configure the printer for sharing. Start by clicking the Share this Printer button.

5. After asking for permission Vista will redraw the Properties dialog box. Click the Share this Printer box.

6. Vista will propose a name for the shared printer that you can keep or change. Click OK to continue.

7. The shared printer's icon will change to include two little people in its lower-left corner.

8. Other users on the network will see the shared printer in their available printer lists when they use the Add printer Wizard and search for shared printers. The actual steps for connecting vary slightly for different Windows versions.

Sharing Other Hardware

You can share other devices—a camera memory card reader, for example—over your network by right-clicking on them, choosing Sharing..., and following Vista's instructions as it walks you through the sharing setup process. Here's how to share a card reader:

1. Right-click on it from your Computer explorer and select Share... as shown in Figure 10.7.

2. Vista treats the card reader like a disk drive, so click the Advanced Sharing button to reveal the additional options shown in Figure 10.8.

FIGURE 10.7

You can share things besides printers over your network.

FIGURE 10.8

Chose the sharing options and name the devices so that others will recognize it when they see it on the network.

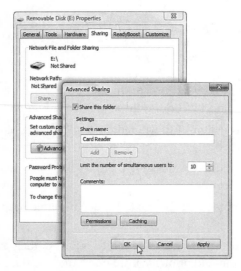

The Absolute Minimum

If you have more than one computer, it's worthwhile to set up a home network so that you can more easily share data and hardware resources (such as a printer or an Internet connection). Setting up a home network has been greatly simplified in Windows Vista. In particular, look into the following features:

- To set up a network, you need multiple computers or other network devices with supported network connections (typically an Ethernet connector or Wi-Fi wireless support). You also need a device (or devices) to let them all communicate with each other. Either a separate broadband mode and router/switch or, even better, an all-in-one broadband modem, router, switch, and wireless device.

- Windows Vista includes a Network Setup feature that automates simple setups and guides you step by step through the process of more complex operations.

- After a network is set up, you and other authorized users can share files. To do so, you must enable file sharing.

- You can also share a printer (thereby printing to the networked printer) or other device (such as a camera card reader), as well as an Internet connection.

- Security is a big issue for networking. Make sure that you turn on and keep on firewall protection (see Chapter 8, "Ensuring Security and Privacy"). Remember to enable wireless security features, such as encryption. These are often tuned off when you purchase a new device.

PART III

DIGITAL MEDIA

11

PLAYING MUSIC, DVDS, AND GAMES

Windows Vista includes what some might argue is an overwhelming array of entertainment features that can turn your PC into a boom box, music mixer, radio, video player, television, PVR box (like a TiVo), and even a movie editor and DVD authoring tool. This chapter covers the basics of these entertainment elements.

Playing Audio CDs with Windows Media Player

It's easy to play audio CDs on your computer using Vista. In addition to playing music you can adjust the volume, view visualizations (abstract patterns that change with the audio content), download track and performer information for the CD, and more.

The first time you place a CD or other disc containing entertainment media into your computer's CD/DVD or optical drive Vista asks if you would like to play it, and it might give you a choice of players as well as other options. For example, inserting a music CD for the first time displays the AutoPlay dialog box shown in Figure 11.1. Click on the desired player you want to use or action you want to take.

FIGURE 11.1

You can control how media files are handled by selecting options here.

Placing (leaving) a checkmark in the Always do this for audio CDs box shown in Figure 11.1 tells Vista to automatically use the option you selected (Media Player in this case) to play CDs, henceforth.

If the CD Doesn't Play Automatically

If the CD does not play automatically when you insert it, your drive might not be set up for AutoPlay, so, do the following:

1. Choose Computer from the Start Menu.
2. Right-click on the CD as shown in Figure 11.2.
3. Choose Play to Play the CD or Open AutoPlay to display the dialog box shown in Figure 11.1, so you can enable AutoPlay for CDs.

When playing a CD using Vista's Media Player, if you are connected to the Internet Vista downloads the title, a thumbnail photo of the disc cover, artist, performer, and track information, and it displays all this as the disc plays. For example, in the next section in Figure 11.3,

caution

You can use many different programs to play music, and your computer might be set up to use a program other than Vista's Media Player as the default. Popular media players include RealPlayer, MusicMatch Jukebox, and iTunes. If you use one of these programs, you can accomplish the same tasks covered in this chapter. For the exact steps to follow, consult your particular program's online help.

Vista is telling us about a disc called *The Quiet Earth: Dusk*. The name of the track being played is displayed ("The Tides of Time"). You also see the length of each track in minutes and seconds. The current song is highlighted in the playlist.

If you see generic names (Track 1, Track 2, and so on), you can often download the track information by connecting to the Internet. Some obscure discs and discs you or your friends create do not have track information downloadable from the Web. However, you can manually enter information for any music track on your computer.

FIGURE 11.2

Right-click on a CD (or other media disc) icon to play it or open the AutoPlay dialog box.

Working with Windows Media Player Controls

The Media Player window provides several buttons for controlling the playback of the CD. These controls let you adjust the volume, skip tracks, and start and stop the playback. Hovering your mouse over the controls displays tips telling you each control's function. Figure 11.3 identifies the basic controls. With these controls (moving from left to right), you can do any of the following:

- To play a particular track, double-click it in the track list.
- To play the next track, click Next. To play the previous track, click Previous.
- To change the volume, drag the volume control. You might also want to adjust the volume button on your computer's external speakers.
- To mute the music (say when you get a phone call), click the Mute button.

Go to the URGE online music store

FIGURE 11.3

You can use the controls in the Windows Media Player window to play a different track, change the volume, and more.

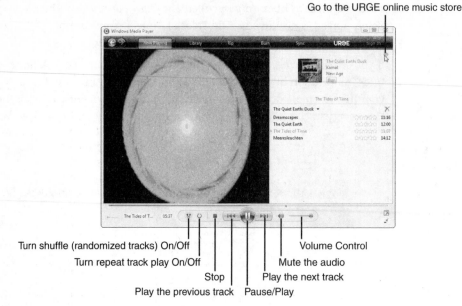

Turn shuffle (randomized tracks) On/Off

Turn repeat track play On/Off

Stop

Play the previous track

Pause/Play

Play the next track

Mute the audio

Volume Control

■ To stop the playback, click Stop. If you stop and want to restart, click the Play button again.

■ To pause the playback, click Pause. To restart, click the Play button. (The Pause button becomes the Play button.)

■ If you want to shuffle the order the tracks are played, click the Turn shuffle on button. (This button is a toggle; click it again to turn shuffle off.)

■ To keep the music playing, but hide the Media Player window, click its Minimize button.

■ To stop the music and close Media Player, click the Close button.

tip

See the next two sections for help on changing the Player colors and switching the Player skin.

Changing the Appearance of the Window

You can change the appearance of the Media Player window in numerous ways. For example you can change the color scheme or select completely different designs called *skins*. There are many free skins available for download—some of them are pretty outrageous and fun.

These are what personal computing is all about. You can experiment and pick the style you like.

To change the player's appearance, follow these steps:

1. Open the Windows Media Player from the Start menu.

2. Right-click anywhere on the bottom of the Player to reveal pop-up menus like those shown in Figure 11.4.

3. Right-click on the bottom border of the Media Player window, select the View menu and choose Skin Chooser to see a list of available skins, and select one.

4. Click Apply Skin. Your newly designed player appears. Figure 11.5 shows an example of an alternate skin. Cool, huh?

To change the player's color scheme, follow these steps:

1. Open the Media Player from the Start Menu.

2. Click the down arrow underneath the Now Playing tab.

3. Open the Enhancements submenu and select Color Chooser to see a set of sliders you can use for color adjustments to the window's elements (see Figure 11.6).

tip

You can click the More Skins button in the Skin Chooser to go online and select from other Windows Media Player skins.

tip

With some of the skins, the control buttons are not easy to figure out. If you use a new skin, you might need to experiment to figure out which button does what. Also, remember you can display a button's name by placing the mouse pointer on the edge of the button as seen in Figure 11.6.

FIGURE 11.4

Right-click near the bottom left of the Player to reveal menus for changing the look of the Windows Media Player window and more.

FIGURE 11.5
FIGURE 11.5
One of perhaps
hundreds of free
Media Player
skins available
online.

FIGURE 11.6
Use the sliders to
change the color
scheme.

Changing the Visualization

In addition to changing the appearance
of the player, you can choose from several
visualizations. A *visualization* is a moving
graphic image displayed during audio, making
music or even spoken words a more multimedia experience. Again, pick the style you
like best. You might want to vary them
according to your mood.

To select a visualization, do the following:

1. Open the Media Player from the Start
   menu.

note

You can also access the
Visualizations menu by
clicking the down arrow underneath the Now Playing tab.

2. Right-click in the visualization area of the Player window to reveal pop-up menus like those shown in Figure 11.7.

3. Choose a new visualization from the available menus and submenus.

FIGURE 11.7
Right-click in the visualization area to select different styles.

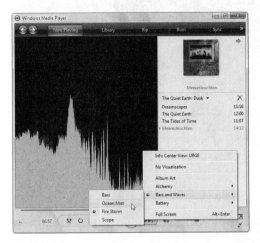

Playing Music and Videos from the Internet

In addition to enjoying audio CDs, you can go online to collect and play music. You can also listen to online radio or play videos using Windows Media Player. This section discusses these Windows Media Player features.

Finding Music Online

Windows Media Player conveniently provides access to its new music site, Urge. Urge does require that you sign up for an account; however, after you sign up you can find music and also videos and other links (see Figure 11.8). Click the Urge button in the Media Player and follow the directions to get started.

After you are logged on, you can browse Urge's entire catalog of music. You can even choose to sample music from this site. For instance, you can listen to the sample tracks of a new CD to see if you want to purchase it.

tip

If you are not connected, you are prompted to log on to your Internet provider so that you can access the online site.

Buying Music Online

You can also download free or purchased music from this site. To do so, click the link for the song you want to download. New songs are often listed on the start page, but you can also use other links to view current songs. Figure 11.8, for instance, shows some songs that were available for downloading.

FIGURE 11.8
Microsoft Urge is where Bill Gates would like you to buy your tunes and more.

Viewing Video Files

The Windows Media Player is not just for playing music. You can also view video clips and animations. These might be files sent to you (such as a video clip of a friend's wedding), files you have created, or files you have downloaded from the Internet, such as movie trailers. To playback a video, double-click the video file.

You can also access online sites and view clips from these sites. To playback an online clip, click the link for that particular video. For instance, www.youtube.com has an endless supply of entertaining (and sometimes disturbing) free video you can watch online.

Using and Synching Other Media Players

In addition to Urge, you can find many other sites devoted to music where you can get information about CDs and artists, hear sound clips of tracks, purchase discs, and download music, audio books, and more to your computer. Popular sites include iTunes.com, MusicMatch.com, and Realplayer.com.

You can sometimes download free music, such as promotional songs. You can also purchase and download specific songs or entire albums. At iTunes, for instance, you pay $.99 for each song. If you use another player, follow the specific instructions for using that player to purchase, download, play, and handle music files.

caution

One hassle is that sites usually require you to use their player to play their music files. For instance, you must download and use the iTunes Player to play (and copy to a CD) music files from iTunes.com.

Ripping Music to Your PC and Recording Your Own CDs

With Windows Media Player (and other players), you can create your own digital juke-box. You can transfer or "rip" music from your CD collection to digital music files that reside on your computer's hard drive. You can then playback any of your ripped music using customized playlists. If you have a playlist you particularly like, you can record or "burn" it to a recordable CD (called a CD-R) or portable digital music player.

For instance, you might create a CD with party tunes for an upcoming event. Or you might create a CD for a friend, sharing your latest favorite songs. You can create a CD from any songs on your computer. This section covers the basics of ripping and burning music using Windows Media Player.

Ripping (Copying) Music Files

If you want to use Windows Media Player as your ultimate digital jukebox, all your music (and video) files need to be stored in Media Player's Library, which is to say, all your music and video must be stored on your hard drive. This includes music you have downloaded from Urge or another online music vendor using Windows Media Player, any music already on your computer (such as sample songs that might be included with Windows Media Player), and songs you have copied to the Media Library from your CD collection.

To copy music from existing music CDs to your Library in Media Player, follow these steps:

1. Insert the music CD into the CD drive; when the player appears, stop its playback (if it starts playing automatically).

2. Click the Rip button to display and select the tracks you want to copy from the CD. To select a track, make sure its checkbox is checked. If you don't want to include a track, uncheck its checkbox (see Figure 11.9).

FIGURE 11.9

Select the songs you want to copy (rip) from the CD.

3. When all the tracks you want to rip are selected, click the Start Rip button to copy the music files to your hard dive.

By default, the files you rip to your PC are copied from the music CD to the Music folder for your user account (click Start, Music to see this folder). Windows Media Player also puts the ripped music data into your media Library. It does take time to rip tracks from a CD (maybe a minute per song, depending on the speed of your drive and the length of each track), but you see a progress report as Vista rips away, letting you know things are progressing.

After the process is complete, you're free to use Windows Media Player to play the music you've ripped directly from your hard dive; no CD required!

caution

When copying any media files, be sure that you understand the legal ramifications of copyright protection. You are allowed to copy music to your hard drive when it is from a CD that you've purchased. However, you are not allowed to copy music you don't own, nor does the law permit you to circumvent any built-in copy-protection mechanisms a disc might have, even if you have no intent of infringing on anyone's copyright.

Creating a Playlist

Playlists let you specify which songs you want to play in which order. Think of them as ways to create your own personal radio station. For example, you can create a playlist for exercising, another for relaxing, and so on. To do so, follow these steps:

1. Open the Windows Media Player, and select the Library tab. You should see a listing in the Navigation pane on the left side of the window listing various parts of your music library (see Figure 11.10).

2. Click the Create Playlist entry in the Navigation pane (refer to Figure 11.10) and then type a name for the playlist.

3. Click on the name of your newly created playlist to open a List pane on the right side of the Media Player window (in Figure 11.11 you see List pane for a playlist I've called "Road Trip").

4. Next, click on the Songs entry located below the Library heading in the Navigation pane. This reveals a detailed

note

If you don't see icons along the left of the screen similar to those in Figure 11.11, Media Player might be operating in a special condensed mode. Hold down the Ctrl key and press the 1 key. This puts Media player back into "Full" mode. (If you want to go back to the condensed window you can press Ctrl+2.)

listing of every song in your media library. To add songs to your playlist, select and drag them to the List pane on the right (see Figure 11.12).

5. When you've added all the desired tracks, click the Save Playlist button in the List pane.

FIGURE 11.10

Place the Windows player in Full mode (Ctrl+1) to see the lists on the left.

FIGURE 11.11

Click the playlist you want to create or edit.

Using and Editing Playlists

Use your playlists to hear just the songs you want, in the order you want them, right on your computer; you can also copy songs to a CD (the topic of the next section).

To listen to a playlist on your computer just double-click its name in the Media Player's Navigation pane. You can rearrange songs anytime you like by dragging them around your playlist. Don't worry, deleting songs from a playlist does not delete them from your library, just from the list.

Remember to click the Save Playlist button after making changes to your lists!

tip

You can also reorder the way songs are displayed in the Music Library by clicking on the headings in the Library section of the Navigation pane. For example to sort music by Genre, click on its label and all the Blues songs will appear together, and so on. Clicking on Artists arranges the Library by artist, and so on.

FIGURE 11.12

Drag songs from your Library to the new playlist.

Navigation pane   Songs and albums in your music library

List pane

Burning Songs to a CD

You can copy songs to a CD either using a playlist or by simply dragging the desired songs manually. Here's how to put songs on blank CDs using either method:

1. In Windows Media Player, click the Burn tab near the top of the player's window (see Figure 11.13).

2. Insert a blank audio CD.

3. Drag individual songs or albums from your music Library to the Burn List on the right side of the screen. If you want to burn a saved playlist, just drag it to the Burn List from the Navigation pane. Media Player shows you how much space remains on the blank disk as you work (51 minutes remains in Figure 11.13).

FIGURE 11.13

Drag individual songs, albums, or playlists to the left window pane.

4. When ready, click Start Burn. The songs are copied to the CD.

You can also copy the playlists from your computer to a portable music player, such as an MP3 player. To do so, connect your player and then select the Sync tab. It works almost exactly like the Burn tab except that you drag your music to the "Sync List" and then click the Start Sync button to transfer music to your portable digital audio player.

ABOUT DIGITAL MUSIC FILE FORMATS

Digital music can be recorded in a variety of different formats. The two primary formats that Windows Media Player supports are MP3 (MPEG 3) and WMA (Windows Media Audio). By default, Media Player records to the WMA format, but you can change that by selecting the down arrow under the Rip tab and choosing a new option from the Format menu.

Although WMA files works with most applications and portable players, MP3 is by far the most universal format. Where WMA, for example, does not work with Apple's popular iPod, but MP3 files do.

There are other proprietary formats, most notably the AAC (Advanced Audio Coding) format that Apple's iPod supports. To play AAC files in Vista, however, you need to download a media player application that supports it, such as Apple's iTunes.

Playing a DVD

Popping a DVD into a DVD-compatible drive on your computer launches the Media Player and lets you watch and control the video. If you have the Home Premium or Ultimate editions of Vista you have the option of playing your DVDs using Windows Media Center instead of using Windows Media Player. (Generally, you only use the Media Center option if you have your PC connected to your TV.) Figure 11.14 shows the Windows Media Player at work, and Figure 11.15 shows the Media Center in use.

Pausing and Restarting a DVD Playback

You stop, start, and navigate DVDs the same way you do audio discs. Some DVDs also contain onscreen menu choices you can select by pointing and clicking onscreen with your mouse.

tip

Many new keyboards (particularly notebook keyboards) have media control buttons on them that replicate the onscreen Play, Stop, Pause, Volume, and other controls. In many cases, these keys simply work just as they're intended. If you find that they don't work with Windows Media Player or Media Center, consult your computer's documentation (or the documentation for your keyboard, if you purchased it separately) for additional information.

Creating Home Movies

Vista comes with a completely revamped version of Windows Movie Maker that lets you combine video clips you have gathered from the Web, shot with your camcorder, and otherwise acquired. You can trim the clips, add a variety of cool transitions between the clips, and add music, voice-over tracks, titles, and much more. Then you can publish your finished work on the Internet, and create DVDs complete with menus and other features formerly out of reach to all but the wealthy few. Figure 11.16 gives you just a taste of this powerful program. Dive into the onscreen help for the program to learn more. It's simple to use and addicting.

FIGURE 11.16

Vista's Movie
maker lets you
create edited
videos for the
Web, DVDs, and
more.

Playing Games

Vista consolidates games into their own separate world, and parents can now use a
variety of game rating systems to decide which games are appropriate for each of
their children. In addition, by setting up individual user accounts for each child (see
Chapter 16, "Setting Up Windows Vista for Multiple Users"), parents can specify
which children can play which games and even control when and how long games
can be played. Figure 11.17 shows the Games Explorer.

FIGURE 11.17

Vista's new
Games Explorer
gives you easy
access to all the
games installed
on your PC.

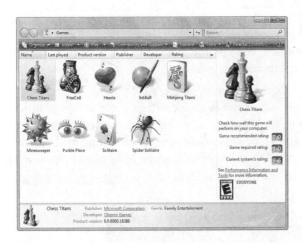

If games are designed according to Microsoft's specifications, when installed they
show up in the Game Explorer, reached by choosing Games on the Start Menu. By
selecting a game in the Games Explorer, Vista brings up as much information as it
has about the game, including its publisher, ESRB rating (these work like movie or
TV ratings), and when it was last played.

To play a game using the Games Explorer, just double-click it. (Note that although the games that come with Windows Vista play immediately upon being launched, most games require their CD or DVD to be inserted in your disc drive before they launch.)

Windows Media Center

The lines between televisions, home stereos, still cameras, and other forms of entertainment are blurring. It's not unusual to see new computers advertised with built-in television tuners, for example.

Many people hook their computers up to their home theater systems so that they can listen to their MP3 playlists through high-quality audio components and operate their PC using their big screen TV as their primary display. In fact, digital photos can look absolutely stunning on a plasma television monitor, and "slideshow" software can make watching the photos more fun.

If you own an edition of Vista that supports Windows Media Center (that is, if you have either Vista Home Premium or Vista Ultimate), and if your computer is properly equipped (first and foremost you need a connector that can connect to your TV), then Media Center features can become the hub of your home entertainment experience.

> **tip**
>
> There are special remote controls designed with Media Center in mind. If you use Media Center as part of your home theater, it's well worth getting a remote that specifically works with Media Center. To increase your level of control, get a wireless mouse and keyboard so that you're not tied to being just a few feet from your PC when using Media Center.

It's even possible to have your TV-connected computer record television shows to a disk so that you can time shift programs, pause and rewind them, skip commercials, and so on, similar to the way people use their TiVo boxes. Figure 11.18 shows the main screen for the Media Center with its unique navigation (navigating in Windows Media Center is a bit different from the usual ways you interact with Windows Vista and can take some getting used to).

FIGURE 11.18

Vista's Media Center (available only in Premium editions) lets your properly equipped PC become a television with a TiVo like recorder and much more.

Much More to Explore!

As you can see from this chapter, Vista is opening up many new ways to entertain ourselves with our computers. Take some time to explore and experiment with these new features. You won't break anything and can broaden your horizons.

THE ABSOLUTE MINIMUM

This chapter explores some of the ways you can use Windows Vista as an entertainment system. You can play audio CDs, go online and view video clips, play music tracks, and more. When working with entertainment media, keep these key points in mind:

- To use the media features, you must have the proper hardware, and you must have the hardware set up. To play music, you need speakers or earphones.

- You can play virtually all audio CDs, DVDs, MP3 and MP4 files, and online streaming media using the Windows Media Player (and Media Center if you have a Premium edition). When playing discs, you can select a different track, adjust the volume, view visualizations, and more.

- If you want to personalize your Media Player, you can do so by selecting skins, changing colors, selecting different display and view options, and more. Experiment!

- You can use Windows Media Player to copy (rip) music from audio CDs to your computer's disk-based music library. You can then create playlists from all of your various tracks. You can playback these lists or use them to create your own custom CDs or download selections to portable players.

- Create your own edited videos and DVDs with Vista's improved Movie Maker complete with titles, music, professional looking transitions, and more.

- Vista Home Premium and Vista Ultimate come with Windows Media Center, a collection of entertainment features worth exploring. Although not a requirement, many of these features work best when your computer is hooked up to external consumer devices, such as plasma screens, stereo components, and so on.

12

WORKING WITH PHOTOGRAPHS

Digital cameras have become more and more popular and affordable. One reason is that they provide some additional benefits over traditional cameras. This chapter examines the basics of setting up a digital camera to work with Windows Vista and working with the picture files. You can print or email the pictures or order prints of the pictures from online photo services.

In addition to using a camera, you can also scan images from a book or scan an existing photograph and use these pictures. For instance, you might scan in old family photographs so that you have a safe digital copy. You might scan in copies of receipts to save. (In some ways, a scanner can be a lot like a copier, only you can edit scanned images.) You can edit, print, and share these photos, just as you can with digital photos captured with a camera. This chapter also examines using a scanner.

Using a Digital Camera

A digital camera works basically the same way as a regular camera, and the features available on a particular camera are similar. That is, to take a picture with a digital camera, you point and shoot. Instead of film, though, the digital camera saves the image in its internal memory or on a special memory card. You can then copy the pictures from the camera's memory or its card to your computer for editing, printing, emailing, and so on.

You can find a wide range of cameras. High-end cameras provide higher quality pictures and have extra features, such as swappable lenses, zoom features, and so on. With some cameras, you can even shoot and store a short video.

The exact steps for using your particular camera vary depending on the model you have. Consult the documentation that came with the hardware to learn how to take pictures. Taking pictures isn't difficult, but you need to learn about the special features of the camera including the following:

note

Cameras range in price from under $100 to several thousand dollars. You can find reviews of digital cameras in several camera and computer publications and websites. Before shopping, read the reviews so that you know what key features you need and what the price range is for those features.

- Some cameras let you shoot pictures at different resolutions (quality or sharpness of the image). You usually select the resolution from the camera's menu system or with a dial on the camera. Quality affects how the pictures look and how big the file is (how much memory is used to store the image). The higher the quality, the more memory it takes and the fewer pictures you can store at one time on your camera.

- Most cameras enable you to preview the picture immediately after you take it. Don't like it? Delete it and reshoot the picture. This is one of the great benefits of a digital camera. You no longer waste film on "bad" pictures. Your camera has methods for scrolling through the pictures stored in memory and deleting any images you choose not to keep.

- Digital cameras don't use film. As mentioned, the images are stored in the camera's internal memory or on a memory card (often called a SmartMedia or CompactFlash card). When the memory is full, you can download the pictures to your computer via a cable and then delete the images from the camera's memory. You can then take your next batch of pictures. Your camera most likely came with a cable used to attach the camera to your computer, although some newer cameras have support for wireless connections to your PC. Also, a photo program for transferring, viewing, and even editing the pictures might come with the camera. Although these also vary from camera to camera, it's important to keep in mind that Vista comes with a capable program in Windows Photo Gallery.

Some cameras can save pictures to a floppy disk or CD directly. For instance, Sony's Mavica line offers these capabilities.

- You can print your pictures on a regular printer (the quality will be so-so) or on a special photo printer with special photo paper. Also, you can order prints online from printing services, and you can take your camera storage media (the memory card) to regular film service sites and have them developed. You learn more about this in the section "Printing Pictures on a Printer" later in this chapter.

Using a Scanner

Another way to work with photos and other illustrations is with a scanner. With a scanner, you can take any image—photographs, drawings, documents, and so on—and scan the image, saving it as a file on your computer. Many scanners come with software that enables you to work with the image after it's scanned. Similar to pictures, you can then modify, print, and email the image. You can even include the image within a document. For instance, you can scan a picture of your family and insert it in your annual Christmas letter. (The next section covers the basics of setting up a camera or scanner.)

Setting Up and Connecting Your Digital Camera or Scanner

Windows Vista recognizes common cameras and scanners, so often you need only to attach the device to your computer and Windows Vista recognizes the new hardware and sets it up automatically. You know this is happening because Windows Vista prompts you with messages in the notification tray that pops up and tells you that the device has been recognized and configured to work with Vista. Thereafter when you connect the device, AutoPlay runs and prompts you to decide on an action. For instance, with a camera, you can select to import pictures or take no action.

If you have a camera or scanner that Windows Vista does not recognize, you can set it up manually using the Scanner and Camera Installation Wizard. Follow these steps:

1. Open the Windows Control Panel (click Start, Control Panel), click the Hardware and Sound link, and then click the link for Scanners and Cameras. You see the list of installed devices on your computer (see Figure 12.1).

2. Click Add Device. This starts the Scanner and Camera Installation Wizard.

3. If prompted to confirm permission to make this change, click Allow.

tip

In many cases, you can download drivers from the camera or scanner manufacturer's website to your PC. To use downloaded drivers you still click the Have Disk button, but instead of choosing a floppy, CD, or DVD drive to find the files, navigate to the folder where you downloaded the files.

FIGURE 12.1

You can view installed cameras and scanners and select to install new ones starting from this Control Panel window.

4. You are prompted to select the device you want to add based on a list of manufacturers and models (see Figure 12.2). Select the manufacturer and then the model of your device. Click Next.

Or

If your particular device is not listed, find the CD, DVD, or floppy disk that came with the scanner or camera. (This disc usually contains the configuration files, called drivers, Vista needs to recognize your device.) Click the Have Disk button and then select the

caution

If you are unable to locate a driver for your camera or scanner that is compatible with Vista, you are unable to connect the device. Try looking for a driver later. As Vista is on the market longer, camera and scanner companies will most likely update their drivers so that the device will work with Vista. Initially, though, you might have to wait.

drive to which you've inserted the disc (if necessary use the Browse button to specify the drive). After Windows Vista has located the driver, click Next.

5. Type a name for the device and then click Next.

6. In the final confirmation dialog box, click the Finish button.

FIGURE 12.2

You can use a wizard to help you set up a camera or scaner manually.

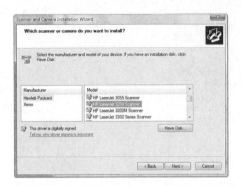

Getting the Digital Image from the Camera or Scanner to Your Computer

After you take your pictures, you need to copy them from the camera to the computer. To capture a scanned image, you need to use your scanner and the program provided for scanning the image. This section gives you an overview of how these tasks work, but keep in mind the actual process varies depending on your particular camera or scanner, so follow those instructions. (This section helps you understand what's generally involved and how simple the process usually is in case you are considering getting a camera or scanner.)

Transferring Pictures from a Digital Camera

The first step in working with pictures is copying them from your camera to your computer. The basic mechanics of using a digital camera is that you take the pictures and then download them to your computer. The steps vary depending on your camera setup, but the general process for transferring pictures is as follows:

1. Connect the camera to your computer via a cable. Usually the type of cable used is called a USB cable. In some cases you might have to remove the camera's memory card and connect it your computer via a connector specific to the type of memory card. (It depends on how your particular digital camera was designed. Check your camera manual if you are unsure.)

2. After the camera is connected, Vista should recognize your camera or memory card and display available options for transferring the images to your computer (see Figure 12.3).

3. Select any options for the download. For instance, you might choose to delete the pictures from the camera's memory after downloading. As another option, you might select to download only some of the images or all the images. Follow the specific instructions for your camera using your manual or online help as a guide.

FIGURE 12.3

When you connect a device, like a camera, AutoPlay usually runs and prompts you to select what action to take.

Importing Images Using Windows Photo Gallery

As another option, you can use Windows Vista new Windows Photo Gallery to import pictures. Follow these steps:

1. Connect the camera to your computer via a cable.
2. Click Start, All Programs, and then Windows Photo Gallery. (You learn more about Windows Photo Gallery later in this chapter.)
3. Click File and then Import from Camera or Scanner.
4. Select the camera and click Import (see Figure 12.4).

FIGURE 12.4

You can manually import images using Windows Photo Gallery.

5. Optionally, type a tag that will be applied to all imported pictures (see Figure 12.5). You learn more about tags in "Adding Tags to Pictures" later in this chapter.
6. Click Import and the pictures are imported.

FIGURE 12.5
You can tag pictures as you import them.

Scanning Images

In general, if you have a flatbed scanner (like a copy machine), you insert the picture or document you want to scan and then use the commands in the scanner program window to start the scan. The options vary. For instance, you're often able to select either a black-and-white scan or color scan as well as the quality of the scan. Because the available program options vary, you need to check your own particular program for specific instructions.

After the document is scanned into the scan program, you have options for modifying, saving, and working with the image using the program provided with the scanner. For instance, you might be able to crop, rotate, add text, and more. You can also print, email, rename, and insert the image into documents. See the section "Managing Picture Files Using the Windows Photo Gallery" in this chapter for more information.

> **tip**
>
> You aren't limited to scanning just pictures. You can scan newspaper articles, bank statements, receipts, and other document types. This section focuses on pictures because these are most likely the type of image you work with that need editing changes. Keep in mind that you can also make changes to more "document" type files.

Using Windows Pictures Folder

Windows includes a Pictures folder which is listed on the Start menu and in the Navigation pane. It's a good idea to store all your pictures in this one folder because you have such fast access to it from several places. You can also work with the pictures in this file, doing file management (see Figure 12.6). That is, you can rename, delete, copy, and otherwise do file-management tasks from this Explorer. Treat the pictures as any other file. (See Chapter 3, "Managing Files," for more information on working with files.) Keep these tips in mind:

- Picture files can be large. You usually don't want to permanently store them on your hard disk. Instead, you can work with them and then print or email them. After that task is done, you can consider a more efficient storage media. For instance, you can copy them to a CD or DVD. (Chapter 3 details how to copy several files to a CD.)

■ You might also simply want to delete the picture files. (If you keep all your picture negatives from a traditional camera, you'll want to save them to another media. If you throw out the negatives after receiving your prints, you might want to delete some if not all of the picture files.) To delete a picture, select the file, click the Delete button, and then click Yes to confirm the deletion.

FIGURE 12.6

View the pictures stored in Windows Pictures folder.

In addition, Windows has provided the new Windows Photo Gallery that pulls pictures and other media into one Explorer. Because this Explorer offers more features, it's the main focus for working with picture files and is the topic of the next section.

Managing Picture Files Using the Windows Photo Gallery

To help you keep your pictures organized, Windows Vista has added the Windows Photo Gallery. It organizes your pictures and videos all in one spot and gives you many ways to access them, including by folder, by ratings (if you have tagged them), by date taken, or recently imported. The Photo Gallery also includes some basic options for editing your photos. You can rotate them, fix red eye, crop the picture, adjust the color, and more.

Viewing Pictures in the Windows Photo Gallery

To view the Windows Photo Gallery, follow these steps:

1. Click Start, All Programs, and then Windows Photo Gallery.

2. Use the options in the Navigation pane to navigate to the folder that contains the images you want to view. After you select a type of folder to display, you see the pictures in that folder (see Figure 12.7).

FIGURE 12.7

You can view pictures in Windows Vista's new Windows Photo Gallery.

Navigation pane

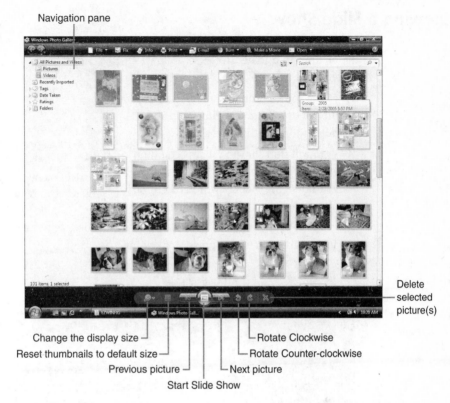

Delete selected picture(s)

Change the display size

Reset thumbnails to default size

Previous picture

Start Slide Show

Rotate Clockwise

Rotate Counter-clockwise

Next picture

3. To view a close-up of a particular picture, double-click it (see Figure 12.8).

4. To return to the Gallery, click Back to Gallery.

FIGURE 12.8

You can open a picture to get a better, closer view of the picture.

Viewing a Slide Show

You can also display a running slide show of all the pictures in a folder. To do so, follow these steps:

1. In the control panel at the bottom of the window, click the Play Slide Show button to start the slide show.

2. Vista will start showing slides beginning with whichever one was selected when you stared the slide show. You can bring up onscreen controls for the slide show by moving the mouse (see Figure 12.9).

3. To stop the slide show, press any key on your keyboard.

tip

If you want to display the next picture more quickly, click the mouse button. You can also right-click the screen during the slideshow to display a shortcut menu. From this menu, you can choose to pause the show, shuffle (show in random order), select the speed, and exit.

FIGURE 12.9

Use the onscreen controls to control how the Windows Photo Gallery slide show feature works.

Current slide

Slide Show controls

Fixing Photographs

You have a few options for editing your pictures using Windows Photo Gallery. You can fix red eye, rotate the picture counterclockwise or clockwise, add a caption, and adjust the colors. Follow these steps to make a change:

1. Open the picture you want to edit.

2. To add a caption to the picture, click <Add Caption> (see Figure 12.10). Then type a caption.

3. To make adjustments to the color or exposure, click the Fix button in the command bar. You see the options for fixing the picture (see Figure 12.11).

4. Do any of the following:

To have Windows automatically make adjustments, click the Auto Adjust option. Click Undo if you don't like the changes. (You can also redo any action that you've undone.)

FIGURE 12.10

You can add a caption to a photo to provide a descriptive title.

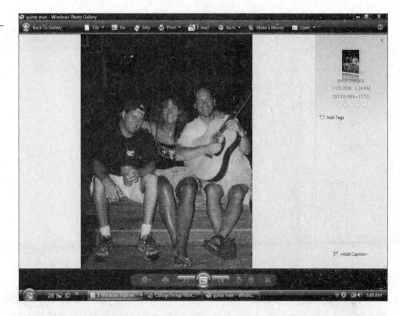

FIGURE 12.11

You can use the available options to adjust the color or fix red eye in Windows Photo Gallery.

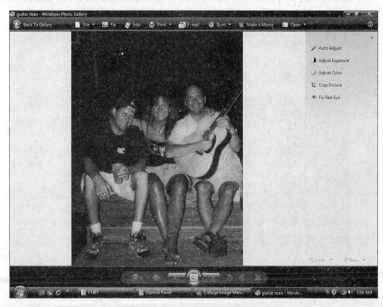

To adjust the exposure or color, click either Adjust Exposure or Adjust Color and then use the drag bars to make changes. For exposure, you can adjust the brightness and contrast (see Figure 12.12). For color, you can adjust the color temperature, tint, and saturation.

To crop the picture, click Crop Picture; a box appears in the photo (see Figure 12.13). Use the box so that it surrounds the area you want to include in the photo. Then click Apply.

FIGURE 12.12

You can change the brightness or contrast of a picture to improve its quality.

FIGURE 12.13

You can crop the picture to key in on a certain area or to get rid of distracting outside elements.

Area to crop to

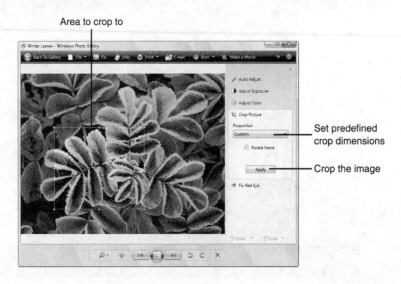

Set predefined crop dimensions

Crop the image

To fix red eye in a photo, click Fix Red Eye and follow the instructions on how to fix red eye for the photos.

Adding Tags to Pictures

You can add tags to help further identify pictures; this helps find pictures and group similar pictures. To add a tag, follow these steps:

1. Open the picture file to which you want to add a tag (just double-click it in Photo Gallery).

2. Click Add Tags.

3. In the Tags box, type the word(s) or phrase(s) you want to use as a tag. To add more than one tag, separate each with a comma.

4. To rate the file, click the stars to assign a rating (see Figure 12.14).

5. Click Back to Gallery to return to other pictures. (You can follow these same steps to add tags or ratings to them.)

tip

To rotate the picture, click the Rotate Counterclockwise or Rotate Clockwise buttons in the bottom pane of the Windows Photo Gallery (refer to Figure 12.7).

tip

If you don't have software or if you want a more sophisticated program, you can purchase a picture-editing program. These range from simple—Adobe's $99 Photoshop Elements—to complex—the complete Adobe Photoshop. You can find other programs besides those created by Adobe, although Adobe is the most popular.

FIGURE 12.14

You can add tags and ratings to a picture.

Picture rating

Tags

Description of image

Once you've added tags, you can use the Navigation pane to sort and organize your photos. Try any of the following:

- The Navigation pane lists the various categories. If the options for that category are not displayed, click the arrow next to the category. For instance, if all the tags are hidden, click the arrow next to Tags in the Navigation pane to display a list of all tags.

- If you used a star rating and want to display only photos with a certain number of stars, click the number of stars under Ratings in the Navigation pane.

- If you added tags and want to view photos with a specific tag, click the specific tag under Tags in the Navigation pane.

- If you want to display pictures by the date taken, click the specific date range (usually by year) under Date Taken.

- To navigate to other picture-related folders, click the specific folder under Folders.

> **note**
>
> The Windows Photo Gallery also lets you access any videos you have stored on your computer as well as public pictures or videos. Use the folders in the Navigation pane to select other Photo Gallery options. You can also select to view recently imported pictures, pictures with their tags, pictures arranged by date taken, and pictures arranged by ratings. Simply select the appropriate folder.

Adding, Printing, and Emailing Pictures

After your pictures are organized, renamed, and touched up (as needed), you can add them to a document or print them on a regular printer or a special photo printer. You can also order prints online through a film service company. To add a picture to a document, you need to follow the specific instructions for that program, but this section gives you an idea of how to perform this task.

Inserting a Picture into a Document

You might want to insert some images into a document. For instance, you might include product pictures in a catalog. Or, as mentioned, you might include family photos in a Christmas letter. As another example, you might insert images into a web document if you want to display them as part of your website.

To insert a picture in a document, look for the appropriate command in the Insert menu. In Word, for instance, you can click the Insert, Picture command. Then select From File or From Scanner or Camera to insert an image from a camera or scanner. Sometimes you can copy a picture to Vista's clipboard (select the picture in your Pictures folder and press Ctrl+C) and then paste it into an open document (by pressing Ctrl+V). If that doesn't work, check with the specific program documentation or online help for the specifics on inserting scanned images.

Printing Pictures on a Printer

Follow these steps to print pictures:

1. Open Windows Photo Gallery.

2. Select the pictures you want to print.

3. Click the Print button and then select Print from the drop-down list.

4. If needed, make any changes to the print options (see Figure 12.15). For instance, you can display the drop-down list and select the printer you want to use. You can select the paper size and quality or resolution of the printed image. You can also select the number of copies to print.

5. Along the right side, scroll through the list of available print layouts and select the one you want for your pictures. Basically these are picture sizes, such as 4×6 or 5×7. If possible, Windows prints as many pictures as will fit on the page (depending on the picture size).

6. Click the Print button. Your pictures are sent to your printer.

tip

If you have more than one page of pictures, you can use the scroll button to scroll to other pages to see how these pages will look when printed.

tip

You won't get photo quality pictures with a regular computer printer. You can, though, purchase special photo printers and photo paper. Expect to pay from $100 to $800 or more for a special photo printer. Some new printers are good for both document, color, and photo printing. Visit computer retail stores to see the various options. The best way to pick a printer? Check the actual printouts from various printers to find one with an acceptable print quality.

FIGURE 12.15
Select the print options from this dialog box.

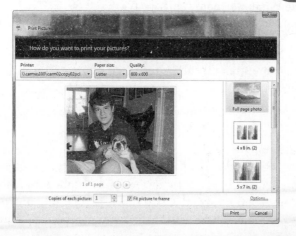

Ordering Photo Prints from the Internet

If you don't get the quality you want from your printer, you can also select to order photo-printing service quality prints from the Internet. Depending on the print service you select, the pricing and options vary, as will the steps you follow. Expect to pay a small shipping charge. For payment, you must supply a credit card number and shipping information. Pictures usually arrive in a few of days. Some services offer several free prints as a trial run.

To order copies from the Internet, you must be connected to it. If you are not connected, you are prompted to do so. When connected, follow these steps to order prints:

1. Open Windows Photo Gallery.

2. Select the pictures you want to print.

3. Click the down arrow next to the Print button and click Order prints.

4. Select the printing company you want to use and then follow the prompts to send your pictures, select the quantity and size, and make other choices.

Emailing Pictures

It's fun to share pictures with friends and family. In addition to printing, you can also email pictures. You might, for instance, email a picture of your new puppy to your friends. You might email pictures from a family reunion to your family members that live out of town. Follow these steps:

1. Open the Windows Photo Gallery.

2. Select the picture(s) you want to email.

3. Click the E-mail button.

4. Select a picture size and click Attach (see Figure 12.16). You then see an email message window.

FIGURE 12.16

You can attach picture files to an email message.

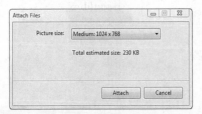

5. Complete the email (recipient, subject, and any message) and send the message. Photo Gallery uses whichever email program is you default to create the email. By default, this is usually Windows Mail. See Chapter 6, "Sending and Receiving Email," for more information on email.

THE ABSOLUTE MINIMUM

This chapter examines some of the fun and exciting things you can do with digital images. Keep these key points in mind:

- You can purchase a digital camera and use it with your computer. A digital camera offers many advantages. You can preview your images after you shoot them, deleting or reshooting as needed. You don't need to purchase film. You can edit the pictures before printing, and you can print, email, or order prints online.

- In addition to cameras, another common imaging device is a scanner. You can use this hardware component to scan in photos, illustrations, documents, and other types of visual or textual information.

- When you attach your camera or scanner, Windows Vista should query it and set it up automatically. If not, you can run the Scanner and Camera Installation Wizard to set up the camera manually.

- Different cameras have different features and work differently. The basics of taking a picture are the same: point and shoot. However, you need to look at your camera's documentation to find out how to change settings, such as image quality and how to preview and handle images.

- You can copy the images from your camera's memory to your computer. You can then work with your pictures. You can make editing changes using Windows Photo Gallery or a photo-editing program.

- You can add tags to a picture file to provide more information; this makes it easier to find the picture and group similar pictures together.

- You can print your pictures on a regular printer or a printer that supports picture printing. Usually you get the best quality when you use a photo printer and special photo paper. You can also order prints online or take your camera's media card to a regular print service bureau and have copies made.

PART IV

CUSTOMIZING YOUR COMPUTER

13

CUSTOMIZING WINDOWS VISTA

Windows Vista provides many customization options that you can use to personalize your computer. Some of these changes are practical. For instance, if you are left-handed, you can change the mouse buttons so that the buttons work for the left hand. If you have trouble seeing the display, you can alter the size (the resolution) of the desktop. If you prefer the taskbar on another part of the desktop, you can move it.

Other changes are purely personal. For instance, you might want to display a picture of your family on your desktop or change your desktop's color. Or you might want to change the sounds that are played for system events (such as a shut down). This chapter examines the most common customization changes. The other chapters in this part of the book cover other customizing options, in particular for setting up programs and for customizing email and Internet Explorer.

Customizing the Taskbar, Notification Area, Toolbars, and Start Menu

The taskbar, although small in size, actually tells you a lot. It lets you know which programs are running and which windows are open. It tells you the time, and shows icons when other activities are going on. For example, if you see a printer icon, you know that your computer is sending data to the printer. If you see a connection icon, you are connected to the Internet.

Customizing the Taskbar

Windows Vista enables you to customize the taskbar and notification area. To make any changes, display the Taskbar and Start Menu Properties dialog box by following these steps:

1. Right-click the taskbar and then click Properties.

2. To hide the taskbar, click the Auto-hide the taskbar check box (see Figure 13.1).

3. To hide the Quick Launch toolbar, uncheck this option.

4. To group similar buttons into a stack, keep Group similar taskbar buttons checked. Or uncheck to turn off this feature.

5. Click the OK button to save any changes.

tip

To access the taskbar while its hidden, put the mouse pointer over the taskbar area, and it reappears.

FIGURE 13.1

You can hide the taskbar if you so choose as well as make other changes.

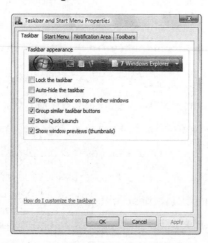

When working with the taskbar, keep these other pointers in mind:

■ You can move the taskbar to another location on the desktop and change its size. To move the taskbar, put the mouse pointer on a blank part of the taskbar and drag it to the location you want. To do so, the taskbar must be unlocked. You can unlock the taskbar by right-clicking it and unchecking the Lock the taskbar option.

- If you want more room to display taskbar icons, you can make it bigger. To resize the taskbar, put the mouse pointer on the border and drag to resize. Note that the taskbar must be unlocked (refer to the preceding bullet).

- If the date and time are incorrect, you can correct them by right-clicking the time display in the taskbar and selecting Adjust Date/Time. Select the correct date and time. You can click on a date in the calendar or display other months or years from the drop-down list to change the date. You can type or edit the correct time in the text box or drag the hands on the clock. When the date and time are correct, click OK. You learn more about adjusting the date and time later in this chapter in the section "Changing the Date and Time."

> **tip**
>
> You can add a password to your account as a security measure. For more information on passwords and setting up other accounts, see Chapter 16, " Setting Up Windows Vista for Multiple Users."

Changing the Notification Area

The notification area appears at the far right of the taskbar and displays icons for programs that are running in the background (like when a document is printing). You also see icons for virus and security programs, and this area displays the clock and volume control. You can modify the notification area to suit your preferences.

Follow these steps:

1. Right-click the taskbar and then click Properties.

2. Click the Notification Area tab (see Figure 13.2).

3. If you want all icons displayed, uncheck the Hide inactive icons check box. (Keep it checked if you want to keep inactive icons hidden.)

4. In the System icons area, check which icons you want displayed. You can select to always show clock, volume, network, and power.

5. Click OK to save any changes.

> **tip**
>
> When inactive icons are hidden or more icons can be displayed, you see a left-pointing arrow next to the notification area. Click this arrow to display additional icons; after a short while it re-hides your inactive icons.

FIGURE 13.2

Customize the Notification Area so that it displays the helpful information you need.

Displaying or Hiding Toolbars

In addition to taskbar buttons and status icons, you can display toolbars in the taskbar. For instance, the Quick Launch toolbar is displayed by default. It enables you to quickly access the Internet and Windows Mail and other commonly used programs. (You can hide it if you want.) You can also display toolbars for Windows Media Player, Internet Address, and others.

To display other toolbars, follow these steps:

1. Right-click the taskbar and then click Properties.

2. Click the Toolbars tab (see Figure 13.3).

tip

Enabling the Windows Media Player toolbar does not have any visible affect on your desktop until you open and minimize Windows Media Player. When you do that instead of minimizing to a taskbar button, Media Player turns itself into a toolbar on your taskbar that you can use to control it without having it displayed on your desktop.

FIGURE 13.3

Want access to other toolbars? Add them to your taskbar.

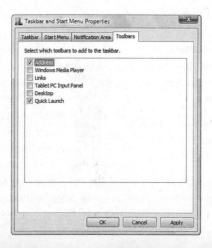

3. Check which toolbars you want displayed and then click OK. The toolbar(s) you selected is displayed. By default, only the Quick Launch toolbar is turned on.

Customizing the Start Menu

In addition to the taskbar, notification area, and toolbars, you also have several options for what appears on the Start menu. You can select whether recently opened files and programs appear.

Follow these steps to customize the Start menu:

1. Right-click a blank area of the taskbar and click Properties.
2. Click the Start Menu tab (this tab may be selected by default).
3. Check (or uncheck) the options for displaying recently opened files or programs (see Figure 13.4).

FIGURE 13.4

You can display (or hide) recently opened files or programs.

4. To make additional changes, make sure the default Start menu is selected and then click the Customize button next to this option.
5. In the list of options, scroll through and view and make changes to how the Start menu appears (see Figure 13.5). For instance, you can check items that you want displayed, such as a Favorites menu or the Run command. For the most part, these changes are more for the advanced user, but you can see what choices are available.
6. Use the spin arrows or type the number of recently used programs you want displayed on the Start menu.
7. Select whether you want your shortcuts for your default Internet or E-mail programs to appear on the Start menu. If the option is checked, it appears. Uncheck it to turn it off. You can also select which programs are used by displaying the drop-down list and selecting the program you want

to use. (This feature is available if you have more than one email or Internet program.)

8. Click OK when you have completed your changes.

FIGURE 13.5

You can customize aspects of the Start menu.

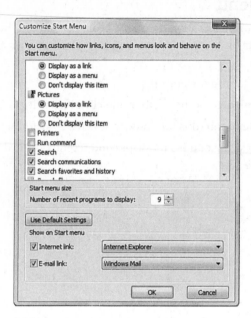

In addition to these changes, keep these options in mind:

- To return to the default settings, return to the Customize menu and click the Use Default Settings button.

- The Classic Menu is a menu that looks like the Start menu from previous versions of Windows. You can elect to use this style of menu and customize it. Because most users have now gotten used to the new style, most users don't mess around with changing to a now outdated and different Start menu. You can select this menu from the Start Menu tab and then to make changes, click the Customize button next to the option. The customization changes are not detailed here because most users stick with the standard Start menu, especially beginners.

Customizing the Desktop

You have several choices for customizing the desktop. You can use a desktop theme, change the color scheme, display an image or different color, use a screen saver, and more. You make these changes from the Personalization Control Panel, which you can access by right-clicking the desktop and selecting Personalize (see Figure 13.6).

FIGURE 13.6

You can make many changes to the visual aspects of Vista using this window.

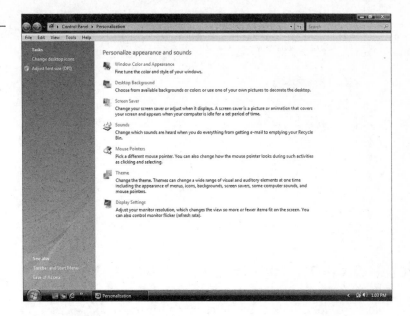

The following sections describe how to make changes to these options.

Using a Desktop Theme

Desktop themes consist of background, sounds, icons, and other elements. Windows Vista offers numerous color-coordinated themes to choose from; alternatively, you can create your own.

To use a desktop theme, follow these steps:

1. Right-click an empty spot on your desktop and select Personalize from the pop-up menu that appears.

2. Click Theme.

3. In the Theme Settings dialog box, display the Theme drop-down list and select a theme (see Figure 13.7).

4. Click OK to apply the theme.

> **tip**
>
> If you make any changes to any of the other settings discussed in this chapter (such as displaying an image), Windows creates a "modified theme" and lists this as the selected theme on the Themes tab. You can save it by clicking the Save As button and typing a name for this theme. Then click the Save button. The theme is added to the Themes drop-down list. If you want to return to the default theme, select Windows Vista from the theme drop-down list.

FIGURE 13.7

You can select a theme or combination of customization changes that relate to the desktop.

Changing the Color Scheme

Windows Vista enables you to change the sets of colors used for certain onscreen elements, such as the title bar, background, and so on. These sets of colors are called *schemes*, and you can select colors that work best for you and your monitor. Lighter colors might, for example, make working in some Windows applications easier on your eyes. On the other hand, you might prefer bright and lively colors. You can also select an option for Windows and buttons as well as a font size.

To make a change to the desktop color scheme, follow these steps:

1. Right-click an empty spot on your desktop and select Personalize from the pop-up menu that appears.

2. In the Personalization Control Panel, click Window Color and Appearance.

3. Select the color you want to use (see Figure 13.8).

4. To turn on or off Windows Vista transparent windows, check or uncheck Enable transparency. If enabled, you can adjust the amount of transparency by dragging the Transparency slider bar.

5. Click OK.

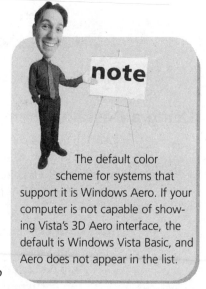

note

The default color scheme for systems that support it is Windows Aero. If your computer is not capable of showing Vista's 3D Aero interface, the default is Windows Vista Basic, and Aero does not appear in the list.

tip

To select a custom color, click Show color mixer and then select a color from the color palette wheel that appears.

FIGURE 13.8

FIGURE 13.8

You can select a different color scheme to change the appearance of your desktop.

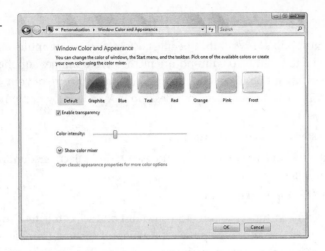

Changing the Desktop Background Color

Another way to personalize your desktop in Windows is to apply a background color. You might choose a different color to make desktop items stand out, or you might choose a different color just because you like it. (Note: The next section examines how to add an image to the desktop.) To make a change, follow these steps:

1. Right-click an empty spot on your desktop and select Personalize from the pop-up menu that appears.

2. Click Desktop Background.

3. If necessary, select Solid Colors from the Picture Location drop-down list.

4. To select a solid color, select a color from the palette and click OK (see Figure 13.9).

FIGURE 13.9

You can use a different color for Windows Vista's background.

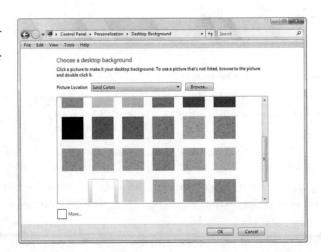

Displaying an Image on Your Desktop

One of the most popular ways that people customize their computers is to add a desktop image. It might be a calm nature picture (from images supplied with Windows), or it might be a personal picture, such as a picture of your child, grandchild, or pet. You can personalize your desktop in Windows by applying a background image.

Follow these steps to make a change:

1. Right-click an empty spot on your desktop and select Personalize from the pop-up menu that appears.

2. Click Desktop Background.

3. Display the Picture Location drop-down list and select the item you want to use as your background. You can select wallpapers, pictures (sample pictures, public pictures, and your pictures), and solid colors (covered in the preceding section). Figure 13.10, for instance, shows some of the sample pictures available.

FIGURE 13.10

Add some pizzazz to your desktop by displaying a desktop image.

4. Select the image you want.

5. Select how the image should be positioned (one big image, the image repeated as thumbnails, or the image in a slide protector).

6. Click OK.

When making changes to the desktop image, keep these tips in mind:

- Depending on what type of background you select, you see different options. You can select the one that suits your needs or likes. You can also experiment to see how each choice looks.

- When you select an image, you can select how it is positioned. You might want one big image, several small repeating images, or an image in a slide frame to fill the screen. These options are listed under the image choices. Click the option button for the one you want.

■ To display one of your own images, select Pictures as the background and then click the Browse button. Navigate to the folder that contains the image, select it, and click Open (see Figure 13.11). Then select the picture from the list of options in the Desktop Background Control Panel and click OK.

FIGURE 13.11

You can select a picture file of your own to use as the background image

Using a Screen Saver

Screen savers are another desktop option. Are they necessary? Not really. On older monitors, an image could be burned into the monitor if the same text or image was displayed for long periods of time. This is not a problem with current monitors. That is, unless you have your computer connected to a plasma display. Mostly, screen savers simply provide some extra spice and a small bit of security for your computer when it is idle.

To use a screen saver, follow these steps:

1. Right-click an empty spot on your desktop and select Personalize from the pop-up menu that appears.

2. Click Screen Saver.

3. Display the Screen Saver drop-down list and select the screen saver you want to use.

4. In the Wait text box, type the number of minutes you want Windows to wait before it starts the screen saver (see Figure 13.12).

5. Click the OK button. The next time your computer is idle for the amount of time specified in step 4, the screen saver is activated. To deactivate the screen saver, press the spacebar to redisplay the screen.

When working with screen savers, keep these pointers in mind:

- To see what the screen saver looks like when it is displayed on the full screen, click the Preview button. Windows displays the saver on the entire screen. Click the mouse button or press the spacebar to turn off the preview.

- You can find screen savers online or for sale in electronic or computer stores. For instance, if you want to display your favorite rapper, you can probably find a screen saver of that person.

- Some screen savers enable you to set options for how they work (3D text, for instance). If these are available, click the Settings button. The options vary depending on the screen saver. Make your choices and click the OK button.

Setting Resolution and Color Settings

The term *resolution* refers to many different things that relate to computers and computer equipment. You might hear resolution as a measure of the quality of a printer, scanner, or camera, for instance. However, in Windows terms, resolution refers to how big or small the images are, and these are measured in pixels, such as 1280×1024. The larger the number, the smaller (and finer) the image. You can change the resolution as another desktop option.

In addition, you can change the number of colors displayed onscreen. To make these changes, follow these steps:

caution

Although a higher resolution is an indicator of a higher quality image, you also need to consider the physical size of your display. Running a high resolution on a small display (such as 1280×1024 on a 15-inch screen) results in text and icons that are small and difficult to read.

1. Right-click an empty spot on your desktop and select Personalize from the pop-up menu that appears.

2. Click Display Settings. You see the available options (see Figure 13.13).

3. To change the size of the images onscreen, drag the resolution bar from left to right. (Make sure you review the following note about what changes Windows Vista will make.)

4. To change the number of colors used for the display, click the Colors drop-down list and choose the number you want. Generally, you want this option set to Highest (32 bit).

5. Click OK.

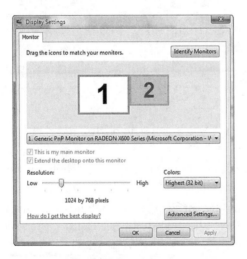

FIGURE 13.13
You can change the size of the items on your desktop by changing its resolution.

Customizing the Mouse

Most PC mice have at least two buttons: a left and right button. The buttons are used for different purposes. The left mouse button is used for most tasks: clicking, dragging, opening menus, selecting commands, selecting text, and so on. The right mouse button is used for less-common tasks. A common use of the right mouse button is to display a shortcut menu.

If you are left-handed, you can change your mouse so that the buttons are reversed: Right does the main options and left does the shortcut menu—much more convenient for you! You can also make other changes to the mouse, including adjusting its double-click speed or changing how the cursors appear. Again, these changes are a mix of practical issues (such as the left-handed change) as well as personal issues (such as the pointer schemes).

To customize your mouse, follow these steps:

1. Right-click an empty spot on your desktop and select Personalize from the pop-up menu that appears.

2. Click Mouse Pointers.

3. If necessary, click the Buttons tab. You see the options for changing how the mouse buttons work (see Figure 13.14).

FIGURE 13.14

Use the Buttons tab to make changes to—you guessed it—how the buttons work.

4. To switch from a right-handed mouse to a left-handed mouse, click Switch primary and secondary buttons.

5. Drag the Double-click speed slider to make the double-click speed faster or slower, depending on your needs.

6. If you want to use a different set of mouse pointers, click the Pointers tab. Then display the Scheme drop-down list (see Figure 13.15) and select a mouse pointer scheme.

7. Click the Pointer Options tab (see Figure 13.16). Use the options to set a pointer speed (drag to make it faster or slower), to have Windows automatically snap the pointer to the default button, and make visibility changes, such as displaying a trail, hiding the pointer while typing, and showing the location of pointer by pressing the Ctrl key.

8. Click OK when you are done making changes.

tip

If you have a mouse with a scroll wheel (most do), you can use the Wheel tab to make adjustments. You can also view hardware information about your mouse by clicking the Hardware tab.

FIGURE 13.15

You can change how the various Windows Vista pointers look to an entirely different set of pointers.

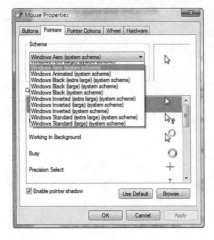

FIGURE 13.16

If the mouse moves too quickly (or slowly) change the pointer speed. You can also make other changes.

Customizing Sounds

Windows plays certain sounds for key system events, such as exiting windows, new mail, log on and log off, and others. You can change these sounds.

To select a different sound scheme, follow these steps:

1. Right-click an empty spot on your desktop and select Personalize from the pop-up menu that appears.

2. Click Sound Effects. If needed, click the Sounds tab.

3. To select a sound scheme, display the Sound Scheme drop-down list and select a scheme or set of sounds (see Figure 13.17).

4. Click OK.

FIGURE 13.17

Select a different set of sounds to alert you to key system events.

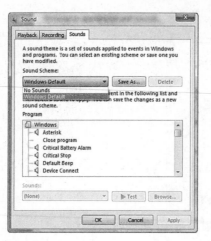

Here are some additional ideas and suggestions for working with sounds:

- To hear a preview of the sound, click the Test button.
- If the sound you want to use is not listed in the Sounds list, click the Browse button. A standard Browse dialog box opens, enabling you to locate and select the sound file you want to use. Sounds must be recorded in the WAV (Wave) sound format for Vista to use them.
- If you don't want a sound played for an event, select that event and choose (None) from the Sounds list.
- You can also change the sound for individual events by selecting the Program event from the list and then displaying the Sounds list and selecting the sound to play.
- If you select a whole set of different sounds, save it as a sound scheme. Click Save As to save the new scheme. Type a name to save the new scheme.
- If an event does not have a sound icon next to it, a sound is not played. You can assign sounds to these items by selecting them and then selecting a sound.

Changing the Date and Time

The notification area always displays the time. (Here's a tip, you can also place the pointer over the time in the taskbar to display the current date.) If your system clock is wrong, you should correct it because Windows stamps the time and date on every file you save.

To make a change, follow these steps:

1. Click the time clock in the Notification area.
2. In the window that appears, click the Change Date and Time Settings link to open the window shown in Figure 13.18.

3. Click Change date and time. If prompted, click Continue to authorize this change.

4. Click the correct date in the calendar (see Figure 13.19). To change the month, click either the right- or left-facing arrows. You can also click the name of the month to "zoom out" the display to show a list of months or even years that you can select.

5. Enter the correct time. You can click on the correct time using the clock or use the time spin boxes to enter the correct time.

6. Click OK to close the Date and Time Settings dialog box.

7. Click OK to close the Date and Time dialog box.

note

As long as you've configured Vista to use the correct time zone and you have an Internet connection, Vista's time should remain accurate. That's because, when connected to the Internet, Vista verifies the data and time online. If the time is incorrect, it might be because you didn't configure Windows to keep the time in sync. Also, an incorrect time or date could be a sign that your battery is going bad. See whether the problem persists and if so, consider replacing your system battery.

FIGURE 13.18
You see the current time settings.

FIGURE 13.19
If your date and time are wrong, adjust them so that file dates are correct.

The Absolute Minimum

This chapter examines some of the many changes you can make to personalize Windows to suit your preferences. In particular, keep the following tips in mind:

- You can make changes to all of the elements of the desktop starting with the taskbar, notification area, Start menu, and toolbars.

- Making a change to the desktop is most often just for the look of it. To access most desktop changes, right-click a blank part of the desktop and select Personalize. You can select a theme for the display, choose a background image, use a screen saver, or change the appearance (color, font, placement) of window elements.

- You can change both how the mouse works and how the mouse pointers appear by using the Mouse Control Panel icon.

- Another common change is using a different sound scheme or selecting different sounds for key system events, such as logging on or logging off.

- If the date and time on your computer are wrong, update them so that they are correct.

14

SETTING UP PROGRAMS

In Chapter 1, "Getting Started with Windows Vista," you learned the basics of how to start a program. In addition to using the Start menu to start programs, you can create shortcut icons to programs. You also can change the Start menu, for example, *pinning* commonly used programs to the main menu (the left side of the menu with Internet and Email). Finally, you can install new programs and uninstall programs you do not use. This chapter covers all these methods for customizing and setting up programs on your computer.

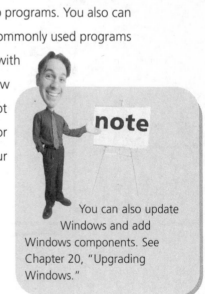

You can also update Windows and add Windows components. See Chapter 20, "Upgrading Windows."

Creating a Shortcut to a Program

You can create shortcuts and place them on the desktop to provide quick access to programs. You can then double-click a program shortcut to quickly start that program. Perform the following steps:

1. Display the program file on the Start menu.

2. Right-click the file and then click the Send To command. From the submenu, click the Desktop (create shortcut) command (see Figure 14.1), or drag the program icon from the Start menu to the desktop.

Windows adds the shortcut to your desktop. In this case, a shortcut to Windows Mail has been added (see Figure 14.2). Notice that it has a small arrow in the left corner. This indicates the icon is a shortcut icon. The icon is not the program itself, but a link to the program.

tip

You can follow these same steps to create a shortcut to a file or folder. Open the drive and folder where the folder or file is stored. Then right-click and select Send To, Desktop (create shortcut). When you double-click a file shortcut that file is opened in the associated program. For instance, if you double-click a shortcut to a Word file, the document is opened, and Word is started. If you double-click a folder shortcut, the contents of that folder are displayed.

FIGURE 14.1

You can use a command to create a shortcut menu.

FIGURE 14.2

The icon is added to your desktop.

New program shortcut

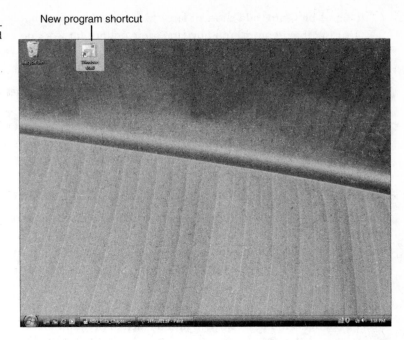

After you add the shortcut icon, you can do any of the following:

■ By default, Windows Vista uses the program name for the shortcut, but you can also rename the shortcut icon. To do so, right-click the shortcut, select Rename, type a new name, and press Enter.

■ Remember that you can move icons around on the desktop. See Chapter 1 for more information.

■ You can delete a program shortcut icon. Right-click the icon and select Delete. Confirm the deletion by clicking the Yes button in the dialog box that appears (see Figure 14.3). Keep in mind, as the confirmation message tells you, that when you delete the shortcut icon, you are not deleting the program itself, just the pointer to the program. If you want to get rid of the program (remove it from your computer), you must uninstall the program. See "Uninstalling Applications" later in this chapter.

FIGURE 14.3

When you delete a shortcut from the desktop, Windows Vista asks you to confirm that action before proceeding.

- Some programs add shortcut icons to your desktop automatically when you install the program. You have the same options for working with these icons: You can rename them, move them, delete them, and double-click them.

- The purpose of the desktop is to provide quick access to your most commonly used programs (files and folders also). If your desktop becomes too cluttered with icons, you defeat the purpose of having fast access. You can clean up your desktop, getting rid of program icons you don't use that often. You can find information on this process in Chapter 18, "Improving Your Computer's Performance."

Adding and Rearranging Programs on the Start Menu

When you install most programs, they are added automatically to the Start menu. You can then start those programs by clicking Start and then All Programs. Windows Vista also enables you to *pin* a program to your Start menu. When you pin a program, it is always listed at the top left of the Start menu (with the Internet and E-mail programs).

To pin a program to the Start menu, display the program for which you want to create a shortcut. You don't have to find the actual program file. You can use the program name listed in the Start menu, either on the left side (commonly used programs) or on the All Programs list. Next, right-click the program name and click the Pin to Start Menu command (see Figure 14.4).

FIGURE 14.4

You can use the Start menu to list the program you want to pin.

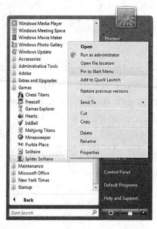

The program is added to your Start menu. Figure 14.5, for instance, shows Spider Solitaire pinned to the menu (listed on the top-left part of the Start menu). You don't have to use the All Programs command to find this program; it appears on the opening Start menu (until you unpin it).

FIGURE 14.5

You can pin commonly used programs to the Start menu so that the program is always listed.

All applications listed above the divider line are pinned

Unpinning a Program from the Start Menu

If you don't want the program listed anymore (at least on the top part of the Start menu), you can remove it by unpinning it. To unpin a program, follow these steps:

1. Click Start to display the Start menu.

2. Right-click the program you want to unpin. You see the shortcut menu.

3. Click Unpin from Start menu. The program is no longer listed on that part of the Start menu. (The program name still appears in the All Programs list.)

Note that you cannot unpin Internet or E-mail, but you can hide them by customizing the Start menu as covered in Chapter 13, "Customizing Windows Vista."

Rearranging Programs on the Start Menu

Another way to change the Start menu is to change the order of the programs listed. You can rearrange the order of the programs. To do so, click the item you want to move and then drag it to the new location in the Start menu.

You can also remove programs from the most frequently used list. To do so, right-click the program and then click Remove from this list. The program is removed.

Installing Programs

When you bought your computer, it most likely came with certain programs already installed. Depending on the brand and model, you might have received some free programs—an antivirus program, for example. These programs should already be installed and set up on your computer.

tip

For more help with installing programs, open the Windows Control Panel (click Start, Control Panel). Click the Programs link. Under the Programs and Features heading, click the How to Install a Program link. Windows Vista can help you out from there.

If you want to add new programs, you can purchase the programs you want and then install them on your system. Most programs provide an installation program that automatically checks your system (to see if you have room for the new program and to see whether you have an existing version), copies the appropriate files, and sets up its related program icons on the Start menu. You can just sit back and click, click, click through the installation routine. Different programs employ different installation processes. That is, the steps vary from one program to another. However, installing programs is usually fairly automated.

The first thing to do is start the installation program. Depending on your particular program, this might happen automatically. If not, you can use can activate manually.

Using the Automatic Install

To start the installation automatically, insert the program disc. Usually, the program has an autoplay feature that automatically prompts you to run the setup or installation process (see Figure 14.6). When you select the setup option, you see your options for installing the program. Follow the specific instructions for the program to complete the installation process. For what to expect when installing programs, see "Understanding What Happens During a Program Install" later in this chapter.

note

If you downloaded the program from the Internet all you have to do is locate the location on your hard drive to which you downloaded it and double-click the program to activate its install process. By default downloaded programs are placed in the Downloads folder in your user account's root folder. (Just click your username on the Start menu to open the folder.)

FIGURE 14.6

When you insert a program disc, Windows displays the AutoPlay options, including running the setup program.

If the AutoPlay doesn't start automatically, you can look for the install program. Follow these steps:

1. Insert the CD or DVD that contains the program you want to install.

2. Click Start, Computer.

3. Right-click the drive that contains the program disc and then click Explore.

4. Look for a file named Setup, Autorun, Install, or something similar and double-click this file; this should start the installation program.

Understanding What Happens During a Program Install

Once launched, the installation program prompts you to make selections, which vary from program to program. Here are some basic choices you can expect:

- You might be asked to accept the license agreement before proceeding with the installation. This is a legal document that says how you can use the program, under what circumstances, and so on. (Typically, you are agreeing to use the program on one PC and not to make illegal copies or share it with others.) Accept the agreement by clicking the appropriate option. If you don't intend to adhere to the agreement, you should not install the program.

- You might be prompted to select a type of installation. You can usually select a standard or customized installation. With a customized installation, you can select, for instance, which program components are installed. Most of the time the standard installation is good enough. As you use and learn more about the program, you can always add other program components (that might not have been installed with the standard installation).

- You might be prompted to select the drive and folder used to store the program files. You might also be prompted to pick or create a new program folder for the program icons. In most cases, the default settings are the ones you should go with.

Each installation is different. Make your choices and click Next to go from one step to the next.

Setting Default Programs

Windows, by default, uses certain default programs for applications such as your email program, your Internet browser, and others. You may use the defaults, or if you have other programs you prefer to use, you can set these as the defaults.

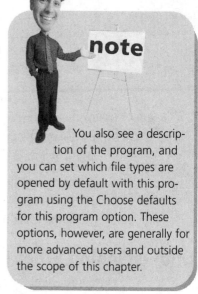

To make these changes, follow these steps:

1. Click Start and then Default Programs.

2. Click Set your default programs (see Figure 14.7).

3. Select the program type for which you want to set the default program (see Figure 14.8).

4. Click Set this program as default.

5. Click OK.

note

You also see a description of the program, and you can set which file types are opened by default with this program using the Choose defaults for this program option. These options, however, are generally for more advanced users and outside the scope of this chapter.

FIGURE 14.7
This option enables you to see and select default programs.

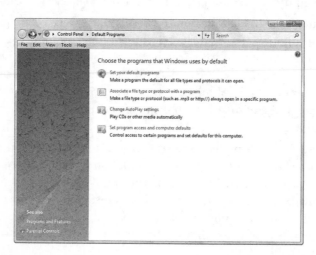

FIGURE 14.8
You see a list of
installed pro-
grams you can
use.

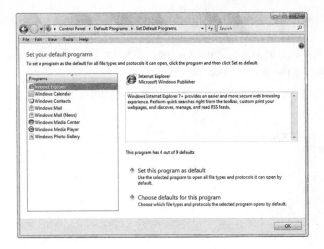

FIGURE 14.8
You see a list of
installed pro-
grams you can
use.

Uninstalling Applications

If you don't use a program, you can remove it from your system. Doing so frees up
disk space. You can simply delete the program file(s), but these files are not always
stored in one location. A program installation might store files in other places on
your hard drive: for instance, in the Windows folder. Therefore, use Windows Vista's
feature for uninstalling when possible.

Follow these steps:

1. Click Start and then Control Panel.

2. Under the Programs section, click the Uninstall a program link
   (see Figure 14.9).

FIGURE 14.9
Use this Control
Panel icon
to uninstall
programs.

Click link to uninstall a program

3. Select the program you want to uninstall. Depending on what it supports you'll either see an Uninstall/Change button or separate Uninstall and Change buttons (see Figure 14.10). Click the Uninstall or Uninstall/Change button in the command bar.

4. If prompted, click Yes to uninstall the program.

FIGURE 14.10

From here you can select which program to uninstall.

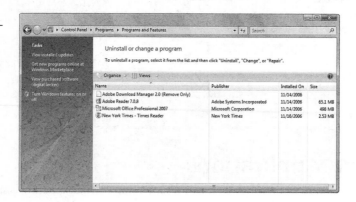

When uninstalling programs, keep these tips in mind:

- If prompted to restart the computer, do so.

- The steps for uninstalling the program vary from program to program. Sometimes a program has its own uninstall routine and clicking Uninstall/Change (the button might be combined for this type of program) starts this uninstall process. Simply follow the onscreen instructions.

- For information about installing or uninstalling certain Windows features, see Chapter 20.

- If you have any folders that contain your documents within the program folders, be sure to move them to another folder for safekeeping (if you want to keep them). While most applications, when removed, leave files and folders the user has created in place, some do not. (And others give you a choice whether to keep user-created files or not.)

Removing Programs Manually

If the preceding method doesn't work (perhaps your program isn't listed or won't be removed), you have to use a different method to remove it. You can try using the program disc.

You might be able to run an uninstall program from the program disc. Insert the disc and see whether options for uninstalling the program are displayed on the install menu. Look for a Setup, Install, or Uninstall icon. Double-click this icon and follow the steps for uninstalling. (Sometimes the Install and Setup programs display a menu, and one of the choices is to uninstall the program.)

tip

You can purchase programs to keep track of what programs you have installed, where they are, and what changes they have made to your system. You can use such a program to uninstall programs.

THE ABSOLUTE MINIMUM

This chapter examines some of the ways you can customize the Start menu and how to install new programs and get rid of programs you no longer need. Here are the key points to remember from this chapter:

- For fast access to commonly used programs, files, or folders, add a shortcut icon to the desktop. When you double-click a program shortcut icon, you start the program. When you double-click a file shortcut icon, you open the associated program and that document. Double-clicking a folder shortcut icon displays its contents.

- You can change how the Start menu appears. You can pin commonly used programs to the top-left pane. You can rearrange the order of programs on the menu.

- When you purchase a new program, you can run the installation program to install the program onto your system. Most programs provide a step-by-step guide for installing the program, and this installation program copies the files to your computer and adds the program to the Start menu.

- To uninstall a program, use the Programs link in the Control Panel.

- Many people use a different mail or Internet browser program. If you are one of these people, you can select the default program that is listed on the menu.

15

CUSTOMIZING EMAIL AND WORKING WITH CONTACTS

Windows Vista is versatile and provides many options for changing how it works. For instance, you can customize how your email is handled. Like other chapters in this part, this chapter covers customization. In this particular case, you learn how to customize Windows Mail so that it works how you want it to work.

The chapter also covers Contacts (formerly known as the Address Book). You learn how this separate accessory program can help you keep track of email addresses and more.

note

You can read about other accessory programs included with Windows Vista in Chapter 21, "Using Windows Accessory Programs."

Setting Mail Options

As mentioned in Chapter 6, "Sending and Receiving Email," you have several options for controlling how messages are sent, received, formatted, and so on. To access all these settings, follow these steps:

1. Click Start, Windows Mail. (If Windows Mail is not your default email program you can instead open it from the All Programs folder.)

2. Click Tools and then click the Options command. You see the General tab of the Options dialog box (see Figure 15.1). From this tab, you can select to play sounds when messages arrive, and choose between a host of other options. For example, you can select how often Windows Mail checks for new messages and whether outgoing messages are sent each time you start the program.

FIGURE 15.1

You have a wealth of options for handling email messages.

3. Make your selections.

4. Click any of the other tabs and then make additional selections. You can do any of the following:

   On the General tab, you can decide whether a sound is played when new messages arrive by checking/unchecking the Play sound when new messages arrive option. You can also select when new messages are sent and received. Check/uncheck Send and receive messages at startup. In addition, select the interval messages are checked in the Check for new messages every xx minutes spin box (xx is the number of minutes).

   Click the Read tab and select read options, such as how long messages are displayed in the preview pane before the message is marked read. The default is 5 seconds (see Figure 15.2), but you can change the interval using the spin box for Mark message read after displaying for xx seconds (xx is the number of seconds).

FIGURE 15.2
Use the Read tab to set read options such as how long messages are displayed as read (appear in bold-face).

You can request a receipt that confirms that a recipient has received a message. Set receipt options from the Receipts tab. You can, for instance, request a receipt for all sent messages.

Click the Send tab (see Figure 15.3) and specify whether a copy of all sent items are stored in the Sent Items folder (check/uncheck the Save copy of sent messages in the 'Sent Items' folder option), when messages are sent (check/uncheck Send messages immediately), the format for your messages (select HTML or Plain Text in the Mail Sending Format area), and other options, such as whether people you reply to are automatically added to your Contacts list (check/uncheck Automatically put people I reply to in my Contacts list folder).

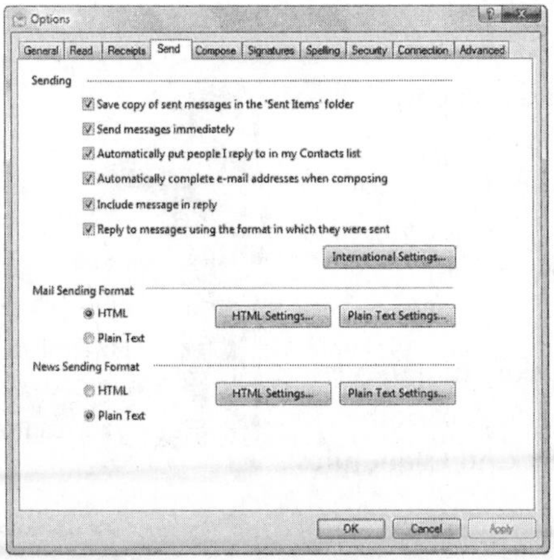

> **caution**
>
> You can also select a stationery, but this option is enabled only if you use HTML mail. Because some readers might have problems displaying a lot of formatting and stationery, use formatting with caution.

FIGURE 15.3
Use the Send tab to select options about how messages are sent.

Use the Compose tab to select formatting options for your email. You can select a particular font by clicking the Font Settings button next to Mail and then selecting the default font you want to use (see Figure 15.4).

To select whether messages are automatically spell checked and set your spell check options, use the Spelling tab (see Figure 15.5). To have Windows Mail automatically check the spelling, check Always check spelling before sending. You can choose to ignore words in uppercase, words with numbers, the original text, and Internet addresses when performing the spell check by checking the appropriate option.

tip

To check the spelling manually, click the Spelling button in the mail window. Windows Mail checks the words in your email against words in its dictionary and flags any words it does not find. Like with word processing spell checkers, you can choose to replace the word with a suggested word, make a manual correction, ignore the misspelled word (for instance, names and technical terms might be flagged but might be spelled correctly), or add the word to the dictionary (so that it won't be flagged in the future).

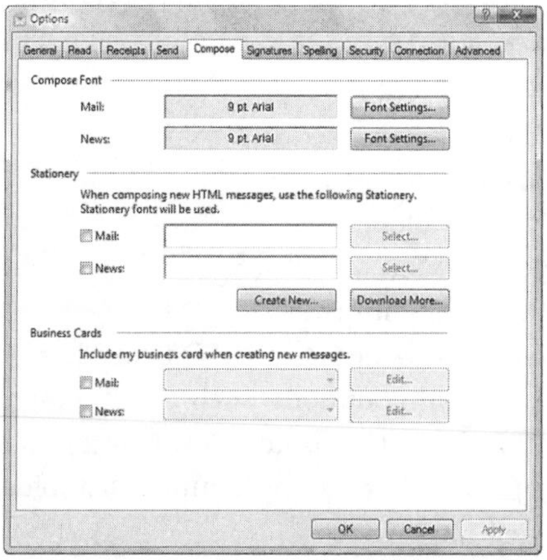

FIGURE 15.4

Use the Compose tab to set up the look of your email messages.

Use the Security tab to set security options, such as message encryption. This tab also includes an option that warns you if another application tries to send mail as you (without your knowledge).

If you want to create a signature that is added to your sent messages, click the Signature tab. Then check Add signatures

tip

You can also change what items are displayed in the Windows Mail window. Use the commands on the View menu to turn on or off the various program window features.

to all outgoing messages. (None of the other options will be available until you check this check box.) In the Signatures text box, type your name, title, email address, or any other sign-off information you want to include for your email messages. Click OK.

On the Connection tab, you can, as just one example, have Windows Mail hang up or end your connection after messages are sent and received. This is only applicable to users who have a dial-up connection to the Internet.

5. When you are finished making changes, click OK to close the dialog box.

In addition to customizing, Windows Mail includes filters that help deal with spam (junk mail) and phishing filters (programs that ask for personal information and then use it for illegal purposes). You learn more about the security features of Windows Mail in Chapter 8, "Ensuring Security and Privacy."

FIGURE 15.5
Use the Spelling tab to control when and how your email messages are spell-checked.

Working with Contacts

One of the most useful things you can do to customize your email is to set up your Contacts. Rather than type an address each time, you can display the Contacts and select a name from the Contacts. This method is not only easier and quicker, but also less error-prone.

You can also use the Contacts to set up a contact group so that you can easily send one message to several people without creating multiple messages or selecting several addresses.

Finally, you can, if you want to put in the effort, store a lot more information for a contact. And if you do so, you can then use this Contacts file in mail merges in other applications, such as Microsoft Word Access.

The following sections cover these Contacts options.

EXPORTING AND IMPORTING CONTACTS

If you upgraded to Windows Vista and have your old Contacts (either on another computer or stored as a file on your PC), you can import it to Windows Vista. Then you don't have to re-create the list you so painstakingly created before.

To export your contacts from your mail program, check your mail program help system. In Outlook Express, for instance, use the File, Export, Contacts command. Note that to import contacts, Windows Mail accepts only certain mail file formats, so be sure to select one of these. The most common is the default for Outlook Express, a .wab file.

To import Contacts, from the Contacts window, click Import in the command bar. Select the type of contacts to import and click Import. Next select the file that contains your contacts and click Open. Your addresses are imported.

Adding New Contacts

Often you use your computer to keep in touch with others either using email, the telephone, or regular mail. In previous versions of Windows, you used the Address Book. Windows Vista includes Contacts, and you can use it to keep track of as much or little information as you like about friends, family, co-workers, and clients.

Follow these steps to add a new contact:

1. Click Start, All Programs, and then Windows Contacts. You see the contact window (see Figure 15.6).

2. To add a new contact, click New Contact in the command bar. You see a blank contact form.

3. For each of the fields, enter the appropriate information. For instance on the Name and E-mail tab, shown in Figure 15.7, enter the name and email address (the most commonly stored information). You learn more about using the other tabs later in this chapter.

tip

A nickname is a shorthand reference to a contact. You can type this shorter name when creating a new mail message.

4. Click OK to add the contact. Although you can use Contacts just for email, this accessory program is actually much more versatile than that. You can use it to enter and keep track of much more information. See the section "Using the Contacts to Keep Track of More Than Just Emails" for more information.

tip

The easiest way to add an email address to your Contacts is to pick up the address from an existing message. This saves you from having to type the information. Display the message with the name you want to add to your Contacts. Then right-click the name and select Add to Contacts. Make any change to the dialog boxes and click OK to add the contact.

FIGURE 15.6

From the main Contact window, you see a list of contacts you have added.

FIGURE 15.7

You can enter as much or as little information for your contacts as you choose when you add a new contact.

Editing Contact Information

Contact information frequently changes; people move, change jobs, or get new cell phone numbers or email addresses. To keep your Contacts up-to-date, you can edit the information.

To edit a contact, follow these steps:

1. Open Windows Contacts.

2. Double-click the contact you want to edit. You see that person's contact information (see Figure 15.8).

3. Click the appropriate tab and then make any changes. For instance, click the Work tab to make changes to office information.

4. Click OK to save the changes.

FIGURE 15.8

People change email addresses, move, add new phones, and make other changes, and you need to make sure you have the most recent information.

Creating Contact Groups

For some projects, you might work with a group of individuals. Rather than communicate individually with each member, you can create a group of contacts. You can then send them email messages, for instance, as a group. It's a great way to create a community, and it makes communicating among the group much easier.

To create a contact group, first make sure you've entered all the contact information you want to include in the group. (You can add new contacts on the fly, but it's easier if all the contacts are already entered in your Contacts list.)

Then follow these steps:

1. Start Windows Contacts.

2. Click the New Contact Group.

3. Type a name for the group in the Group Name text box (see Figure 15.9). You might use a project name, company name, department name, team name, or some other name that identifies the group.

4. Click the Add to Contact Group button. You see the list of your contacts.

tip

As mentioned, you can add new members on the fly. To do so, click the Create New Contact button when setting up the group. Then create the new contact.

FIGURE 15.9

Type a name that describes this group of people.

5. To add a contact to the group, select it in the list and then click the Add button. The person is added to the group list.

6. Continue to add members until the group is complete (see Figure 15.10).

7. When all the members are added, click OK. The group is listed in the Contact list.

You can also click the Close button to close the list of contacts.

FIGURE 15.10

When all the members are added, your group is complete.

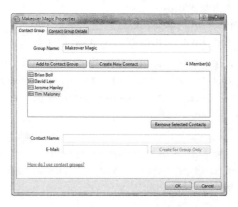

Tips for Working with Contact Groups

Just like you need to keep individual contacts up-to-date, you need to make changes to your contact groups. Keep these pointers in mind:

- When you want to send a message to all members in this group, you can click the To button in the new mail message window and then select the group from the Contacts.

- If you edit an individual entry for a member, the list is updated automatically.

- To add a member to the list, display your Contacts list and then double-click your group. Add the new member using the same process you did when first adding members: click Add to Contact group, select the contact, and click Add.

- If you want to delete members from the list, display your Contact group and then double-click your group. Select the contact to delete and click the Remove Selected Contacts button. Click OK to close the Contact Group.

- To delete the entire group, select it in the Contacts Explorer, click Delete in the command bar, and then confirm the deletion by clicking Yes.

- If your contact group has a set location, you can enter address information, notes as well as a web page. To do so, click the Contact Group Details tab and enter any information. Then click OK.

Working with Contacts

From your Contacts, you have lots of options. You can do any of the following:

- You can create an email message by selecting a contact, click the E-mail Message button to send an email message, complete the message, and click Send. See Chapter 6 for more information.

- To delete a contact, from your Contacts list, select the contact you want to delete. Select the contact and then click Delete in the command bar. Confirm the deletion by clicking Yes.

- To print a list of your contacts, click Print in the command bar. (You might have to click the double arrows at the end of the command bar if not all options are displayed.) Click Print, make any changes to the print options, and then click Print to print the list.

- To find a contact, in the Search text box, type any identifying information such as the person's name, part of his or her email address, or company information. Any matching entries are displayed (see Figure 15.11). You can double-click the entry to open the contact information.

tip

Just like in other Explorers, you can change the view using the Views button. You can also use the Preview pane to view information about a selected contact or contact group.

FIGURE 15.11

You can search for a contact, helpful if you have an especially large contact list.

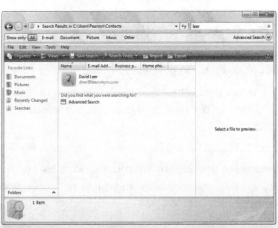

Using the Contacts to Keep Track of More than Just Emails

In addition to keeping track of email addresses, you can also add other information for each contact, including address, phone numbers (phone, fax, cell), business information (company, title, web page), personal information (spouse, children, birthday), and notes. To add other information, follow these steps:

1. Open the Contacts by clicking Start, All Programs, and then click Windows Contacts. You see the list of contacts in the Contacts Explorer.

2. Double-click the contact for which you want to add more information. The Properties dialog box for that contact is displayed. The Name and E-mail tab is displayed by default.

3. Click the Home tab. You see the various fields of information you can enter (see Figure 15.12). Complete any or all of the fields.

4. Click any of the other tabs and complete any or all of the fields for that category. For instance, click Work to enter company information (see Figure 15.13).

5. Click OK when you are finished entering information.

FIGURE 15.12

You can keep track of other information, such as home address and phone numbers.

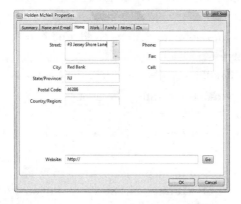

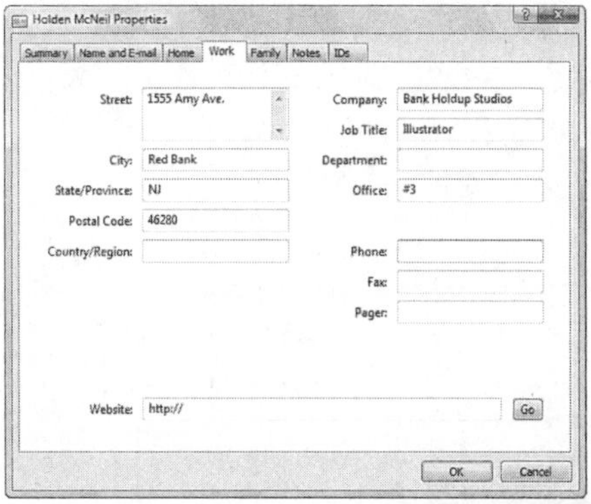

FIGURE 15.13

In addition to home information, you can add work-related information as well.

In addition to the tabs covered here, you can also use these tabs:

- The Family tab includes information about birthdays, anniversaries, and spouse and children names.

- Use the Notes tab to enter notes about conversations or other details about this contact.

- Use the IDs tab to associate a digital ID with the email address. A digital ID helps prove your identity when sending emails.

- The Summary tab includes key information pulled from all the various tabs; you can change this tab only by changing information on the other tabs.

THE ABSOLUTE MINIMUM

This chapter examines the many ways you can customize email to suit your preferences. This chapter also examines how to use Contacts (the new replacement for the Address Book in previous versions) to keep track of more than just emails and to organize members into groups to make group communication easier. In particular, keep these main points in mind:

- You can control how messages are sent, received, and handled using the Windows Mail options.

- To make addressing email messages easier, use the Contacts list.

- Keep your contact up-to-date by editing if one of your contacts has new contact information.

- If you frequently send email messages to a set of people, create a contact group.

- You can use the Contacts list to keep track of more than just an email list. You can also keep track of addresses, business information, and personal information.

16

SETTING UP WINDOWS VISTA FOR MULTIPLE USERS

If more than one person uses your computer, you might want to personalize certain Windows settings for each user. For example, all family members can have their own desktop design, Start menu, Favorites folder, Documents folder, and so on. Each time users log on, all of their personalized settings go into effect making the computer assume different "personalities" for each operator. Implementing this kind of functionality requires the use of individual accounts for each user. Having multiple accounts, one for each of the computer's users, also provide an additional measure of security, because you can assign different passwords to each account, restricting access to each other's stuff.

Perhaps more importantly, different users can be granted different levels of computer *access*, controlling what each specific user can and cannot do. For example, in your home you might decide that only parents can add and delete programs and operate the computer at all times of the day and night. With separate user accounts for each adult and each child you can adequately restrict computer use at specific times, and even restrict use to running only selected programs.

Why have separate accounts for each child? If you have multiple children, odds are they're not all the same age. What might be an appropriate use of your home computer for one might not be so for another. This comes in especially handy when you want to restrict your children's game play to only age-appropriate games.

Vista adds another new twist to this concept by making it possible to *temporarily elevate* a user's status. This means that with your approval, users, who otherwise could not, can receive temporary permission to install a program, and so on.

This chapter covers the basics of logging on and off, setting up accounts, modifying accounts, establishing parental controls, and temporarily elevating account status.

> **caution**
>
> Multiple accounts do add to a computer's complexity, making backups, document sharing, and other tasks slightly more complex. If you are a beginner, consider putting off multiple account setups until you feel comfortable with your computer and Vista; then start with just one additional account before assigning everyone in the house their own account. It's easier to add a third and fourth account later than it is to unravel a clutter of unwanted, multiple Documents folders, and so on.

Logging On and Off

When you power up your computer you need to *log on* if you have assigned a password or if your computer has multiple accounts. If you have established multiple accounts more than one person can be logged in simultaneously, making it quicker to switch from user-to-user without restarting your computer—in order to briefly check email, for example. Here are the options and some recommendations.

Logging On

When you turn on your computer you see at least one account name and icon. If the computer has multiple accounts set up you see them all listed and you can click your account icon to log on. If accounts on the computer have been assigned passwords (as recommended and explained later in this chapter), you need to enter your password to log in. The Log On screen also shows which other users, if any, are already logged in.

After you log on, any personalized settings, such as a customized desktop, wallpaper, Favorites list, and others, are loaded, and you see Windows Vista just the way you left it. You can get to work.

> **tip**
>
> When sharing a computer it's a good idea to log off when you are finished with both for security purposes and to speed up computing for other users.

Logging Off

Powering-down your computer logs you off. Use the Power controls on the Start menu. You can also log off by visiting the Start menu and choosing Log Off. This logs off the active user (the user whose desktop is displayed when you use the Log Off command).

Switching Users

If one or more users have logged onto the same computer using different accounts, and you simply want to switch from one account to another, you can do so without logging off. For instance, if you're already logged on and your spouse needs to briefly gain access to her user account (to check email, for example), you can simply tell Vista you want to switch users and let your spouse log on without having to log off of your own account. To switch users, follow these steps:

1. Click Start.
2. Click the right-facing arrow next to the Lock button at the bottom of the Start menu.
3. Choose Switch User from the resulting pop-up menu.
4. Vista returns you to the log on screen where you see a list of available accounts.
5. Click the account to which you want to switch. (You also need to type the password if the account is password protected.) The chosen account becomes active.

That's all there is to it. In the case of this example, when finished, your spouse can log out, which allows you to switch back to your account, or your spouse can also use the Switch User option, which leaves both accounts logged on.

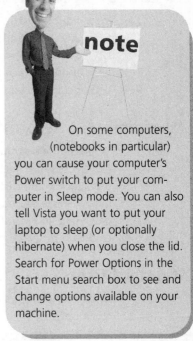

note

On some computers, (notebooks in particular) you can cause your computer's Power switch to put your computer in Sleep mode. You can also tell Vista you want to put your laptop to sleep (or optionally hibernate) when you close the lid. Search for Power Options in the Start menu search box to see and change options available on your machine.

note

Be patient when telling Vista you want to switch users. Because Vista must record the status of an open account to your PC's hard drive before it lets you switch to another user, it can take a while to get to the log on screen.

Types of Accounts and Their Privileges

Vista handles account types, and therefore *account privileges*, slightly differently from previous Windows versions. Many of these changes have been made for security purposes. However, many have also been implemented to improve the experience of having multiple users access the same computer. There are four types of user accounts. Let's take a look.

Administrator Account

Administrator accounts enable the user to have complete control of Windows Vista (within reason). Each computer needs at least one Administrator account with full privileges so that the person in charge of the computer can add and delete programs, make full backups, add new hardware, install and update drivers, and so on. When you install Vista the first account created is an Administrator account.

Standard Users

In Windows Vista, Standard User accounts are given only the privileges required to perform such everyday tasks as changing the clock's time zone, changing power management settings, adding printers and other devices that already have the required drivers installed on the computer, and installing critical Windows Updates. Microsoft also refers to Standard Users as "least-privileged users."

The Guest Account

Vista also permits adding a Guest account, which has even fewer privileges than a Standard User account, but the Guest account is disabled by default. You might want to enable it if you have visitors you would like to let use your computer but not access your files.

> **tip**
>
> It's a good idea to set up most users, even the primary user of the system, as Standard Users because this provides the most security. It's harder for hackers and malicious programs to infiltrate a computer when its user is logged on as a Standard User. As I talk about at the end of this chapter, in the "Temporarily Elevating Account Status" section, it is possible to perform almost any action with a Standard account, as long as the user knows the name and password of another administrator account.

Setting Up a New User Account

When you first install and use Windows Vista, you are prompted to provide names for each account you know you want to include on your PC. You can add names for each person using the computer (and then later go back and modify the accounts) or you can create one primary account and add any other accounts later, as described here.

After you log into an account, any changes you make to certain settings (Favorites List, display, mouse, and so on) are saved with that particular account. Settings in other accounts remain unchanged.

Follow these steps to set up a new account:

1. Click Start and then click Control Panel.

2. Click the Add or Remove User Accounts link in the User Accounts and Family Safety section of the Control Panel window. Any accounts you created are listed in the resulting dialog box (see Figure 16.1). In this example there's one account—the Administrator, Curly, and the aforementioned Guest account, which is disabled by default.

FIGURE 16.1

You can use this Control Panel option to modify existing accounts and set up new accounts.

3. Click the Create a new account link. You are first prompted to type a name. As the prompt explains, "This name will appear on the Welcome screen and on the Start menu" (see Figure 16.2).

4. Type a name for the account.

5. Choose Standard user or Administrator level. Unless you have specific reasons to do otherwise, both Vista (notice the link at the bottom of the window in Figure 16.2) and I recommend you opt to create a Standard user account.

6. Click the Create Account button.

You see the new account name in the resulting Manage Account dialog box. It has a standard Vista-chosen icon. In Figure 16.3 we've added an account called Larry and Vista has assigned him the fireworks icon.

FIGURE 16.2

The name identi-
fies the account
and displays
when you start
Windows Vista.

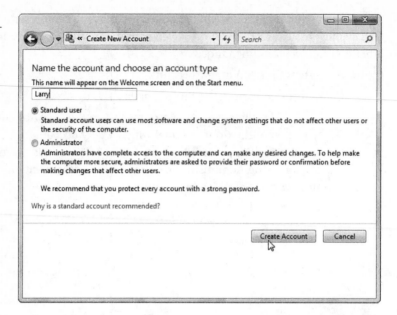

FIGURE 16.3

A second
Standard User
account has been
added and a
standard icon
was automati-
cally assigned.

Changing Account Settings or Removing an Account

As the needs and preferences of your computer's users change, you might need to make changes to an existing user account. Maybe you want to change an account's type from Administrator to Standard User. Maybe one of the users wants a new password or user icon. Whatever the case, Vista enables you to change your account settings (and those of other users if you have access to an Administrator account) from the User Accounts area of the Control Panel (see Figure 16.4).

The screen you see is for the currently logged on account. You can specify a password for that account, change the picture, and so on.

To modify an account, follow these steps:

1. Log into the account you want to modify. (You can also modify any user account from an Administrator account. Just select the Manage another account link shown in Figure 16.4.)

> **tip**
>
> Click on the user account icon at the top of the Start menu to more quickly reach the Account Settings screen.

FIGURE 16.4

Here's where you modify accounts. Reach this screen from the Control Panel.

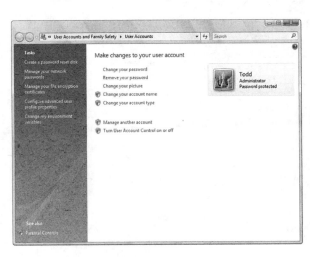

2. Click Start and then click Control Panel.

3. Click User Accounts and Family Safety in the Control Panel window and then the User Accounts link. You see available options for the account (refer to Figure 16.4).

4. Select the change you want to make (account picture, password, and so on).

5. You can then make changes as described in the following sections.

6. When you are finished making changes, close the Control Panel windows.

Changing the Account Name

To change the name of the account, click Change Your Account Name. In the screen that appears, type a new name and then click the Change Name button. The new account name shows up on the Welcome screen and Start menu.

Adding or Changing a Password

If you want to improve security on your computer (and you should), you can assign a different password to each account. Users must type their passwords to log into their accounts.

To create a password, visit the User Accounts area in the Control Panel area illustrated in Figure 16.4 and click Create a password for your account. If there is already a password assigned to the account, you see a link that reads "Change your password."

When creating a password you see several text boxes (shown in Figure 16.5). Type the password you want to use in the first text box. Type it again to confirm in the second text box. Finally, type an optional hint to help you remember the password. If you're changing a password instead of creating one there is one additional field from what's shown here because you first have to provide the account's old password before entering a new one.

FIGURE 16.5

Assign account passwords for added security.

When you've completed all three text box entries, click the Create password button. (It says Change password if that's what you're actually doing.) Clicking the button enables password protection for the account or updates the existing password to the new one.

EFFECTIVE PASSWORDS

Vista passwords are case sensitive, so "nuk" is not the same as "Nuk." The password screen has a link that can help you create strong, hard to guess passwords. In general they should be eight characters or longer and include a combination of uppercase and lowercase letters and a combination of letters and numbers. A password should not be your name, the word "password," or other common words found in the dictionary. It also helps if the password contains some unusual characters such as an exclamation point or tilde. For example, "nuk" is a terrible password, whereas "nuk-Nuk-12!" is much better and not much harder to remember.

Removing a Password

You can remove a password. To do so, log into the account and click the User Accounts link in the User Accounts and Family Safety area in the Control Panel window. Then click the Remove your password link.

To remove an account password you must also provide the account's current password. After you do that, you can click the Remove password button to confirm the deletion.

Changing a Picture

Windows Vista assigns a graphic icon to each account (a dog, a goldfish, a robot, a chess set, and others). If you don't like the graphic selected for your account, you can use one of the other icons supplied with Windows Vista. If none of these suits your fancy, you can use other graphic images. For instance, you might use actual pictures of users for their accounts.

caution

Keep in mind that doing so also removes any passwords you have saved for your Internet browsing. When you type a new password into Internet Explorer it asks whether you want it to remember that password automatically. If you click Yes, the password is stored with your account. Deleting the account password also deletes all these passwords.

To use a different picture for an account, follow these steps:

1. Click Change your picture from the User Accounts page.

2. Select from one of the available pictures or click Browse for more pictures to select another picture (for instance, a photograph) stored in another location (see Figure 16.6).

3. If you're choosing a graphic from a new location, open the folder that contains the image (refer to Figure 16.6), select the image, and then click Open.

4. Whether you use a custom graphic or select one of the default images that Vista provides, click the Change Picture button to assign the new image to your account.

Deleting an Account

If someone no longer uses the computer (perhaps he got his own!), you can delete accounts. Doing so frees up the disk space taken by this person's user account settings and documents. (You do have the option of saving the documents or deleting them.)

FIGURE 16.6

You can select
from several
images included
with Windows
Vista or browse
for others on
your disk(s).

To delete an account, follow these steps:

1. Log in as an administrator and go to the
   User Accounts section of the Control Panel.

2. Click the Manage Accounts link and
   select the account you want to remove
   (see Figure 16.7).

3. Click Delete the Account link (refer to
   Figure 16.4).

4. You are prompted to keep or delete the
   files (see Figure 16.8). Answer by clicking
   Keep Files or Delete Files. Keeping an
   account's files moves the Desktop design,
   Documents folder's contents, Favorites
   folder, Music folder, Pictures folder, and
   Videos folder to a desktop folder named
   after the user being deleted.

note

You can reach the Users
folder from File Explorer.
Click Start, Computer. From the
File Explorer window that appears,
double-click the Local Disk (C:) and
double-click the Users folder that
appears in the Explorer window.

FIGURE 16.7

You can delete
outdated or
unused accounts.

FIGURE 16.8
You are asked if you want to save or delete the account's documents, favorites, and other settings.

5. You are next prompted to confirm the deletion.

Strictly speaking, after a user account is removed, it can't be recreated. However, if you elected to keep a deleted user account's files, you can create a new account under the same username and move the saved files to the new account's folder in the Users folder.

Parental Controls

Among Vista's most useful new features are a diverse set of user account controls designed to give parents complete decision-making authority over what their children can do on a computer.

If you have Administrator rights you can set up parental controls for other user accounts. To turn these controls on you need to first log on using an Administrator account. Then navigate to the User Accounts and Family Safety area of the Control Panel, and click the link, Set Up Parental Controls for Any User, which is located under the Parental Control area. Click it and then choose the account you want to control to see a screen similar to Figure 16.9. Click the On, enforce current settings button to enable Parental Controls.

caution

Obviously if your Administrator accounts don't have passwords, anyone can log in as an Administrator and change their own restrictions, or remove everyone's restrictions entirely. To be the boss you need good passwords. And don't write them on sticky notes stuck to the computer!

FIGURE 16.9

Controlling user

access.

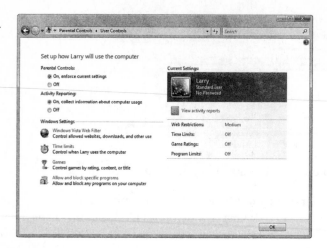

After you enable Vista's Parental Controls for a user account there's a variety of tools at your disposal to help you control how your kids use your PC.

Activity Monitoring

Vista makes it possible to play "Big Brother." You can monitor users' browsing activities and see what they have been doing by turning on Activity Reporting. Just select the On, collect information about computer usage button under the Activity Reporting section of the User Controls window (refer to Figure 16.9).

After this feature is turned on, Vista monitors all activities for the applicable user. To view an activity report, such as the one shown in Figure 16.10, click the View Activity Reports link.

Web Restrictions

Most parents know that there's a lot of content on the Web that's not appropriate for young children. Using Vista, web restrictions can be enabled that block specific sites, use automated tools Microsoft has developed to block inappropriate web content for you, and prevent web downloading of files. These are all imperfect tools and simply engaging them does not keep your family away from everything you might want them to avoid. They can also inadvertently block useful web content.

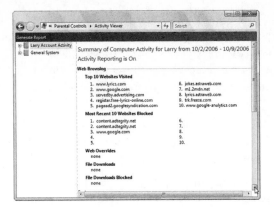

For example, with Web controls enabled a Google search for the relatively harmless
music group Bare Naked Ladies is blocked. However, if a blocked user searches on
"Lyrics," and then picks from the dozens of music lyric sites, it's pretty easy to
search for and find the group Bare Naked Ladies, get what they want, so to speak,
including, by the way, links to adult joke sites found on the lyrics sites.

In fact, if you look back at Figure 16.10, although you can't tell from the report,
Larry read an adult joke at the website numbered 6, which he found through a link
from a song lyrics site.

The point is, on some level you must face the fact that your kids are going to see
things on the Internet you'd rather they didn't. Vista's web content filter is not a
cure all. However, it can make your job as a parent considerably easier. Take this
feature for a spin yourself before enabling it for your family to see if it does the job
for you and fits your lifestyles.

You can specify a specific list of sites a user can visit, (this is an almost excessively
limiting option); or you can create a list of blocked sites, (equally frustrating and
very time-consuming), or you can choose from Microsoft's High, Medium, or
Custom settings (see Figure 16.11).

FIGURE 16.11

Set and explore
Web Restrictions
here.

According to Microsoft the High restriction setting lets users see *"Children's sites [which] include content that is understandable and usable by children, and that is appropriate for them. The language of a children's site is typically aimed at 8 to 12 year-olds, and the concepts presented are accessible to younger minds. When you choose this level, you permit your child to see children's sites, as well as any website that you add to the list of allowed websites."*

The Medium restriction setting, again quoting its creators restricts *"based on web content categories. This lets your child explore the wide range of information on the Internet, but not see content that is inappropriate."*

Again, your definition of inappropriate might differ from Microsoft's and you will need to do some testing, thinking like an eight-year-old, or whatever when you surf.

The Custom setting lists specific "content categories" and lets you allow or restrict them. Category examples include pornography, mature content, tobacco, and so on. You can also specify particular sites to block by choosing the Custom setting.

Time Restrictions

For kids, using a computer when they're not supposed to can be a tempting proposition. Maybe your daughter wants to try to play a game past her bedtime, for example. Fortunately, you can take that temptation away by telling Vista when a user is allowed or not allowed to log on to the computer.

You can specify time restrictions by clicking the Time Limits link on the User Controls page (refer to Figure 16.9). The dialog box that appears is similar to the one in Figure 16.12. In this example, computer use is pretty severely restricted to anytime Saturday or Sunday and from 6 p.m. to 10 p.m. Monday through Friday and 4 p.m. to 10 p.m. on Friday.

FIGURE 16.12

Restricting time.

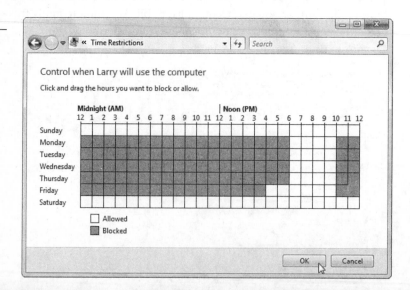

To set your own time restrictions, click or drag on a block of time to darken and thereby restrict computer access to the time limits you desire. Each account can have its own schedule.

Restricting Game Usage

You can use the Parental Controls feature to completely prevent users from playing games, or specify specific games that can or cannot be played. You can also enable one of multiple game rating systems and let the computer manage game access for you using industry "standards." Begin by clicking the games link in the parental Controls explorer. You will see something similar to Figure 16.13.

FIGURE 16.13
There are many ways to restrict gaming.

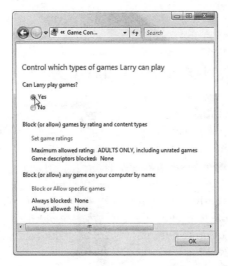

First you need to decide if you want to block or allow unrated games. Then you need to choose an industry game rating level that pleases you and is appropriate for the user. Remember, each user of the computer can have his or her own account and thus his or her own customized restrictions.

Preventing Access to Specific Games

Another alternative is to block specific programs by using the Game Overrides feature. Reach this feature by clicking the Block or Allow specific games link in the Game Controls. It's shown in Figure 16.14. Spider Solitaire is being blocked. Spiders give Larry nightmares.

FIGURE 16.14
Block specific
games here.

FIGURE 16.14
Block specific
games here.

Temporarily Elevating Account Status

From time-to-time Standard Users need the ability to perform an action that's normally restricted, such as install a new program. Fortunately, you don't have to go through the hassle of logging off the Standard User in favor of an Administrator account or switching users, as long as someone with an administrator's password is available to provide the Standard User with authorization to execute an action that's normally restricted.

Whenever a Standard User tries to perform an action not permitted for that account type, they see a dialog asking for an Administrator's password. All you have to do is provide that password and Vista executes the action without a hitch. As the Administrator you obviously want to type the password yourself rather than sharing it verbally.

tip

The ability to temporarily elevate an account's status to perform an action makes it much easier for all users to stick with Standard User accounts, rather than have anyone log on strictly as an Administrator. Even if you are that administrator for your PC, you might find it preferable to use a Standard User account for everyday use and keep your Administrator account separate.

THE ABSOLUTE MINIMUM

User accounts are a handy way to let multiple users have a personalized version of Windows Vista that suits how that person uses the computer (how the desktop appears, the list of favorite sites, and so on). They also improve security and frustrate hackers and malicious programs, particularly if you install good passwords. For this purpose, Windows enables you to create user accounts. You can use this feature to do the following:

- You can set up accounts for each person who uses the computer, selecting an account name, picture, and type.

- When you turn on the computer, all user accounts are displayed. You can log on to your account.

- When you are done using the computer, you should log off. Then another user can log on. You can have several persons logged on at the same time and simply switch users, but it's best to conserve system resources by logging off. Use the Log Off button on the Start menu to log off.

- Any changes made to Windows settings are saved each time a person logs off.

- You can modify user accounts as needed, changing the name, type, or picture. You can also assign a password and delete unneeded accounts.

- Vista provides parental controls that can help you monitor and restrict users, but these are by no means perfect, and not necessarily desirable in some settings.

PART V

MAINTAINING YOUR PC

17

SAFEGUARDING YOUR WORK

Many beginning computer users are understandably skittish about using the computer. They think they are going to "break" it. Really, there's not much you can do to ruin your computer, but you should take some precautions to guard your data. With the cost of backing up data plummeting, chances are the information on many computers is worth ten times the hardware cost, and recreating lost data, if it's even possible, costs much more than protecting it.

Another safety issue is checking a disk for problems and repairing them. This chapter covers checking a disk for errors and how Vista can help you work around them.

You also learn about using System Restore, useful for going "back in time" on your computer. You can use this to troubleshoot many of the problems that might pop up when you make changes to your computer.

tip

Another important security issue is protecting your computer while using the Internet. Internet security issues are covered in Chapter 7, "Browsing the Internet."

Most of these tasks are easily accomplished using Vista's handy new Backup and Restore Center, as I'll discuss in this chapter.

Backing Up Your Work

The most important thing you can do to safe-guard your data is to back it up! Yes, it can be time-consuming. Yes, it is a hassle. True, many of us fail to do it. However, the most valuable thing isn't the computer itself; it's the data on it. Re-creating lost data like documents and spreadsheets is not easy and in many instances, such as with digital photos and home movies, it's flat out impossible. Say, for instance, you store all your chapters for your next great book. Can you re-create them? Sure, you can re-rip your CD collection or regurgitate the items on a to-do list, but if a hard drive failure claims your digital family photos—births, graduations, and all—they're gone forever if you haven't backed them up.

> ## caution
>
> It's not enough to simply make additional copies of your files. They need to be stored in a safe place away from the computer used to create them. Computers get stolen, are washed away in floods, destroyed by lighting strikes, and die of old age. Your best bet is to never store backup copies of data on the computer containing the original files, and you should preferably store the backups in another ZIP code if you can arrange it.

We take for granted the accessibility of our data. Take your Contacts list, for example. With it, you can easily send email to all your friends, colleagues, and relatives. Without it, do you really know by heart all the email addresses in that simple file?

That's why backing up your data is so critical. You should get in the habit of backing up your entire system at regular intervals and backing up your documents (data files) even more frequently.

Selecting Backup Equipment

To back up your files, you need backup media and a backup program. Media is the place you store your data. Before the hard drives on computers became so big, it was common to back up data on floppy disks. Now backing up your system to floppy disks would be ludicrous (although you can use floppy disks as a quick method to back up small files, if your computer has a floppy drive in it).

Instead, beginners most commonly back up to a recordable DVD or CD. Many businesses still back up their drives to tape and there are backup tape drives you can purchase for your home PC.

> ## tip
>
> Rather than using floppies for smaller backup tasks, many users have turned to inexpensive USB thumb drives. These drives are small enough to hang on a key-chain, and they can hold anywhere from a single CD's worth of data to capacities rivaling that of recordable DVDs!

Another increasingly popular option is to back up your entire system disk to an external hard drive, such as the one shown in Figure 17.1. Some of these drives even come with their own backup software and one-touch buttons that run the entire backup process for you whenever you push the button. Most of these drives connect to your computer via a USB 2.0 or FireWire port. Some even support both interfaces.

Today's external hard drives hold anywhere from 60GB to a whopping 400GB or more of data. With that kind of capacity there's plenty of space for most users to back up their data. It's also much faster than backing up to a tape drive or burning a CD or DVD.

FIGURE 17.1

External hard disks are great backup media. This one from Maxtor has a one-touch backup button.

Finally, Internet-based backup services, once only affordable for large businesses, are becoming inexpensive enough to deserve your consideration for your personal or small business computer. Perform an Internet search for "online backups" to keep an eye on developments in this area. (Google.com is a good search engine if you don't already have a favorite.)

Choosing Backup Software?

Although you can manually locate and copy files to perform an effective backup, it's easier to use a dedicated backup program. These programs not only perform the backup, but they also provide options for selecting which files are backed up and when.

In the past some versions of Windows have included a built-in backup program and some haven't, but even those versions that did received a lukewarm response from many users for not offering enough features. Windows Vista includes a preinstalled and much improved backup program that, for casual users, might be all you need.

You can also purchase third-party backup programs, and as mentioned, some backup hardware devices (external hard drives, tape drives, and so on) come with their own specialized software.

You can find many—sometimes even free—backup programs by visiting the freeware or shareware sites on the Internet. Some popular programs include Monday Backup, Winbacker, Sysback (for backing up system files), and Backup Pro.

However, because Vista's new backup feature, called the Backup and Restore Center, is already installed and easy to use, perhaps you should give it a try first.

TIPS FOR BACKING UP

Here are some tips to make backing up more efficient:

- If you don't perform routine backups of your entire computer, you should at least make manual copies of all your data files. You can make a backup of important data files by copying them to a USB flash drive or to a DVD or CD (if you have a drive that can read and write data). See Chapter 3, "Managing Files," for information on copying data.

- Consider doing a complete backup at least once a year and before any major system change (such as upgrading to a new operating system).

- You don't have to back up your program files (except during your complete system backup) because you can always reinstall them from the original program discs. Do, though, back up your data files more than once a year. You might consider daily or weekly intervals. I guarantee you the minute you think you don't need a backup will become the minute you do.

- To facilitate backing up data files, create and store files in a solid organizational structure. You might store all data files within subfolders in the Users folder. You can then concentrate on this folder when creating data file backups. Some programs choose their own file locations when saving your data. You need to know where these files are stored and which ones to back up. Read the documentation and online help for programs that collect important data.

Using Vista's Backup and Restore Center

You can either launch the Backup and Restore Center from Vista's Welcome Center, type "backup" in the Start Menu's Search box and launch the Center when it appears in the Start menu, or click Start, All Programs, Maintenance, Backup and Restore Center. When it opens, you will see something like Figure 17.2.

The Backup and Restore Center gives you the option of either backing up your entire computer or just selected files and folders. Obviously, if you want to backup the entire computer you need a backup device or collection of writeable DVDs capable of holding the entire contents of your computer. This can easily exceed 100GB or more these days and might not be worth the time and effort you put into it. In most cases, the best thing to do is just back up selected files instead.

FIGURE 17.2

The new Backup and Restore Center makes it easy to protect your data and recover from problems.

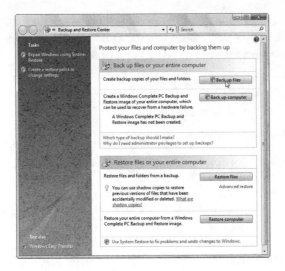

When you start a backup the program asks you to specify a destination for the backup files. As you can see from Figure 17.3, you can choose to backup to an external drive (hard disk or recordable disc) or to a network location. The options available to you in the On a Hard Disk, CD or DVD field includes only those storage devices that Vista has determined are connected to your PC. If you choose to back up to a networked location, you can use the Browse button to locate and specify another PC's drive or networked storage device.

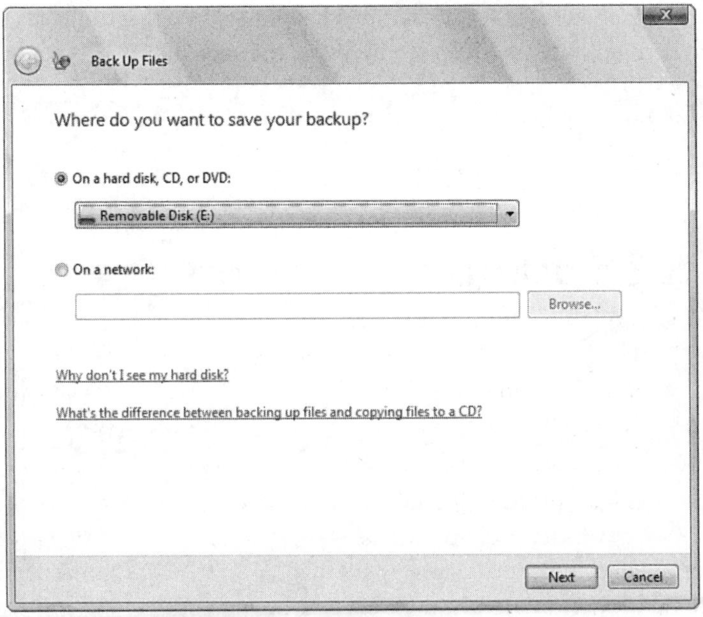

FIGURE 17.3

The Backup and Restore Center suggests destinations for the backed up files.

Back Up Files

Where do you want to save your backup?

◉ On a hard disk, CD, or DVD:

    Removable Disk (E:)

○ On a network:

                                                          Browse...

Why don't I see my hard disk?

What's the difference between backing up files and copying files to a CD?

Next   Cancel

When you click the Next button you are given a choice of file types to back up. Hovering over the names of the choices explains what is backed up (see Figure 17.4). Choose just the file types you want to protect and click Next.

FIGURE 17.4

Choose the desired file types to back up.

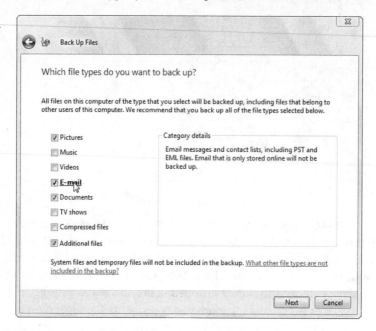

Next, Vista asks you to specify how often you want the backups to be made and at what time of day (see Figure 17.5). When you save the settings for the first time Vista does an initial backup regardless of the schedule.

FIGURE 17.5

Scheduling regular backups and running the first one.

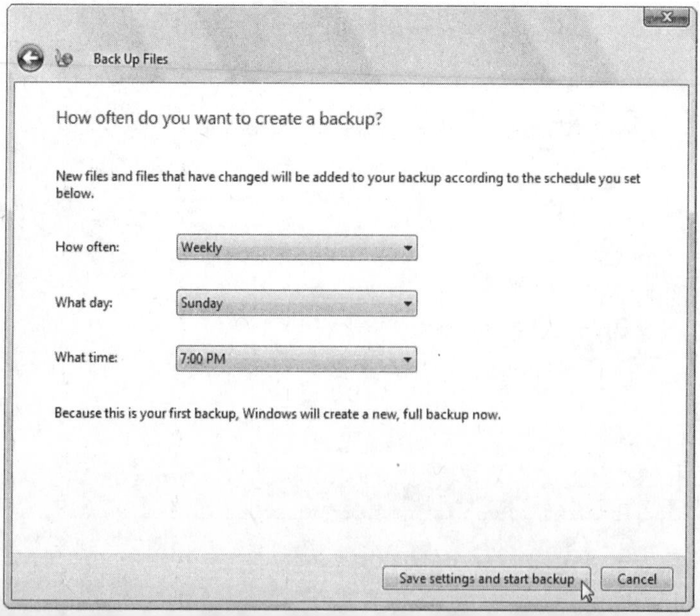

After you click the Save settings and start backup button, the backup begins and you see the progress onscreen as shown in Figure 17.6. When the backup is done you'll see a success message.

FIGURE 17.6
A backup in progress. You'll see the file-names displayed as they are copied.

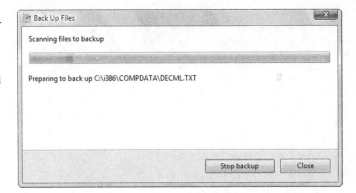

Restoring Files from a Backup

Ideally, you'll never have to restore a backup. However, if you use your PC long enough, sooner or later you'll need of it. As you've probably guessed already, you can use the Backup and Restore Center (refer to Figure 17.2) to recover damaged or lost files. The first thing to do is make sure the media containing the backup files is available to your computer (insert the DVD, connect the external drive containing the backups, and so on). After you're ready, use the following steps:

1. Launch the Backup and Restore Center as before by visiting the Welcome Center or by searching for "backup" in the Start Menu Search box.

2. Click the Restore Files button when you see the Backup and Restore Center. You are asked if you want to restore from the last backup or an earlier one. Indicate your choice, which will depend upon what has happened to your files. You want the most-recent backup without the problem—the one before your computer was infected with a virus, for example.

3. You are presented with a list of potential folders and files to restore, similar to the one shown in Figure 17.7. Choose the ones you want. The items you choose

note

If you haven't made backup data available to your PC neither option in the Restore File window is enabled. The only thing you are able to do is Cancel or select one of the links for Other Options. (These links connect to Vista's System Restore feature, the Recycle Bin, and a help file about using Vista's backup program.)

show up in the Restore files list. Click Next when you have selected everything you want to restore.

FIGURE 17.7
Restoring files.

4. Vista will ask if you want to overwrite the old data or place it in a new location on your computer. If you're trying to replace damaged or missing files, it's probably best to overwrite the old data. After making your choice, click the Start Restore button.

5. The backup software begins the restoration process, and asks you how to handle any conflicts it discovers. For instance it asks if you want newer files replaced with older ones from the backups. You might want to replace some but not all of the new files with old ones, so pick and choose carefully.

Checking a Disk for Errors

In addition to backing up your data, you should also periodically check your disk for errors. It's not uncommon for parts of your hard disk to get damaged even though the drive as a whole appears to be functioning normally. When this happens, you might see an error message when you try to open or save a file.

To scan the disk for damage and fix any problems, you can use a handy system tool called Check Disk that is included with Windows Vista. Follow these steps to use this program:

1. Choose Computer from the Start menu.

2. Right-click the drive you want to check for errors and select Properties. If you

note

Although Vista does a much better job of automatically looking for disk problems than previous versions of Windows, you can also run the diagnostic whenever you choose.

have just one hard drive, it is named drive C. Some computers have more than one hard drive. If so, right-click the desired drive to select it.

3. Click the Tools tab. You see the system tools for working with hard drives (see Figure 17.8).

4. Click the Check Now button in the Error-checking section of the Tools tab. After confirming that you want to run the test, you see the available options for running the scan. You can select whether errors are automatically fixed and whether the scan checks and repairs bad sectors. Under most circumstances it's best to select both (see Figure 17.9).

tip

You can use this same dialog box to clean up your disk (get rid of files you don't need). For information on disk-performance options, see Chapter 18, "Improving Your Computer's Performance."

FIGURE 17.8

You can access the Check Disk program from the Tools tab.

5. Click Start to start the check.

6. If the program finds an error, a dialog box appears explaining the error. Read the error message and choose the option you want to perform. For instance, the check might find errors in how data is stored (such as sector errors, invalid file dates, and bad sectors). Click OK to continue for each message you receive. Windows Vista takes care of fixing or working around any errors it finds.

7. When the disk check is complete, click OK.

Using System Restore

Occasionally when you add new programs or hardware to your PC, you might find that your system stops working properly. Trying to troubleshoot a problem such as this can be difficult. To help, Windows Vista includes an improved version of System Restore. This utility enables you to roll back core system files to a previous state in the hope that any changes that are causing the problems are undone.

For instance, suppose that you installed an updated driver for your graphics card, and now your computer is not working properly. You can go "back in time" to before you installed the software to get your computer working properly again. Using System Restore enables you to preserve recent work, such as saved documents, email messages, history lists, or favorites lists.

You can then step through whatever created the problem again to see if you can pinpoint and resolve it.

Understanding Restore Points

Vista's System Restore monitors changes to your system and creates *restore points* automatically. There are several types of restore points:

- The *initial system checkpoint* is created the first time you start your computer after Vista is installed (don't select this restore point unless you want to wipe your computer clean of everything you've done on it since installing Vista).

- Windows automatically creates *System checkpoints* every day and night and immediately before any significant event, such as installing new hardware or software.

- *Manually created restore points* are those restore points you create yourself (covered later in this section).

- *Restore operation restore points* track restoration operations themselves, enabling you to undo them.

All of this can be accomplished from the System Restore dialog box shown in Figure 17.10. You can reach System Restore quickly by typing System Restore in the Start Menu Search box and picking it from the menu or clicking Start, All Programs, Accessories, System Tools, System Restore.

FIGURE 17.10

The System
Restore window.

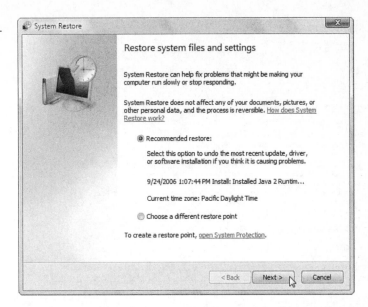

Restoring Your System

When something does go wrong and you wish you could get in a time machine
and go back to happy times when you could check your email and you could use
your printer, try reverting to a restore point, preferably the most recent one made
prior to your system's newfound problems. Follow these steps to do so:

1. Open System Restore as discussed in the previous section.

2. Vista is eerily good at suggesting a useful restore point, usually displaying
   the last important change you have made (installed a new program, for
   example). In Figure 17.10, in the previous section, System Restore has suggested a rollback to before Java 2
   Runtime was installed. If this is the
   correct point, simply click the Next
   button. Vista will do the restoration.

3. To choose a different point, click the
   Choose a different restore point button
   and then click Next. You will see a list
   of possible points similar to the one in
   Figure 17.11. Pick the one you want and
   Click Next to accomplish the restoration. Read and follow any onscreen
   prompts. Note that saved documents
   and email are not affected and you can
   reverse the actions of a system restore.

tip

If you want to undo the
restore, you can do so.
Follow the same steps to
open the System Restore
window. You now have an
option for undoing the
restore. Select this option
and then follow the onscreen
prompts, clicking Next to go from
step to step.

FIGURE 17.11

Restoring Vista to
better times.

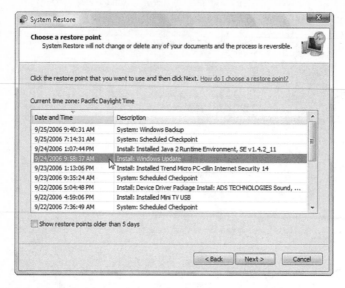

FIGURE 17.11

Restoring Vista to
better times.

Setting a System Restore Point

In addition to the restore points that the system sets automatically, you can manually set a restore point to the current point in time. Then you are guaranteed a
go-back-in-time point to when you know things were working. To set a system
restore point, follow these steps:

1. With the computer working the way you want it to, open the System Restore
   Explorer as described earlier in this chapter.

2. Click the Open System Protection link near the bottom of the System Restore
   explorer. You'll see a dialog box similar to the one in Figure 17.12.

FIGURE 17.12

You can manu-
ally specify
restore points
for any disks
connected to
your computer.

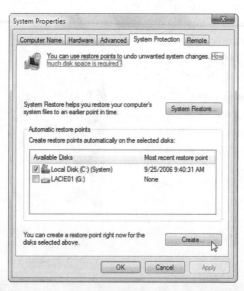

3. Click Create and type a description for the restore point (name it) and click Create a second time. The point is created with the date and time you set the restore.

THE ABSOLUTE MINIMUM

This chapter focuses on how to keep your data and computer secure using a variety of Windows Vista tools and other programs, including a backup program and a virus program. In particular, keep these main points in mind:

- Back up your data: It is the most important and valuable thing on your computer. A computer can be replaced; your data sometimes cannot.

- To back up, you use a backup program, such as Vista's built-in one or something purchased from a third party, as well as backup media (an external hard drive, tape drive, or DVD-R, CD-R, or RW drives). You can select how often to perform the backup and which files are backed up.

- Vista automatically scans your computer for errors. You can also use Windows Vista's Check Disk to do manual scans.

18

IMPROVING YOUR COMPUTER'S PERFORMANCE

Like a shiny new car off the dealer's parking lot, a computer never performs better than when it's fresh out of the box. However, over time you're sure to notice your PC's performance grow sluggish, among other inevitable annoyances. You might find, for example, that your desktop is cluttered with too many icons or that it takes forever for the hard drive to stop thrashing around upon logging into your user account. To keep your computer working as efficiently as possible, every now and then you should use some tools to check and, if needed, optimize the computer's performance. This chapter deals with how to perform routine maintenance on your hard disk and how to use Windows Vista's other tools to enhance your computer's performance.

Displaying Disk Information

Vista displays disk information to give you an idea of the size of your hard disk and how much space is used. This is handy if you think you are running out of room for your files.

When you click Computer in the Start menu, Vista shows you an Explorer window listing all the storage devices connected to your computer. For example, in Figure 18.1 there are three storage devices: the computer's hard drive and a DVD drive. There is also a removable flash memory device plugged into a USB port.

FIGURE 18.1

The Computer shows all connected storage devices and the free space on the hard drive(s).

If you select, for example, the hard drive from the Explorer window and review the Details pane, you'll see that Vista displays the amount of free space available on the hard disk (the 87GB drive in Figure 18.1 has 55.6GB available).

Saving Space Using Disk Cleanup

Like any storage place (think closets, garages, basements), eventually the clutter starts to overwhelm you, and you need

tip

You can easily get more information about this disk drive or any of the other attached storage devices by right-clicking on its icon and selecting Properties. The dialog that appears offers a more graphical look at the amount of used and free space available on the storage device.

to get rid of stuff you don't need. The same is true for your hard disk(s). You should periodically clean out files you don't need. To help with this task, you can clean up some temporary files, empty your Recycle Bin, and find some other clutter that takes up storage space.

Windows makes it easy to get rid of files that you don't need with the Disk Cleanup feature. When you use this wizard, Vista recommends some files for deleting and estimates the space you'll gain. You can select from the list of items suggested for deleting and then have Windows Vista remove these items and regain that space.

To clean up files using the Windows Vista Disk Cleanup Wizard, follow these steps:

1. Reach Computer from the Start menu and right-click on the drive you want to clean up and select Properties (see Figure 18.2)

FIGURE 18.2

Opening the Properties dialog box for any storage device gives additional details about the drive and offers tabs containing more options.

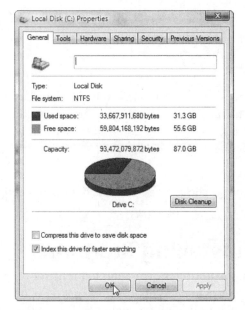

2. Click the Disk Cleanup button shown in Figure 18.2.

3. When asked if you want to clean up just your files, or files for all users of the computer, select the option that meets your needs.

4. Vista will chug and whirr for a while, then present you with a list of possible deletions similar to the one in Figure 18.3. It also estimates the amount of space that might be freed up.

caution

One of the first places Windows looks for space is in the Recycle Bin. Before you permanently delete those files, take a quick peek to make sure that the Recycle Bin doesn't contain any files you need. To view the particular files, select the item in the list and then click the View Files button. You can then confirm that they can be deleted.

FIGURE 18.3

Possible things
you can delete.
Don't get carried
away.

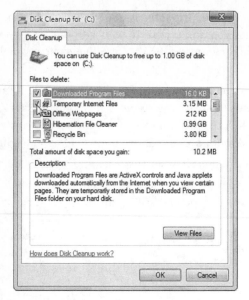

5. Check the items you want to delete. Generally all of the listed files can be safely deleted. Do be sure there is nothing in the Recycle Bin that does not belong there. Uncheck items you do not want to delete. If you are uncertain about a category of items, don't delete them.

6. Click OK.

7. Confirm the deletion by clicking Yes. The files are permanently deleted and that disk space regained.

Saving Space by Uninstalling Programs

Although the Disk Cleanup feature can clear out a fair amount of space on your hard drive, one of the best ways to net even more is to get rid of any old programs you no longer use. For more information on adding and removing programs, see Chapter 14, "Setting Up Programs." You can also remove Windows features that you do not use.

Saving Space by Compressing Files

As mentioned, you'll be surprised how quickly your computer fills up with files, especially if you work with a lot of digital photos, music, or video files. You can delete unneeded files, but some files fall into the category "I want to keep it, but I don't really use it."

With the cost of adding an external hard disk plummeting every day, your best bet might be to simply purchase an additional hard drive, plug it into a USB or FireWire port on the back of your computer and move the rarely used files onto it.

Alternatively, if your computer is capable of writing DVDs or CDs consider moving the rarely used files to discs.

A final, and many think unwise, alternative is to compress files and leave those compressed files on your hard disk; deleting the originals and then expanding the compressed ones when you need them. Chances are you won't have any more room on your hard drive later than you have today, so compression only puts off the problem without solving it.

Nevertheless, compressing large files is a great idea if you need to fit them on a CD or floppy to pop in the mail, or if you want to email big files.

caution

A good rule of thumb is to always have at least 20% of your primary (C:) drive's disk space available. Keep an eye on it. Delete files and consider a hardware upgrade if you're continually running out of space.

Compressing Files

Follow these steps to compress files:

1. Select the file(s) or folder you want to compress.

2. Right-click any of the selected items and then select the Send To command. You see the Send To options (see Figure 18.4).

FIGURE 18.4

You can create a compressed folder from the Send To menu.

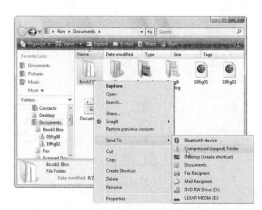

3. Select Compressed (zipped) folder. The files are zipped up and stored in a folder with the default name of the first file or folder you selected. The files still appear in the compressed folder (just double-click it to see them) and you can rename it if you like.

Now you can email the compressed file(s), copy them to a DVD, and so on.

If you decide to free up hard disk space by keeping the compressed file and trashing the originals it's smart to open (double-click) the compressed folder to confirm it contains the correct files and folder. If it does, it's safe to remove the original files and folders from your system.

Uncompress Files

If you need to access these files again, you can uncompress or unzip them as follows:

> **tip**
>
> You can add additional files to the compressed folder. Drag the file icon to the folder icon. The file is added but also appears listed. You can delete the file because it is now stored in the compressed folder.

1. Open the drive and folder that contains the compressed folder. Note that the folder icon has a little zipper indicating that it is a compressed folder (see Figure 18.5).

FIGURE 18.5

Compressed files and folders have zippers on their icons.

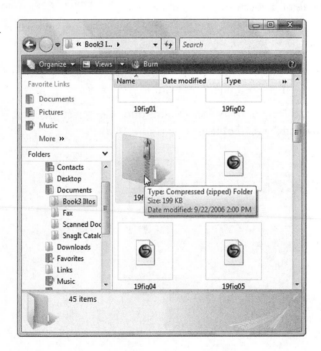

2. Double-click the compressed folder. You see the files within this folder. Note that the files are not uncompressed until you follow the next steps.
3. Select the file(s) you want to unzip and then select the Copy command. You can right-click and select Copy, or you can click Copy the selected items in the task pane.

4. Open the folder where you want to place the uncompressed files. Usually you can click Back to go back to the original folder (the one that contained the compressed folder).

5. Copy the files by right-clicking a blank area of the file window and selecting Paste.

The file(s) are uncompressed, and you can now open and work with them as needed.

> **tip**
>
> There are two other ways to uncompress files or folders. One easy way is to drag files and folders to a new location. You can also right-click a compressed folder and select Extract All. This starts a wizard in Vista that walks you through uncompressing the folder.

Increasing Performance by Defragmenting Your Disk

Another way to improve performance is to *defragment* your disk. To understand how this process improves your disk performance, you first need to have a short introduction to how data is stored on a hard disk.

Understanding the Basics of Disk Storage

When you store data on your computer, you create files with specific names, each stored in a specific location on your disk. To keep files organized, your disk is divided into sections called *sectors*, which are broken down into smaller sections called *clusters*. Each cluster can hold a certain amount of data.

A file is usually larger than one cluster. Therefore, when you save a file, Windows stores it in the first available cluster it can find. If the file is too big to fit in one cluster, Windows goes to the next available cluster, stores more of the file in that cluster, and so on, until the entire file is stored on the disk.

On a well-organized, clean disk there are plenty of contiguous clusters and large files are stored in sequential clusters. If there are not enough contiguous clusters for a file, Windows scatters parts of the file around wherever it can find available clusters, and keeps a "cheat sheet" that tells Windows where all the chunks of each file are stored. Consequently, the data for a single file can end up physically scattered (fragmented) all over your PC's hard disk.

When you open that file again, Windows collects all the pieces of the file, basically putting the file together again. When a file is badly fragmented, it requires the disk drive to spend a lot of time rummaging around the whole disk gathering up data from the widely scattered clusters.

Initially, this does not cause serious performance problems because your disk is mostly empty, and files are usually stored sequentially or at least with all their parts in nearby neighborhoods. However, over time your disk files become more fragmented and you might find that it takes a long time to open a file or start a program.

To speed up access to files and to help prevent potential problems with fragmented files, you can use Disk Defragmenter to *defragment* your disk. Defragmenting basically reorders the files on the disk, putting file parts next to each other if possible and putting all the empty, available clusters together so that when new files are saved, they get a block

tip

Vista automatically defrags your hard disk on a schedule you can alter.

of clusters together. Defragmenting your disk is a general-maintenance job that you should perform every few weeks for best results.

Running Disk Defragmenter

Although Vista automatically defrags without your intervention, you can manually run the defragmentation program on your hard disk any time you like by following these steps:

1. Choose Computer from the Start menu, right-click on the disk you wish to defrag and select Properties (refer to Figure 18.2).

2. Click the Tools tab in the Properties dialog box, as shown in Figure 18.6.

FIGURE 18.6
Use the Tools tab to access disk tools.

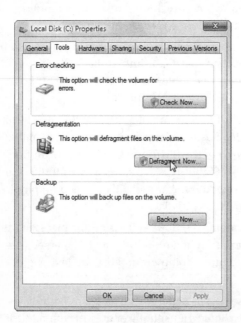

3. Click the Defragment Now button. You are asked for permission to continue, and perhaps for the Administrator's password. From the Disk Defragmenter window you can choose to defragment your drive or modify the automatic defrag schedule.

4. To force a defrag operation click Defragment Now. After the defrag process begins you can click the Cancel Defragmentation button (it replaces the Defragment Now button) to stop the process (which can take up to several hours to complete, depending on the size of your hard drive, free space, and the current level of fragmentation).

5. When the process completes, you can choose to display a report; this report displays detailed information about the disk that was defragmented. Click the Close button to close the report and then the Defragmenter window. Or you can click OK to close the Disk Defragmenter window without viewing the report.

Changing the Defrag Schedule

To change the time of day, day of the week, or frequency of defragmentation operations click the Modify Schedule button (refer to Figure 18.6) and adjust the schedule as shown in Figure 18.7.

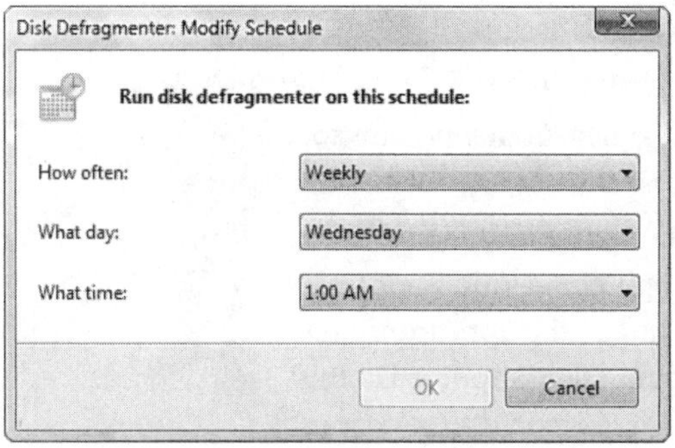

FIGURE 18.7
Modify the defragmentation schedule here.

As you can see you can adjust the frequency, day, and time Vista should use to run an automatic hard disk defrag. The only stipulation is that the system be powered on and not being actively used.

Working with Desktop Icons

In addition to cleaning up files, you might also want to tidy up your desktop. Doing so won't necessarily improve the system performance, but it can help *your* performance—that is, help you find and access the icons on your desktop more efficiently.

Follow these steps:

1. Right-click a blank part of the desktop and open the View shown in Figure 18.8.

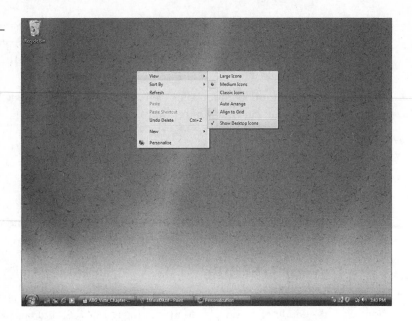

2. To hide desktop icons, click the Show
   Desktop submenu choice to toggle the
   checkmark on (show desktop icons) or
   off (hide desktop icons).

3. You can use the other submenu items to
   arrange the icons and change their style.

4. You can also change Icons, (add
   Computer, Control panel, and so on).
   You can even change the appearance of
   Icons by changing their graphics. Do this
   by visiting Personalization and selecting
   or deselecting items, or using the Change
   Icon button to alter an Icon's appearance.

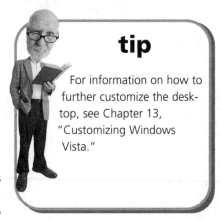

tip

For information on how to
further customize the desktop, see Chapter 13,
"Customizing Windows
Vista."

It needn't be all or nothing at all. If you just want to cleanse your desktop of a few
annoying icons you don't need while preserving the rest, you can right-click on just
about any desktop icon, select Delete, and send it to the trash. You'll be asked to
confirm this action, but after you do, the icons go to the Recycle Bin where you can
retrieve them (before you empty the bin) if you change your mind.

For most users deleting unwanted icons as they start to annoy you and leaving
the desired icons turned on might be a better solution than hiding them all.
Otherwise, if you hide the icons, and then add programs over the years, the
icons installed for those programs will likely appear when you redisplay icons,
creating a potentially cluttered desktop.

Scheduling Maintenance Tasks

Maintenance tasks are easy to overlook. However, the old axiom still holds true: An ounce of prevention is worth a pound of cure. Fortunately, Vista looks out for you, so that you don't have to remember to do easy, but important, system maintenance chores. Vista schedules and runs the most maintenance-important tasks itself. For instance, you can set up the backup program to run once a week (or monthly or daily).

You can schedule maintenance tasks and other tasks, including checking and downloading mail. You basically can run any program at the time and interval you select. This section covers how to add and modify scheduled tasks.

In earlier Windows versions you needed to use a tool called Scheduled tasks to set up things such as automatic defragmentation, system updates, file backups, and so on. Vista has lightened the load for us somewhat by coming preconfigured to do many things on a recommended schedule, and by asking you when you would like to do specific tasks, such as automatic backups the first time you use the program—Backup, and so on.

There is a scheduling tool in Vista (called Task Scheduler) but most beginners should probably avoid messing with it because it contains schedules for important, technical tasks. If you absolutely must satisfy your curiosity about this you can open the Start menu and choose All Programs, Accessories, System Tools, Task Scheduler (or just type "Task Scheduler" into the Start menu's Instant Search box). You can see the Task Scheduler interface in Figure 18.9.

caution

My advice to beginners is "look but don't touch." Unless, of course you know what a CrawlStartPages task is and how often it should run. But then you wouldn't be a beginner, right?

FIGURE 18.9

Schedule specific tasks in the Task Scheduler window.

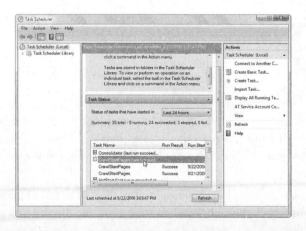

Modifying Scheduled Tasks

The programs found by default in the Task Schedule that you most likely might want to reschedule—Windows Updates, backups, and so on—let you change schedules from within the programs themselves, and are discussed along with their related topics throughout the book. Some programs, such as antivirus packages and email applications, also have scheduling features used to download new versions, fetch the latest email, and so on. You schedule these things from within the programs themselves, not through the Vista Task Scheduler. Consult the programs' documentation or online help for assistance.

tip

If you want to learn how to use the more advanced options available in Task Scheduler you might want to look into a more advanced book, such as *Special Edition Using Windows Vista* (ISBN #0-7897-3472-9), by Bob Cowart and Brian Knittel.

Setting Power Options

Nobody wants to waste energy, and this is particularly true for those of us with battery operated computers. Vista has improved power management features for both battery and AC powered computers. Because portable computers have the most complex and important power setting issues, this section looks at that scenario.

The quickest way to find Vista's Power Options feature is to search for Power Options in the Start menu search bar. You'll see an explorer something like the one in Figure 18.10, but with your computer's power options displayed.

FIGURE 18.10
The Power
Options explorer.

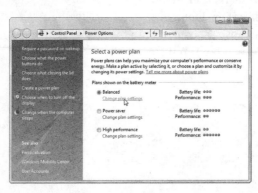

From this one place you can change individual settings for such things as how long the display stays lit while the computer is idle, predefined combinations of settings designed to either save battery power or boost performance at the expense of battery life, and so on.

For example, to define how long the display should stay powered up when the computer is not in use, click the Choose when to turn off the display link and you will see potions similar to those in Figure 18.11. Over time you will develop power settings that suit your work style.

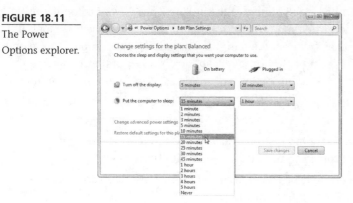

ReadyBoost and ReadyDrive

Vista has an intriguing new feature called ReadyBoost. It works with Vista's SuperFetch feature and lets you use selected external memory devices such as high performance USB thumb drives and flash memory cards to boost your computer's performance by "caching," or temporarily storing copies of frequently used files on these fast, solid state devices. This makes it less necessary for Vista to access your relatively slower hard disk during frequently done tasks.

ReadyBoost

When you plug in an external memory device Vista displays an AutoPlay dialog box containing, among other choices "Speed up my system." If you click on that choice Vista examines the device to see if it is fast enough and has enough free space to work with the ReadyBoost feature. If it does, Vista uses the drive to speed up your system's ability to access stored data.

Note that ReadyBoost encrypts the files placed on your removable device, so you needn't worry about security. And unplugging the device will do no harm, your computer will simply go back to its former, slower self.

ReadyDrive

ReadyDrive is a feature designed to support a new crop of "hybrid" disk drives emerging on the market. These hard disk drives add solid state flash memory to the drive, which enables Vista to use the faster solid state memory to boost efficiency. These drives should be a big help to portable computer users, so if you are shopping for a new notebook computer and performance and battery life are important to you, explore the possibility of adding a hybrid disk drive.

THE ABSOLUTE MINIMUM

In this chapter you learned how to improve the performance of your computer using some of the built-in tools in Windows Vista. You might not need to use these tools if you have a new computer, but keep them in mind as you use the computer more and more. If you notice a drop in performance, take a look at some of the changes you can make to regain that performance. In particular, keep these main points in mind:

- You can view the disk properties of your hard disk to see how much total space you have, how much is used, and how much is free.

- If your drive is becoming too full and you want to remove files, you can help Windows select some commonly unneeded files for removal.

- For files you want to keep (but don't need immediate access to), compress them or move them to other media.

- When performance is really slow, you might need to defragment the drive to optimize performance. Vista does this on a schedule. You can start the defragment process sooner from the Tools tab of the Disk Properties dialog box.

- If your desktop becomes cluttered with too many icons, you can hide them by right-clicking, or perhaps, better yet, right-click and delete the unnecessary ones when they get in your way.

19

UPGRADING YOUR COMPUTER

As you use your computer more and more, you might find that you want to add features to it. For instance, you might purchase a digital camera or music player, such as an iPod. You might add a new printer for printing photographs. As another example, you might change how you connect to the Internet, switching from dial-up to a cable modem, perhaps.

Usually when you install new hardware Vista recognizes the new device as soon as you plug it in, and it walks you through the necessary steps to run it correctly, or even complete the installation automatically without your help and then notify you of its success. Sometimes, however, you need to install software before attaching the hardware to your computer, or answer a series of questions during the installation process to help Vista get up to speed with your new hardware.

For most hardware additions you can use the Hardware and Sound portion of the Control Panel (click Start, Control Panel), or simply plug in the device and follow the onscreen instructions. This chapter provides an overview of how to add many types of computer hardware.

Adding a Printer

Perhaps the most common addition to a computer is a printer. Windows Vista manages print jobs for all of your programs. Therefore, you set up printers in Windows, and then all programs can access and use your printer(s).

In many cases, Windows can automatically set up your printer as soon as you attach it to your computer. However, if that doesn't work, you can perform a manual installation, also discussed in this chapter.

Automatic Setup

On a good day all you need to do is plug in your new printer, wait and watch. Most printers today connect to your PC via its USB port. After you do that, Windows Vista recognizes the presence of a new hardware device and queries it, looking for technical setup details. Vista uses the information it gleans for the installation. As illustrated in Figure 19.1 Vista alerts you that the printer has been found and is being installed. Progress messages pop up from the system tray as the installation progresses. If you get a successful installation message, you are set. You can use your printer and skip the rest of this section!

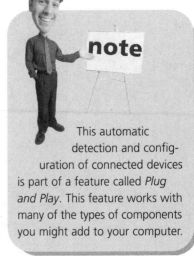

caution

It's important to read the documentation that comes with any new gadget before plugging it into your computer. Not doing so can complicate hardware installation, and might necessitate your listening to music on hold while waiting for tech support. If at any point you find that the information found here conflicts with the installation instructions that came with your new hardware, follow the manufacturer's guidelines.

note

This automatic detection and configuration of connected devices is part of a feature called *Plug and Play*. This feature works with many of the types of components you might add to your computer.

FIGURE 19.1

Often Vista takes care of hardware installations without your intervention. Watch the progress in the lower-right area of your screen.

Installing device driver software
Click here for status.

3:48 PM

Manual Setup Using Vista Drivers

If the automatic setup doesn't work, you can add a printer manually from the Hardware and Sound section of the control panel. You might need to do this if you have a printer that isn't on Vista's Plug and Play list. Cutting edge printers, older printers, or budget printers, for instance, might require manual installation.

One quick way to add a printer manually is to click on the printer icon in the Control Panel and then click the resulting Add a printer link.

After you have connected the printer to your computer using the necessary cable and have rounded up any installation disc(s), perform these steps, following any onscreen prompts carefully:

1. Click Start and then click Control Panel.

2. In the Control Panel window, click the Hardware and Sound link. You should see a window similar to Figure 19.2).

3. Click Add a Printer.

4. For the first step, select to set up a local printer or network printer (see Figure 19.2). For the purposes of this example, let's go with Add a Local Printer.

5. You are prompted to select the printer port (see Figure 19.3). Non Plug and Play printers are most often attached via the LPT1 (also called *parallel*) port. Select the correct port from the drop-down list port and click Next. You see a list of printer manufacturers and printers.

6. Select your printer manufacturer in the list on the left. Then select your particular printer from the list on the right (see Figure 19.4). Click Next.

7. You are next prompted to type a name for the printer. This name is used to identify the printer icon for this printer. Type or accept the suggested name and also select whether you want to make this the default printer by clicking Yes or No. Click Next.

A *driver* is software that tells Windows the specific details of your hardware device, such as how it works and what features it has. The driver enables Windows to communicate with the device and put it to use. Printers, for instance, have drivers as do virtually every other hardware component connected to your system from graphics cards to your keyboard and mouse.

To install a shared printer you need to have your local network or wireless network set up first. See Chapter 10, "Setting Up Windows Vista on a Home Network," for details.

FIGURE 19.2

Installing a
printer from the
Control Panel.

FIGURE 19.3

For our purposes,
a port is a plug
that connects a
device cable to
the computer,
often, but not
always using a
cable.

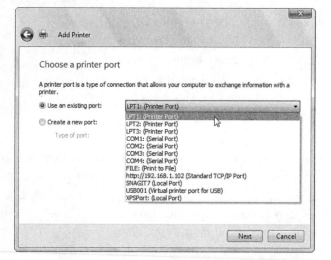

FIGURE 19.4

Windows Vista
lists the printer
models for which
it has drivers.

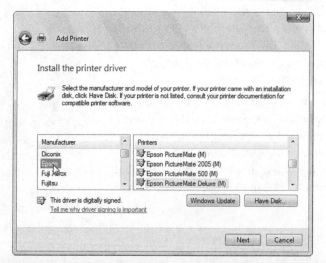

8. You should see a screen similar to Figure 19.5 congratulating you on the successful installation and offering a chance to print a test page. Click the test page button and cross your fingers.

FIGURE 19.5

With luck you'll get the success message and can print a test page.

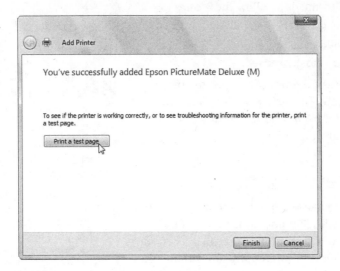

Manual Setup Using the Printer's Drivers

Most printers come with a disc that contains a driver for using the printer. If your printer is not listed in the Add Printer list and running Windows Update does not help, and you have your printer's installation disc, you can install the appropriate driver from the disc by inserting the disc and using the installer's browse button to locate the driver files. Some discs have multiple drivers. Be sure you select the correct model, language, and so on.

You can also find drivers at different Internet sites (for instance, www.WinDrivers.com). You can find the printer driver from the site of the printer maker, from a Windows or Microsoft site, or from a general hardware help site (www.pcguide.com). Check your printer documentation to see what online resources you have. Try searching the Microsoft

note

If your printer is not on the list and you are connected to the Internet click the Windows Update button to see if you can add the necessary driver. Or if you have an installation disc that came with the printer, click the Have Disk button and follow the directions.

site (www.microsoft.com) for printer drivers. Or look for sites in computer articles for general help (www.pcworld.com).

If you have the disc, follow these steps to install the driver from the disc:

1. Follow the preceding "Add a Printer" steps to get started.

2. When prompted to select the printer software, click Have Disc. You are prompted to select the disc that contains the driver.

tip

If your printer fails to print a Vista test page, check the obvious first. Is the printer plugged into both the computer and the power outlet and is it powered up? Is there paper in the supply tray? If there's a way to manually print a test page from your printer menu or buttons try that. The next most likely culprit is the driver, or perhaps you're failing to follow the manufacturer's installation instructions. Reread them.

Installing New Fonts

One of the most common formatting changes you make is changing appearance of the text by using a different font. You can select from business fonts to calligraphy fonts, from fancy fonts to silly fonts. The fonts that are listed within the program are the fonts you have installed in Windows Vista. How do they get there and what fonts do you have? This section answers these questions.

Where Do Fonts Come from?

Fonts come from several sources, and the first source is the printer itself. Every printer comes with built-in fonts that it can print, and these are usually indicated with a printer icon in font lists.

tip

See Chapter 7, "Browsing the Internet," for more help on visiting websites.

In addition to the built-in fonts, Windows itself includes numerous built-in fonts; these fonts are actually TrueType files and they tell the printer how to print that particular font. Other TrueType fonts are installed when you install some programs; the programs themselves also include fonts and when you install the program, you also install the fonts.

As another source, you can purchase fonts and install them within Windows. After they are installed, they become available to all programs. Some sites, such as www.1001fonts.com, provide free fonts. You can download these fonts from the site and add them to your font list. This section covers how to view the fonts you already have on your system and how to add new fonts.

Viewing Your Installed Fonts

Windows Vista lets you view which fonts you have and install new fonts. You do so using the Fonts Control Panel. Follow these steps:

1. Click Start and then click Control Panel.

2. In the Control Panel window, click the Appearance and Personalization link. Click Install and or Remove a font under the Fonts heading or the Fonts heading itself. (You will see a list of installed fonts like the one in Figure 19.6.)

3. To view a font, double-click the font icon as shown in Figure 19.6. You see a sample of the font in various sizes and information about the font (its name, type, version, and file size). Figure 19.7, for instance, shows the information revealed about Aharoni Bold when you double-click on its icon. You can print out these samples if you like using the Print button. The advanced button shows technical information that might be of interest to artists and designers.

4. Click the Close buttons in the upper-right corners of the font sample and explorer windows to close them.

note

When printing, Vista creates an XPS document in the background and sends the XPS image to the printer. Because the doc is an image, it doesn't matter what fonts are used in the document. Your printer will print what's in the image, so it is now almost irrelevant which fonts your printer contains.

FIGURE 19.6

Fonts are stored as files on your computer and indicated with a font icon.

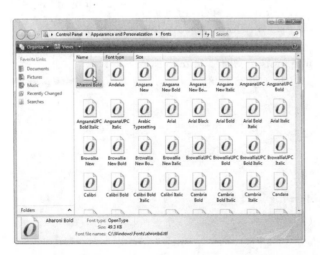

FIGURE 19.7

FIGURE 19.7
Double-click font icons to see how each letter of the alphabet appears in the font and a sample sentence in various sizes.

Installing New Fonts

If you obtain new fonts, you can install them in Windows as follows:

1. Right-click on any blank part of the font list shown back in Figure 19.6 (but not on a font icon) and choose Install New Font from the menu.

2. Select the drive that contains your font files from the Drives drop-down list.

3. If the files are stored within folders, double-click on the folder from the Folders list. Until you open the folder you won't see any fonts displayed. When you open the drive and folder, all the available fonts are listed in the List of fonts list (see Figure 19.8).

> **tip**
>
> To add fonts you have downloaded, you usually copy the fonts from the download location to the Fonts folder. (The path to the Fonts folder is WINDOWS/FONTS.) You might have to uncompress the fonts if they are zipped or compressed into a zip folder first. Check the site for specific directions on installing the font files.

FIGURE 19.8
Many font collections include so many fonts that you probably don't want to install them all. Instead, select the fonts from the collection that you do want to install from this dialog box.

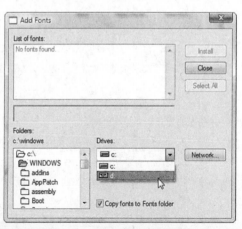

4. Select the font(s) to install. To select multiple fonts, Ctrl+click each font you want to select. To select all fonts, click the Select All button.

5. Be sure the Copy fonts to Fonts folder box is checked, and then click Install to install the selected fonts. You will probably be prompted with a permission screen. Click Continue if you want to install the fonts. The files are copied to the Fonts folder and are then available in all Windows programs.

6. Click the Close button to close the Fonts window.

tip

After you become comfortable with browsing, dragging, and dropping, you can quickly add fonts to Vista by copying and pasting or dragging them from folders into the font list shown in Figure 19.6.

Setting Up New Hardware

As you use your computer, you might find that you want to add new or upgraded components to your system. You might purchase a digital camera or scanner. You might add a rewritable DVD drive or add more system memory (RAM). As another example, you might add one of the many digital music add-ons, such as a portable digital music player.

Sometimes setting up new hardware can be as straightforward as the automatic printer installation described earlier. In the best-case scenario, you simply attach or install the new device, and Windows Vista sets it up automatically.

caution

Remember it's always a good idea to read the documentation that comes with your device *before* connecting it. Some devices need special software installations to precede hardware connections!

This is usually the case for any device that connects to your computer via a USB port, including a mouse, keyboard, scanner, digital audio player, and so on. If that doesn't happen, however, you can always install the device manually. Both methods are covered in this section.

Setting Up New Hardware Automatically

To set up hardware automatically, simply follow the installation instructions for your particular device. For some add-on components, you plug the device into an available connector. For example, most scanners plug into a USB port.

For other hardware, you might have to turn off your computer and remove the system case. For instance, to install a wired or wireless network card or upgrade a graphics card, you have to turn off the power, remove the case, and then plug the cards into an open, matching slot inside the system unit.

In either case, if Windows Vista recognizes the new hardware, it automatically starts the Add Hardware Wizard and queries the device for setup information. It then installs the appropriate driver file and alerts you that the device has been found and installed. You should see alert messages in the system tray as this process is completed. You can then use your device.

Again, the most important thing to do is follow the instructions the manufacturer of the device provided for you. Each device is unique and the instructions provided with them help you navigate most potential bumps in the road.

Using the Manufacturer's Install Program

Usually a hardware component comes with a disc containing its own driver and installation software. If your new device came with a disc, use this disc to install the new hardware. Usually, but not always, you are instructed to connect the device and then insert the disc to start the installation process. Follow the specific instructions for your particular hardware component.

USB is short for *universal serial bus*, and it is a type of port found on all modern computers. You can connect devices to these ports by plugging in the USB cable to an available USB connector on your computer.

There are two "flavors" of USB: the original USB 1.1 and USB 2.0 (also called Hi-Speed USB). Some demanding devices (for example, video cameras and high-performance disk drives) require a USB 2 connection, or at least they work better when plugged into a USB 2.0 port. Newer computers, like the ones most likely to be running Windows Vista, almost all have USB 2.0 ports. Many older computers can be upgraded with a USB 2.0 add-in card. Consider this when purchasing new gear.

Hardware-specific installation discs might also contain accessory programs that you might or might not need to install. Most digital cameras come with photo organizing programs for example. Because Vista does a nice job of this task already, you might choose not to install the extra programs that came with your camera, and only load the necessary drivers if Vista doesn't already have them.

Installing New Hardware Manually

If the Add Hardware Wizard does not start and find your new hardware device automatically or if you do not have a driver from the hardware maker, you can use the Add Hardware Wizard to manually set up the device.

When you begin the process that follows, Vista encourages you to try installing your device using the installation disc that came with it before attempting a manual install on your own; therefore, if possible, and you have not done this already, give that a try before proceeding with the steps that follow.

You can then have Windows search for and install the new device or you can select the device manufacturer and product from a list. Windows Vista includes drivers for many popular hardware components.

Follow these steps to run the Add Hardware Wizard:

caution

If Vista does not automatically install your new device and the installation disc provided also fails to get the device working, consider getting knowledgeable help before attempting a manual installation. The manual installation process is "pushing the envelope" for absolute beginners and will likely frustrate you.

1. Click Start and then Control Panel.

2. Change to Classic view by clicking the Classic view link in the task pane. In the Control Panel window, double-click Add Hardware. You will be asked to confirm the operation, or perhaps to provide an Administrator's password.

3. You see a Welcome screen for the Add Hardware Wizard. Read it and click next to continue or Cancel to use the installation disc that came with your device.

4. Vista asks if you want it to search for uninstalled hardware or if you want to manually select it from a list. Start by letting Vista search for you. See Figure 19.9.

FIGURE 19.9

Vista can look for uninstalled hardware and sometimes takes charge of the installation after it finds it.

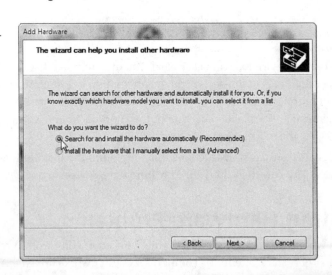

5. Select Add a new hardware device. (Scroll to the end of the list to find this option.) Click Next. You have the choice of letting Windows Vista search for the new device and set it up automatically or to set up the device manually. Try searching first.

6. To have Windows Vista search and install, select this option and click Next. Windows Vista searches for new devices. If the device is found, Windows Vista then installs the new device. Follow the onscreen prompts to install and set up the device. You can skip the remaining steps listed here.

   Or

   If the automatic method failed, Vista tells you; clicking Next takes you to a list similar to the one in Figure 19.10. Clicking the Show All Devices gives you the most comprehensive list. (Vista updates this list over time as part of the automatic update process.)

FIGURE 19.10

Select the make and model of the device you are adding.

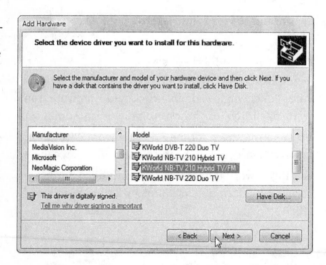

7. Select your device type and click Next. You are prompted to select the manufacturer and model of the device you are attempting to install. Scroll through the list of manufacturers until you see the manufacturer of your device. Then click it. When you see available models from this manufacturer in the Model list scroll and click the model. Now click Next.

8. Follow the onscreen instructions for completing the installation of your device. You can then use your new hardware device.

Troubleshooting Hardware Problems

Sometimes when you add a new device, your computer won't work properly. Perhaps the computer gets stuck or else the component doesn't work correctly. For instance, if your printer driver isn't functioning, your printer might print random characters.

If you are having problems with a particular hardware device, you can use one of Windows Vista's troubleshooters to display common problems and solutions.

Follow these steps to display help on a particular hardware device:

1. Use the search box near the Start button to search for "Device Manager."

2. Click the resulting link.

3. You see the Device Manager listing the categories of hardware devices. Each category has a plus sign next to it. You can click this plus sign to expand the list and see the device(s) installed for each category. Figure 19.11, for instance, shows the expanded Sound, video, and game controllers category.

> **tip**
>
> If your computer gets stuck, you might have to undo the installation of the hardware component. To do so, you might use the System Restore points to restore the system to the settings *before* the installation. Chapter 17, "Safeguarding Your Work," covers using System Restore. Sometimes, simply choosing safe mode when you restart (press the F8 key while the system is booting) and restarting again normally will solve the problem.

FIGURE 19.11

The Device Manager can help troubleshoot and repair some installation problems.

This device is not working properly

4. Problem devices usually have little yellow caution triangles next to them. The USB 2861 Device in Figure 19.11 is an example.

5. Double-click the troublesome device. This launches the Windows Vista Properties dialog box for the device (also shown in Figure 19.11).

6. To activate a Vista troubleshooter, click the Check for solutions... button.

7. Vista looks on your hard disk and on the Internet, if you are connected, for possible solutions to the problem. Review each screen, selecting the appropriate option and clicking Next.

If you are in luck, the device starts to work. If not, you are prompted to report the problem to Microsoft so that they can add it to their list of potential bugs to stomp out. (That doesn't mean you should expect a message from Microsoft if they do identify and fix the problem. This function is intended for them to find and fix widespread problems, as opposed to those found on an individual user level.)

To get one-on-one help, the best thing to do is contact the device's manufacturer or your dealer for technical support. Start with the website, and then try online chat if it's available, or, heaven forbid, dial up some phone help. Good luck!

THE ABSOLUTE MINIMUM

In this chapter you learned about some additional maintenance features available in Windows Vista, in particular the following:

- You need to set up any printers you use with your computer. The easiest way is automatic setup, which works for common printers. You can also set up the printer manually using a printer driver from Windows Vista or an installation disc from your printer maker.

- Fonts enable you to change the appearance of text within a document. The fonts available in your programs are the fonts you have installed through Windows or the ones that were included with your printer. You can view the fonts and add new fonts using the Font Control Panel icon.

- If you add new hardware, you can install it using one of several methods: automatically, using the installation program and files provided with the hardware component, and using the Add New Hardware Wizard.

- You can use the Device Manager to display information about installed hardware and troubleshoot a device if you are having problems.

IN THIS CHAPTER

- Windows Anytime Upgrade
- Using Windows Update
- Installing or Removing Windows Extras
- Moving Files and Settings from Another PC (Easy Transfer)

20

UPGRADING WINDOWS

Windows Vista is constantly evolving, even as you read this book. Microsoft programmers constantly find and fix problems, add new drivers to support the latest hardware innovations, and so on. They also upgrade security features as the hacker wars continue. Windows Vista makes it easy for you to have an up-to-date version of the operating system with little or no intervention on your part.

However, Windows Vista adds another factor to the upgrade landscape, depending on which version of it you're using. With Windows XP you could purchase XP Home or XP Professional (and later the Media Center and Tablet PC editions), but after you made your choice, that's the OS you had. There was no way to switch to a different version without buying it. With Windows Vista, you can upgrade a "lesser" version, like Home Basic, to a more feature-rich version like Home Premium, Business, or the Ultimate Editions.

Finally, you can also make changes to your existing Windows Vista installation. You can review the list of installed Vista components and add or remove them as you see fit. That's the focus of this chapter— upgrading Windows.

Windows Anytime Upgrade

As I discussed in the start of the chapter, Vista has several versions available. Which one you have depends on what you purchased off the shelf or what your computer's manufacturer provided. The type of edition you have might have includes:

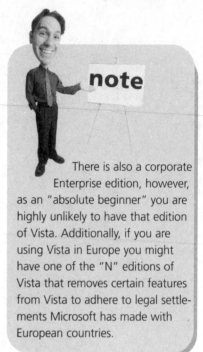

- Windows Vista Home Basic
- Windows Vista Home Premium
- Windows Vista Business
- Windows Vista Ultimate

To find out which edition of Vista you have, all you need to do is open the Start menu, right-click Computer and select Properties. The Window that appears tells you a variety of information about your system, including the version of Vista that you're running.

If you're running a "lesser" version of Vista and want some of the features found in one of the "big-ger" editions, you don't need to run out and buy a new version on the shelf of your local software store. Your current Vista DVD has every version of Windows on it, it's just a question of which one you're licensed to install and upgrading to a bigger edition is a simple manner of employing the Vista's Anytime Upgrade feature.

To activate Windows Anytime Upgrade, open the Start menu and click Control Panel. Select the System and Maintenance link and then click the link that says Windows Anytime Upgrade. From there it's a simple matter of following Microsoft's onscreen directions to purchase an upgraded version of Windows Vista.

Using Windows Update

As I've already indicated, Windows is always evolving. In addition to various individual security updates and program fixes, Microsoft typically offers "Service Packs" every couple of years that combine past Windows Update releases and add a host of new fixes and features. In effect, these Service Packs give you an updated, hopefully more reliable, version of Windows. For example, many if not most Windows XP users are (or ought to be) running version 2002, Service Pack 2.

tip

You can check version information about your edition of Windows by right-clicking Computer from the Start menu and selecting Properties.

At least in the short term, expect Vista to stick with a consistent update process where improvements are made available to users as soon as they are created. As with Windows XP, over time we'll likely see a Service Pack that combines these fixes into a single download so that newly installed versions of Vista won't have to download multiple individual fixes.

The utility Microsoft uses to deliver updates to Windows PCs is called Windows Update. Microsoft specifically designed Windows Update so that average users wouldn't have to worry about remembering to look for and install critical updates that close security holes, fix bugs, or add new features to Vista. Windows Update enables you to let the process happen automatically, leaving you with one less computing chore to worry about.

Although Windows Update can and does work without your intervention, you can and should learn how to interact with it. To gain access to the Windows Update, simply open the Start menu, and select All Programs, Windows Update. This opens the Windows Update window shown in Figure 20.1.

FIGURE 20.1

You can see the status of updates in the Windows Update explorer.

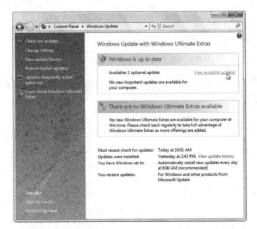

From this window you can see if there are any important or optional updates, and if there are any new features Microsoft would like you to try or, in some cases, purchase. This is also the screen you use to change the automated update settings, view the history of updates for your computer, and learn about new optional features.

To keep your system as up-to-date as possible, you should ensure that critical Windows updates are installed promptly. These updates, as mentioned, fix bugs and provide software

tip

If you're not sure if the list of available updates is accurate, click the Check for Updates link.

patches. A bug is a problem in the software code that causes problems. A patch is a small chunk of programming code that repairs the bug or provides some additional functions for Windows.

There are two ways to install an update. This section covers both of these methods and how to change the notification settings (how and when you are notified about updates).

Running Automatic Updates

If you have an Internet connection established, when Windows Vista is initially installed, critical updates are downloaded and applied automatically. If you don't have an active Internet connection when installing Vista, it will gather and install the updates the next time you connect to the Internet. Unless you have a specific reason to do otherwise, you should leave automatic updates on, and then occasionally confirm that it is working properly by checking to see if there are any available updates that you might want that haven't been downloaded and installed.

Checking for Updates

You can check for updates at any time. For instance, in addition to critical updates, Microsoft also provides optional, non-critical updates and updates that add new features. To check for and install other updates, follow these steps:

1. Click Start, All Programs, Windows Update.

2. From the same Windows Update screen you saw in Figure 20.1, click the View Available Updates link. This takes you to a page that lists any updates that haven't been installed on your system.

3. You will see a list of available updates and if you double-click on them, you can read about them in secondary windows like the one shown in Figure 20.2. The information Window for an update gives you an overview and often provides links to the Internet for more details.

tip

To check for and install automatic updates, you must have an Internet connection. See Chapter 5, "Getting Wired for Communication," for more information on this topic. Given the size of some of Vista's updates, a broadband connection is highly recommended, but not required.

note

Not all updates available from Windows Update are "critical." Over time, there are bound to be some non-critical updates available of which you might want to take advantage.

FIGURE 20.2

When you double-click an available update from the Windows Update window, Vista opens a dialog box with an in-depth description of that update.

4. If you do want the update, or multiple updates, click to place checkmarks next to the desired updates, leaving the unwanted items unchecked, then click Install to begin the process. From there Windows guides you through the update process, most of which is handled without requiring interaction from you.

Hiding Unwanted Update Options

Over time there are bound to be updates available that you have no interest in installing. Maybe they have to do with features of Vista that you don't use, such as extended support for Tablet PCs. To reduce clutter you can hide unwanted updates. Right-click on the update's name and choose Hide update as shown in Figure 20.3. This removes it from the list, but if the update is already downloaded (but not installed) to your system, it does not delete the downloaded file(s) from your computer.

FIGURE 20.3

You can hide unwanted updates.

Viewing Update History

As I mentioned earlier it's a good idea to make sure automatic updates are happening properly. Choosing the View update history link in the Windows Update explorer shows you a screen similar to Figure 20.4.

FIGURE 20.4

You can see a list
of updates by
clicking View
update history in
the Windows
Update explorer.

Double-clicking on items in the list provides more detail. If you don't see recent updates
in the list you should check the automatic update settings; this is discussed next.

Setting Automatic Update Options

If you want to review or change your automatic update settings follow these steps:

1. Click Start, All Programs, and choose Windows Update.

2. From the Windows Update window, click the Change Settings link
   (see Figure 20.5).

FIGURE 20.5

You can see the
current settings
for Automatic
Updates from the
Vista Change
Settings screen
reached from
Windows Update.

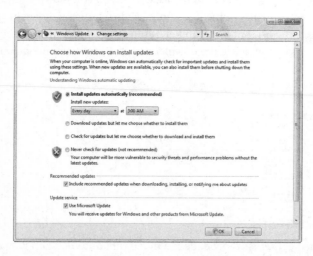

3. The Install updates automatically button should be enabled, and you can
   specify a time for the updates to be applied. This should probably be a time
   when you know your computer will be powered up, but preferably not in
   active use. Using these settings, Vista installs all critical updates automatically.

Alternately you can have updates downloaded but not installed, which makes it your responsibility to apply the updates using the techniques discussed earlier in this chapter.

A third option is to have Vista tell you that updates are available and ask you if you want them downloaded or not. This might work best for someone with a dial-up only connection or if someone who prefers to have the final say over which critical updates are downloaded and installed.

The "never check for updates" option, while available, is not recommended unless you have specific cause to do so.

4. If you also want Windows to advise you of updates to other Microsoft products you have, MS Office, for example, then place a check in the Use Microsoft Update box shown in Figure 20.6.

Installing or Removing Windows Extras

In addition to Windows updates, you might also want to add or remove Windows Extras—new programs or features available from Microsoft that you can get to enhance you computer. Depending on the version of Vista you have, different extras might be available to you. Some are free, and others you will need to pay for.

To see, and possibly add, Vista Extras, follow these steps:

1. Click Start, All Programs, Windows Update to open the Windows Update window.

2. Click the Learn about Windows Extras link. (The exact name of this link will reflect your version of Vista.)

3. You see a list of possible additions and can begin downloading them by clicking the download link shown in Figure 20.6.

FIGURE 20.6
Exploring
Windows Vista
Extras.

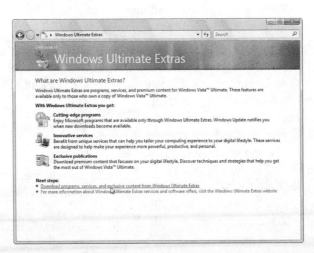

Moving Files and Settings from Another PC (Easy Transfer)

If you have purchased a new computer loaded with Vista and your old computer has Vista, Windows XP, or Windows 2000, you can transfer files, settings, browser favorites, user account information, and other data from your old computer to the new one using a Vista feature called Easy Transfer.

To make this work, the two computers need to be connected by an appropriate cable or both reside on the same network (see Chapter 10, "Setting Up Windows Vista on a Home Network"). Alternately you can move the data using writable DVDs or CDs or even an external hard drive or USB flash drive as long as both the new and the old computers support these media.

The quickest and easiest approach, if you can place your existing and new system close enough, is to use a USB transfer cable similar to the one in Figure 20.7. You can purchase one of these in computer stores or online for under $30.00.

FIGURE 20.7

A typical USB transfer cable.

1. Begin by cleaning up your old computer, eliminating unwanted programs, files, and so on. Run a complete antivirus scan on the old machine using an up-to-date virus scanning program.

2. On the Vista computer to which you want to transfer settings, search for "Easy Transfer" using the Start menu search feature, and pick the program from the resulting list. (You can also find it in the All Programs, Accessories, System Tools folder.) When you see the Windows Easy Transfer explorer shown in Figure 20.8 click the Next button.

caution

It is possible to transfer a virus, worm, or other nasty computer bug from your old computer to the new one. Scan and clean your old computer first.

FIGURE 20.8

Use the Easy
Transfer program
to move your
Windows config-
uration data
from one com-
puter to another

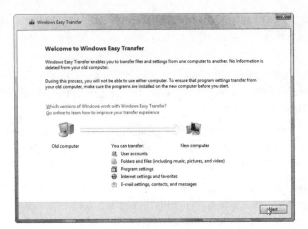

3. You will be asked if you want to start a new transfer or continue one in progress. Click Start a New Transfer.

4. You'll be asked if you are running Easy Transfer on your new or old computer. Pick new.

5. What happens next varies with the type of computers and accessories you are using. Read and follow the onscreen instructions carefully. (If you have a USB transfer cable as previously shown, then select Yes, I have an Easy Transfer Cable.) Otherwise, Windows Easy Transfer will guide you through other options.)

caution

Always start Easy Transfer on your new Vista computer first, not your old one. You want to control things from the new computer

6. Confirm that your settings and files are on the new computer and working before deleting them from your old machine.

Easy Transfer Tips and Strategies

Each person's situation is different, so there are endless possible transfer scenarios. Here are some tips and strategies to consider for situations you are most likely to encounter. You must have Administrator privileges on both machines to use Easy Transfer.

What You Can Transfer

The version of Windows on your old machine determines what you can transfer with Easy Transfer. If your old computer runs Windows XP you can transfer your files, email settings, contacts and messages, program settings, and favorites from the old computer to the new one.

If, instead, you are running Windows 2000 on the old machine you can only transfer files (documents, music photos, and so on) but not favorites and program settings.

If your old machine runs an early, now unsupported operating system such as Windows 98 you will need to *manually* transfer files via CD-ROMs, USB drives, external disk drives, and so on. Vista's Easy transfer won't work with these early Windows versions.

In any case you will need to reinstall *programs* on your new machine using the program's original installation discs. Easy transfer does not move programs from one machine to another.

You can ask Easy transfer to copy everything possible, or narrow what gets transferred by using the Custom choice to select individual files, folders, and so on. This can be quite tedious. You might be best-served by first cleaning up the old computer and then choosing to transfer everything remaining after the housekeeping.

Multiple User Accounts and Easy Transfer

If you have Windows XP or 2000 on your old machine and have multiple user accounts on the old machine, choose All user accounts, files and settings if, (and only if) all of the users of the old machine will be moving to the new one. Otherwise, specify just the desired users when transferring.

Preparing to Transfer

Clean up your old machine, deleting files, programs, photos, videos, and other unwanted items. Run an antivirus and do a spywear scan.

Install the programs you will be using on the *new* machine *before* using Easy Transfer. Otherwise the software installers might over-write the settings you transferred earlier from the old machine.

Ways to Transfer

If you are using a USB transfer cable, (the quickest method), don't connect the two machines with the cable until Easy Transfer instructs you to do so.

If you are using a network connection to do the Transfer, rather than a USB cable, both computers must be on the same network. Start the network-based transfer from the new Vista machine. The new machine will issue an Easy Transfer (security) key. You will need to type this key on the old computer when instructed to do so.

It is possible to use a USB drive with Easy Transfer. Using a large (1G or bigger) drive that can hold all of your files and settings in one pass will simplify things greatly. If you don't have a large USB drive consider purchasing or borrowing one for the transfer.

You cannot use floppy disks to accomplish a transfer with Easy Transfer, but you can use CDs or DVDs to make the transfer. This is much slower than a USB cable or network transfer and should be considered a last resort. You will need a drive capable of writing discs on the old machine and a supply of writeable discs. Easy transfer will estimate the number of discs required.

The Absolute Minimum

To keep your system up-to-date, you should periodically check for and install Windows updates. This chapter covers this topic as well as installing or removing Windows components. Keep these main ideas in mind:

- Vista should install updates automatically by default, but check the history list to verify this.

- To check for updates manually or to select from optional updates, use the Windows Update command.

- If you prefer to control when updates are installed, you can change the Automatic Updates settings. To do so, use the Windows Update feature.

- To review, add, or remove installed Windows Extras, use Vista's Windows Update feature.

- To move files, programs settings, and more from an old computer to your new one use Vista's Easy Transfer program.

PART VI

WINDOWS SPECIAL FEATURES

21

USING WINDOWS ACCESSORY PROGRAMS

Windows Vista includes more than just the necessary tools and programs to be your operating system. Windows Vista also comes packed with several other programs, such as Windows Mail (covered in Chapter 6, "Sending and Receiving Email"), Internet Explorer 7 (covered in Chapter 7, "Browsing the Internet"), Windows Fax and Scan (covered in Chapter 9, "Sending and Receiving Faxes"), Windows Media Player 11 and several built-in games (covered in Chapter 11, "Playing Music, DVDs, and Games"), among several other applications.

This chapter focuses on some of the other accessory programs included with Windows Vista. Although these programs won't replace your need for full-fledged programs, they do serve some simple purposes, and they are great for tinkering around and experimenting. Many everyday PC skills—copying text, selecting a menu command, undoing changes—work the same way in all programs. Use this chapter to explore some of Windows Vista's accessory programs.

Checking Out the Accessories

You can get a good idea of the accessory programs included in Windows Vista by displaying the Accessories folder. To do so, click Start, All Programs, and then Accessories. Some programs are grouped together into a folder (such as System Tools). Others are listed on the menu (see Figure 21.1). To open a folder and display the programs, click the folder name. To start any of these programs, click its name.

FIGURE 21.1

You can view the accessory programs included with Windows Vista.

The following briefly lists the main uses of the Accessories programs and provides references to other chapters where these features are covered.

- Calculator is a basic calculator you can use to calculate mathematical equations. This program is covered later in this chapter.

- Command Prompt is a throw-back to those DOS days. (DOS dates back to computers before Windows 95 and is really applicable to advanced users or those who need to use old programs.) Even within the world of Windows, you might need access to a command prompt. For instance, you might use Command Prompt to run a DOS game or to execute a command for checking your system. This accessory is covered later in this book.

- Notepad is good for text files. You'll find some brief information on this simple program.

- Paint is fun for creating simple illustrations; this program is covered in this chapter.

- Run is used to run commands in Windows. This feature is covered later in this chapter.

- Some features pertain to special setups, such as Network Projector, Tablet PCs, Sound Recorder, Sync Center (used to sync data between two computers), or Remote Desktop Connection (used to enable someone from another location to access your computer, usually for troubleshooting purposes). Some of these accessories require special equipment as well. For instance, with a microphone attached, you can record sounds using Sound Recorder. If you have a Tablet PC, you can use the options found in the Tablet PC folder. You might find some information in tips in other chapters in this book, but these are not main accessory programs and aren't stressed because they are mostly used in special cases.

- The Snipping tool is used to capture screen shots; this program is covered later in this chapter.

- The Welcome Center is displayed when you start Windows and displays common options. You can select any of these options or click the Close button to close the window. You can also access this set of features from the Accessory folder on the Start menu (see Figure 21.2).

FIGURE 21.2
The Welcome Center is displayed when you start Windows and lists common tasks you might want to perform.

- Windows Explorer is just like a regular Explorer with the Folders list displayed. See Chapter 4, "Viewing and Finding Files," for more information.

- Windows Sidebar displays any number of available gadget tools that can deliver news feeds and other customized information on your desktop. This feature is covered later in this chapter.

■ You can use WordPad to create simple text documents. WordPad is described in this chapter.

■ The Ease of Access folder provides access to special features for those with unique needs. For instance, you can display an onscreen keyboard and type from that. You can magnify the screen for those who are far-sighted or have other vision problems, or have it display only in high-contrast colors (useful for users who are color-blind). You can read more on these features in Chapter 22, "Using Ease of Access Features."

■ System tools such as checking a disk for errors or backing up files are covered in Chapters 17 and 18.

Some key programs include Windows Calendar (covered here), Windows Contacts (covered in Chapter 6), Windows Defender (explained in Chapter 8, "Ensuring Security and Privacy"), Windows DVD Maker, Windows Fax and Scan (covered in Chapter 9), Windows Media Player (the topic of Chapter 11), Windows Photo Gallery (covered in Chapter 12, "Working with Photographs"), and others.

Basically if the program is useful for beginning users, that program is covered in this book. You can use the table of contents or index to locate any topic. Some features, which are often not useful for an absolute beginner, are beyond the scope of this book and are not covered. For a complete coverage, you might consider a more comprehensive reference title, such as *Special Edition Using Microsoft Windows Vista* (ISBN: 0-7897-3472-3) by Bob Cowart and Brian Knittel.

Using WordPad

WordPad is a simple word processing program with basic features for typing, editing, and formatting text. If you create simple documents, WordPad might suit you just fine. If you create a lot of documents, consider purchasing a word processing program with a more robust set of features. Popular word processing programs include Microsoft Word and WordPerfect.

This section covers some basic features of WordPad. For more information, consult online help or experiment!

Taking a Look at the Program Window

You start WordPad as you do all other programs: click Start, All Programs, Accessories, and then click WordPad to start the program and display the WordPad window (see Figure 21.3).

Many onscreen features are included in WordPad. You find these same features in other programs. Table 21.1 describes common program elements found in WordPad and other programs.

FIGURE 21.3

The WordPad window includes many features in its program window

Ruler

Title bar   Menu bar   Toolbars

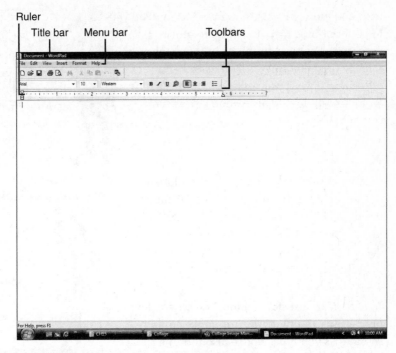

FIGURE 21.3

The WordPad window includes many features in its program window

Table 21.1   Common Program Elements

Item	Description
Title bar	Lists the name of the document and the program. If you have not saved the document, you see a generic name.
Menu bar	Lists the menu names. To select a menu command, click the menu name and then click the menu command.
Toolbars	As a shortcut to commonly used menu commands, most programs include a variety of toolbars. WordPad has a standard toolbar and a separate Format bar, for example. You can use the toolbar buttons to open a document, create a new document, print your work, save your document, and more. Use the Format toolbar to make changes to the appearance of your document. For instance, you can use the Font drop-down list to change the font. Use the Bold button to make text bold.
Ruler	Includes options for setting indents and tabs.

WordPad, as mentioned, is used to create text documents. If you want to create a simple document, WordPad has enough features and options to create a basic document. If you are new to computing, WordPad is a great place to learn skills, such as entering text, copying and moving text, deleting text, changing the appearance of text, and more. The skills you use in WordPad to perform these tasks translate to other programs. That is, you follow the same basic steps to copy text in WordPad as in a full-featured word processing program such as Word for Windows. This section covers some common tasks.

Typing Text

When you start WordPad, you see a blank document onscreen. You also see a flashing insertion point that indicates where text will be inserted when you type. When you edit a document, you can move this insertion point to any place in the document to add or select text.

To enter text, just start typing. You see the text onscreen as you type. You can make editing changes as you type. Notice also that the insertion point moves to the right as you type and that WordPad automatically wraps text to the next line. You do not have to press Enter at the end of the line.

Editing Text

After you have entered text, you might need to go back and make some revisions. The following list covers the basic text-editing skills. Keep in mind that these skills work in most other text programs.

To make a change to text, you start by selecting it. For instance, if you want to move or format a section of text, you select it with the mouse. To select text, click at the start of the text, hold down the mouse pointer, and drag across the text you want to select. The text appears highlighted onscreen (see Figure 21.4).

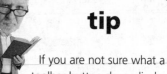

tip

If you are not sure what a toolbar button does, display its ScreenTip name by putting the mouse pointer on the edge of the button. The button name should pop up.

note

When you first open WordPad you cannot move the insertion point because you have not typed any text.

caution

A common mistake is to press Enter at the end of each line, but you should, instead, let WordPad add the line breaks. That way if you add or delete text, WordPad adjusts the line breaks as needed.

Do press Enter when you want to end one paragraph and start another or when you want to insert a blank line.

FIGURE 21.4

The first thing you do in most editing and formatting is select the text you want to modify.

Selected text

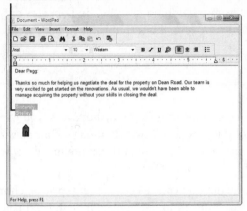

Here are the basic editing tasks:

- To delete text, select the text and press the Delete key. Notice that WordPad adjusts the lines of text. Use this method when you want to delete more than a few characters. You can also delete characters one at a time using the Backspace key, which deletes characters to the left of the insertion point or the Delete key, which deletes characters to the right of the insertion point.

- Moving and copying text uses a cut/copy and paste metaphor; the next section provides the steps for this common task.

- If you make a mistake, you can undo it. Suppose, for instance, that you delete text by mistake. You can undo it by selecting the Edit, Undo command or by using the Undo toolbar button. (The shortcut key for Undo is Ctrl+Z.)

Copying and Moving Text

To copy or move text, follow these steps:

1. Select the text you want to move or copy.

2. To move the text, click Edit, Cut. To copy the text, click Edit, Copy.

3. Move to the location where you want to insert the text; this might be another location in the current document, in another document, or even in another program.

tip

Most programs include multiple ways to perform the same task. Is one better? Not really. You can select the one most suited to your working style. In addition to the menu commands (how most beginners learn), you can also use the Cut, Copy, or Paste toolbar buttons for moving and copying text. Or you can use the shortcut keys: Ctrl+X for Cut, Ctrl+C for Copy, or Ctrl+V for Paste. Finally, you can right-click and select the commands.

4. Click Edit, Paste to paste the text in the new location. When you move text, the text is deleted from the original location and appears only in the new location. When you copy text, the text appears in both locations: the original and the new.

Formatting Text

When you want to make a change to how the text appears, you can use the Format commands or the Format bar. The fastest way to make a change is to use the Format bar, but if you have many changes or if you are unsure of what each button does, use the commands in the Format menu.

From the Format bar or menu, you can select another typeface; change the font size; apply emphasis (bold, italic, or underline); change the text color; change the alignment of paragraph(s) to left, right, or center; and make many other changes.

To make a change select the text to change and perform one of the following actions:

- To apply emphasis (bold, italic, or underline), click the button for that feature.
- To change the typeface, display the Font drop-down list and select the font to use (see Figure 21.5).
- To change the size, display the Size drop-down list and select the size.
- If you want to use a different color, display the color palette and click the color you want to use.

Figure 21.6 shows a document with these types of changes made.

FIGURE 21.5

Use the Font drop-down list to select a different font.

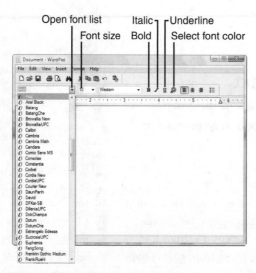

FIGURE 21.6

This document gives you an idea of some of the text formatting changes you can make.

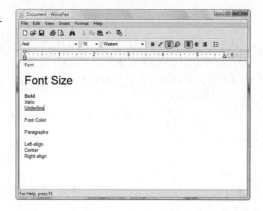

The preceding are text changes. You can also change how the paragraphs are formatted, their alignment, or add bullets to a list. Start by selecting the paragraph(s) you want to change. Then you can do any of the following:

- To change the alignment, click one of the alignment icons: Align Left, Center, or Align Right.
- To add bullets to text, click the Bullets button.

Figure 21.7 shows examples of different paragraph or line alignments.

FIGURE 21.7

You can change how your paragraphs align on the page. For instance, headings are often centered.

Saving Your Work

As you create documents (any document, not just WordPad), you should save and save often. To save a document, use the File, Save As command. Select a folder for the document, type a name, and click the Save button. (For a refresher on saving, opening and printing documents see Chapter 2, "Saving and Printing Your Work.")

tip

You can also use the various commands available in the Format menu. Use the Format, Paragraph command to indent text and select alignment. Use the Format, Bullet Style to change the style of the bullets. Use Format, Tabs to set new tabs in the document.

Using Paint

In addition to a word processing program, Windows Vista includes a drawing program called Paint. You can use Paint to create simple drawings. You can draw lines and shapes, add text, and change the colors. If you make a mistake, you can use the Eraser to erase part of the drawing.

To start Paint, click Start, All Programs, Accessories, and then click Paint. You see the Paint window (see Figure 21.8).

FIGURE 21.8

You can create simple diagrams and drawings using Paint.

Menu bar   Color box

Toolbox

In Paint, you can do any of the following:

- To draw a shape, click the tool in the toolbar. Then click and drag within the drawing area to draw the shape. Figure 21.9 shows a house created with shapes.

- To add color, you can use the Fill With Color tool, the Brush tool, or the Airbrush tool. You can fill any shapes using the Fill With Color Tool. With the Airbrush tool, you can click the tool and then select a splatter size. Then simply drag across the drawing to add color. Figure 21.10 shows using the Brush tool.

FIGURE 21.9

You can draw shapes and combine them to create a drawing in Paint.

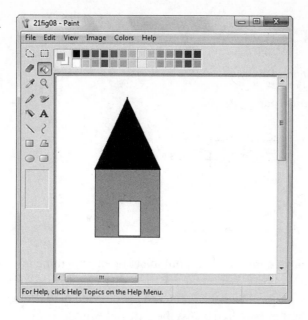

FIGURE 21.10

Use the Brush tool to draw and add color to the page.

■ To draw a text box, use the Text tool. Then type the text you want to include. You can change the font, font size, and font style (bold, italic, or underline) using the Fonts toolbar that is displayed when you are creating a text box. Figure 21.11 shows the process of creating a text box.

FIGURE 21.11

When you create a text box, type the text to include, but you can also make formatting changes to the text.

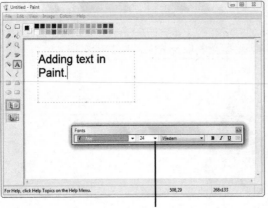

Text toolbox

- If you make a mistake and want to get rid of something you have added, you can use the Eraser tool. Click the Eraser tool and click the size you want the eraser to be. Move the pointer to the drawing area. Hold down the mouse button and drag across the part you want to erase.

- If you want to save your drawing, use the File, Save As command. To open a document you have previously saved, use the File, Open command. For more information on saving and opening a file, see Chapter 2.

Using the Windows Calendar

The Windows Calendar is a new feature to Windows. You can use Calendar to schedule events, appointments, and meetings and to create a Task list. You can also share your Calendar with others so that they can see your availability. Some users even post their calendars on the Internet.

Depending on what you need to find in your Calendar, you can change views. If you to know what's scheduled for a particular day, change to a day view. If you want to look a little farther into the future, you can view a week's list of events. You can also view months in the future.

To start this program and view your calendar, follow these steps:

1. Click Start, All Programs, and then Windows Calendar. You see that date's calendar of events (see Figure 21.12).

2. To change to a different view, click View and then select the view you want to see. Figure 21.13 shows a week view, for instance. (You can hide the Details pane, as shown here, so that you can see more of the schedule part of the calendar; how to make this change is covered in the following bulleted list.)

FIGURE 21.12

View a calendar to see what events you have scheduled.

Calendar   Appointment   Details pane

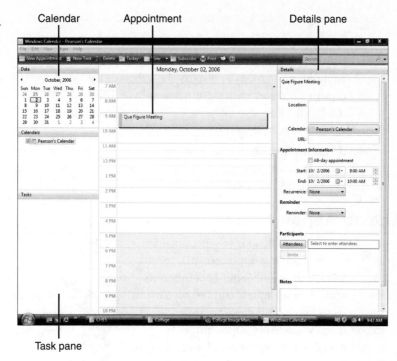

Task pane

FIGURE 21.13

You can change to alternative views when checking out your calendar.

View previous month

View next month

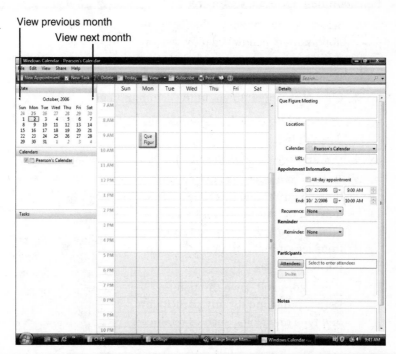

When viewing calendars, keep these tips in mind:

- To view another month, click the scroll button next to the month name. You can scroll backward or forward through the months.

- To make more room to display the calendar and its details, you can hide certain Calendar panes. For instance, you can hide the Navigation Pane or the Details Pane. To do so, open the View menu and then uncheck these options to turn them off.

- If you want to go directly to a particular date, you can do so. Click the View, Go to Date command, select the date from the drop-down calendar or type the date, and click OK.

Scheduling an Appointment

You can use your Calendar to schedule a variety of events including appointments, meetings, events, and so on. Some appointments are one-time events; others can be reoccurring, such as a weekly board meeting. Calendar makes it easy to schedule appointments including all the pertinent details such as start time, duration, location, and more.

tip

If you need to cancel an event, display the appointment, right-click it, and then click Delete. Click Yes to confirm the deletion.

1. Select the day for which you have the appointment. Change to day view if needed. Also, make sure the Details pane is displayed.

2. Click New Appointment in the command bar.

3. In the Details area, type a name for the appointment and, if necessary, enter a location.

4. Use the drop-down arrow or spin boxes to select a start and end time.

5. To set a reminder, display the Reminder drop-down list and then select the amount of time you want to the reminder sound to ring. You can select from zero minutes to two weeks to a particular date.

6. If needed, scroll down through the Details pane and list any participants and type any Notes, such as reminders for the appointment. After you've entered any information about it, the appointment is immediately scheduled (see Figure 21.14).

tip

You can also click the appropriate time and type the appointment directly on the calendar.

FIGURE 21.14

You can type the information about your appointment.

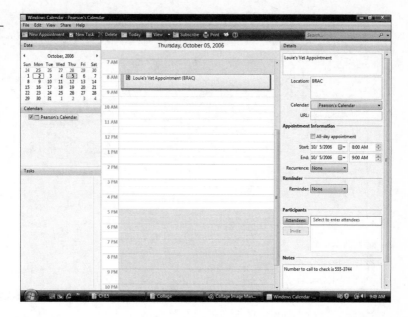

Entering a Task

In addition to events, you can also schedule tasks for your calendar. Doing so helps you keep track of what you need (or hope) to accomplish during a day or time period.

Follow these steps to add a task:

1. Click the New Task button. A new task item is added to the Tasks list.

2. Type a name for the task.

3. To set a priority, display the Priority drop-down list and select a priority: low, medium, high, or none.

tip

To delete a task, right-click it, click Delete, and then click Yes to confirm the deletion. To check off a complete task, click the check mark next to its name.

4. To assign a start date and deadline, use the Start and Due Date drop-down lists to add these.

5. To add a reminder, display the Reminder drop-down list and select the date and time to be reminded.

6. Optionally, add any notes about the task. After you've entered enough information about the task, it's added to the list in Calendar's Task pane (see Figure 21.15).

FIGURE 21.15

Add a task to your Calendar to keep track of those to-do items.

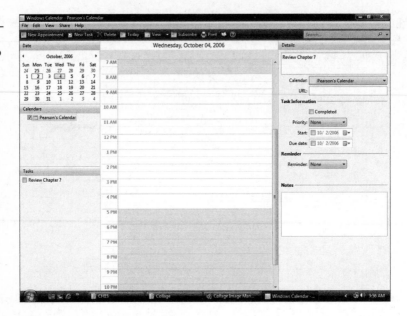

Using the Snipping Tool

You can use the new Snipping Tool to capture part of the screen. Start the program and then follow these steps:

1. Drag the cursor around the part of the screen you want to capture.
   After you select an area, you see it pasted into the Snipping Tool window (see Figure 21.16).

2. After you capture an image, you can do any of the following:

   - To save the snip, click File and then Save As. Follow the same procedure for saving any document. You can save the snip as a PNG, GIF, JPEG, or Single HTML file (various graphic format files).

   - Use the tools to edit the snip, such as adding comments with the pen, erasing parts of the snip, or highlighting parts of the snip.

   - To email the snip, use the Send Snip button or click File, Send To and then select one of the email options.

FIGURE 21.16

You can capture screen shots and partial screen shots.

Image snipped from here...

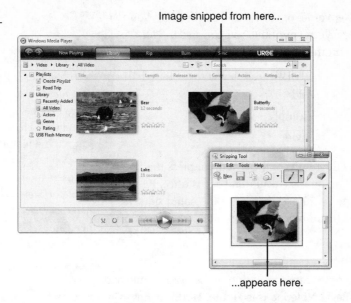

...appears here.

Using Calculator, Notepad, and Run

The previously covered accessory programs are a little more full-featured (yet still simple). There are still a few other mini-programs that are useful. Usage of each of these tools is covered over the next several sections.

Using Calculator

One of my favorite accessory programs is the Calculator. It's easy to pop it open and perform calculations. You can add, subtract, multiply, divide, figure percentages, and more with this handy tool shown in Figure 21.17.

FIGURE 21.17

Use Calculator to perform basic calculations.

To use the calculator, type the first numeric entry. You can type values or operators on the Numeric keypad (press Num Lock first) or on the number keys above the alphabet keys. You can also click the buttons on the calculator. Type the value, operator, value, operator, and so on, until you complete your equation. You can use the following mathematical operators:

-    Subtract
+   Add
*   Multiply
/   Divide

To view the results of the equation, press the equal sign on the calculator. For instance, if you type 5 * 20 and then press the equal sign, you see the results of this equation, which is 100.

> **tip**
>
> The calculator also has memory and percentage features. If you routinely use a handheld calculator, you already know how to use these features. (If not, consult online help.) You can also use a more complex scientific calculator. Start Calculator and then click View, Scientific. You then can use any of these calculation features.

Using Notepad

Another program for editing or viewing simple text (.txt) files is Notepad (see Figure 21.18). It has even fewer features than WordPad, but it is useful for viewing installation or other information files often included with programs (including the HTML code used to build web pages). These are the plain vanilla files of the computer world; anyone can open and read a text file.

You can type a text file and save it. You can also open a text file.

FIGURE 21.18

Notepad is the simplest of text editors.

Using the Run Dialog Box

Sometimes you need to get a program to run that doesn't have a shortcut icon. (And sometimes it's just easier to use the Run dialog rather than rummage through the Start menu to find its shortcut.) Often system diagnostics are executed using the Run dialog box. To use this accessory program, follow these steps:

1. Click Start, All Programs, Accessories, and click Run (or press the Windows Logo+R keys).

2. Type the name of the program you want to run and click OK (see Figure 21.19) to run the program.

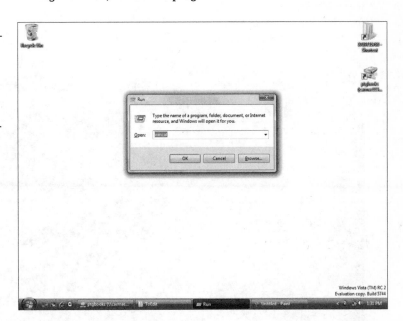

Using Sidebar and Gadgets

New with Windows Vista are mini-applications or gadgets that you can add to your desktop, in a vertical bar called the Sidebar. (On some systems, the Sidebar might be displayed automatically. On others, you'll have to turn it on.) These gadgets provide nuggets of customized information at a glance, such as a Clock, a slideshow that displays pictures, and a news feed that supplies current headlines. You can select which gadgets you want to appear in your sidebar. You can also download and install other gadgets.

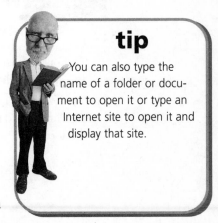

tip

You can also type the name of a folder or document to open it or type an Internet site to open it and display that site.

Here are the key things to keep in mind about Sidebar:

- To open Sidebar open the Start menu and select All Programs, Accessories, Windows Sidebar.

- To close Sidebar, right-click the Sidebar and then click Close Sidebar.

- To add a gadget to Sidebar, right-click the Sidebar and then click Add Gadgets. You see a panel of available gadgets (see Figure 21.20). Double-click the gadget you want to add. To download more gadgets to your computer, click the Get More Gadgets Online link.

FIGURE 21.20

You can display gadgets that provide information at a glance such as Stocks or provide quick access to commonly used tools like Calendar.

Detached gadget

Close gadget

Drag gadget | Configure gadget

Opens Add Gadget window

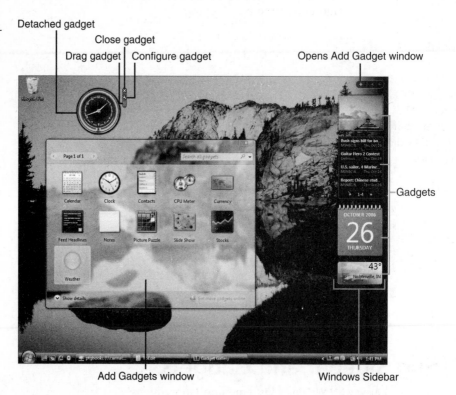

Gadgets

Add Gadgets window

Windows Sidebar

- If you no longer want to display a particular gadget in the Sidebar, you can hide it. Right-click the gadget and then click Close Gadget.

- If you want to move the gadget from the Sidebar to the desktop, right-click the Gadget and then click Detach from Sidebar. Next drag the gadget to the desktop.

The Absolute Minimum

Explore the many extra programs packed in with Windows Vista including the following:

- To create simple text documents, use WordPad.
- Paint is a great way to create simple drawings or graphic documents, such as party invitations. Kids also like to play around in Paint.
- For a quick mathematical problem, use Windows Vista's built-in calculator.
- Keep track of appointments and tasks with the Calendar.
- Use the Windows Sidebar to add gadgets to your desktop that add custom information, like a mini-calendar or weather updates, to your desktop.

22

Using Ease Of Access Features

Microsoft has created Vista's Ease of Access Center for people with special needs, but many of the features you find in the Center can be useful to everyone. For example, some features, designed to help those with vision difficulties, can be used by anyone wanting to magnify portions of a screen for a better look. Other features, created for the hearing impaired, can help everyone working in noisy environments or in places where computer alert sounds might be disruptive. Furthermore, you can customize the keyboard, as well as substitute an onscreen keyboard for your regular one.

This chapter covers the key elements of Vista's Ease of Access features, including the Magnifier for enlarging screen images, the Narrator that reads text from the screen, an onscreen keyboard, and a variety of display, keyboard, sound, and mouse settings designed to help computers adapt to their users and environments.

Using the Ease of Access Center

To open the Ease of Access Center either visit the Control Panel (open the Start menu and click Control Panel) and click the Ease of Access link, or search for "access" in the Start menu's search area, then click the Ease of Access choice. You will see the Ease of Access Center shown in Figure 22.1

FIGURE 22.1

Reach the Ease of Access Center from the Control Panel, or search for "access."

Take a moment to browse the general categories of access assistance listed onscreen. They include the following:

- Using the computer without a display.
- Making the computer (display) easier to see.
- Using the computer sans mouse or keyboard.
- Making the mouse easier to use.
- Making the keyboard easier to use.
- Using text or visual alerts in place of sounds.
- Making it easier to focus on tasks.

Let's start by getting an overview of which features Microsoft thinks help with typical challenges, and then dig into the specifics of those features and their settings later in the chapter.

tip

The first time you launch the Ease of Access Center a voice automatically starts reading the screen aloud to help the visually impaired. You can turn off this voice feature by removing the checkmark from the "Always read this section aloud" box.

Choosing the Right Features for You

You can, of course, simply experiment with the various Ease of Access features on your own, but Vista helps you choose the best ones if you are willing to answer a few personal questions. Click the link called "Get recommendations to make your computer easier to use." You are asked affirm statements that apply to you, for example, "I am hard of hearing."

Using your answers Vista recommends features and their settings. Figure 22.2 shows an example of the personalized recommendations for a hearing impaired user. You can choose the accessibility features and their options right from these recommendation screens by clicking them.

FIGURE 22.2

A typical feature recommendation and settings screen for a hearing impaired user. Click to make choices.

Alternately, to explore the Access features without answering any questions simply click on the various links in the Ease of Access Center (refer to Figure 22.1) to either try out the features or learn more about them.

Four of the most commonly used features, (the Magnifier, On-Screen Keyboard, Narrator, and High Contrast settings) are highlighted near the top of the Center's main screen. All of the available settings are listed below them, organized by the type of help they provide. You might need to scroll to see them all.

Using the Computer Without a Display

Figure 22.3 shows the settings Vista suggests for using a computer without a display. This screen lets you employ the Narrator to read onscreen text aloud. Obviously you need speakers or earphones to use this feature.

FIGURE 22.3

The settings for using the computer without a display.

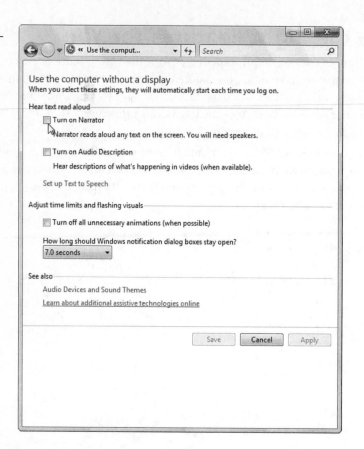

You can also enable narrative audio for videos. PBS and other video producers sometimes employ human readers to add descriptions on secondary audio channels enabling blind users to hear what's happening onscreen. This feature lets you hear those descriptions when they are available.

Finally you can disable unnecessary animations and define how long you want notification dialog boxes to remain open from here.

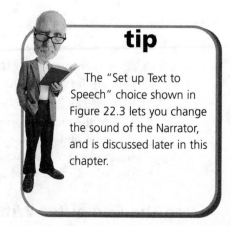

tip

The "Set up Text to Speech" choice shown in Figure 22.3 lets you change the sound of the Narrator, and is discussed later in this chapter.

Making the Computer Screen Easier to See

This set of choices lets you enable high-contrast color schemes and turn on the Narrator, change the size of text and icons, turn on the Magnifier, and create screen images that are easier for you to see. Figure 22.4 shows some of the choices.

As you might have already noticed, a few options you just read about a few paragraphs back are repeated here—the Narrator, for example. Vista tries to recommend the best mix of features to solve particular challenges.

note

The bottom of each Access Center screen contains links to additional computer settings you might want to change and links to online resources.

FIGURE 22.4

Ways to make the computer screen easier to see.

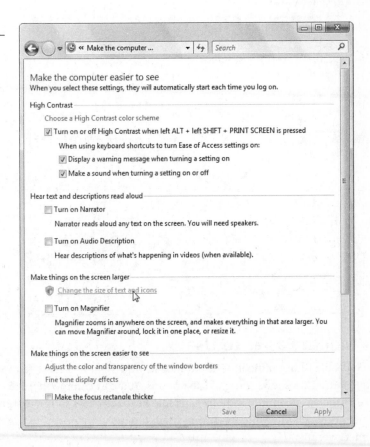

Using the Computer Sans Mouse or Keyboard

Difficult as it might be to imagine, you can use your computer without a mouse or keyboard. The choices shown in Figure 22.5 let you enable onscreen keyboard and mouse features that can be operated with a joystick or other pointing device.

Moreover, if your computer is properly equipped you can use a microphone and Vista's built-in speech recognition software to control your computer and even dictate text rather than typing it. You need to set up the speech recognition features first, and Vista walks you through the steps the first time you try to use the voice recognition feature.

FIGURE 22.5

It's possible to use your computer without a keyboard or mouse, and even talk to it!

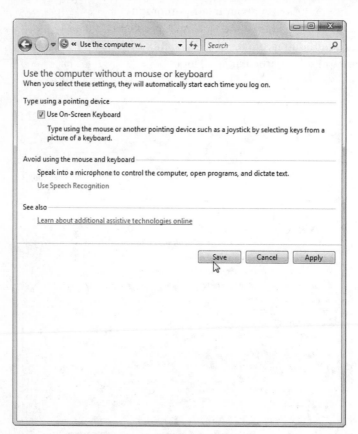

Making the Mouse Easier to Use

Some people find it difficult to use a mouse, and Vista has some features that can help. Figure 22.6 shows some of the options. You can change the size and appearance of the onscreen mouse pointer, create keyboard keys to move the mouse pointer, and activate windows (bring them foremost) by hovering the mouse pointer over them.

FIGURE 22.6

Making the
mouse easier
to use.

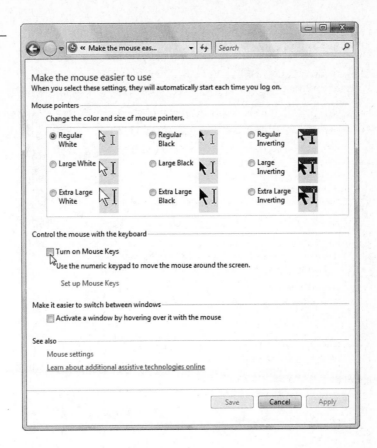

Notice that the "See also" area of this screen has a Mouse settings link. It takes you where you need to go to swap mouse buttons if you are left-handed, change the mouse speed, and so on.

Making the Keyboard Easier to Use

Folks with shaky hands and other motor skill challenges will appreciate the keyboard features shown in Figure 22.7. They make the keyboard friendlier by ignoring accidental brief key repetitions, for example.

Sticky keys can help as well. They make it possible to tap the Ctrl, Alt, and similar keys once and have them activated without continually holding them down.

Other keyboard options generate tones when the Caps Lock, Num Lock, and other keys are hit as an alert in case you accidentally tapped them. I like this one myself.

The mouse key options mentioned earlier appear in this easier keyboarding list as well.

FIGURE 22.7

Making the
keyboard easier
to use.

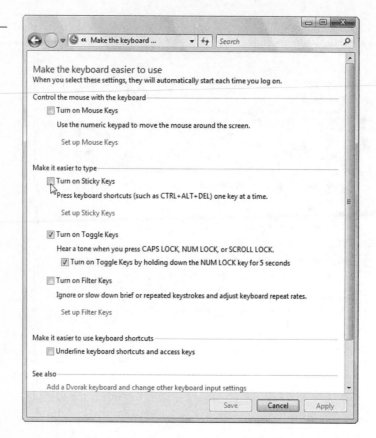

FIGURE 22.7

Making the
keyboard easier
to use.

Using Text or Visual Alerts in Place of Sounds

The Sound Sentry feature displays an onscreen alert whenever Vista beeps or blurts at you. Great for the hearing impaired, this also works for folks in meetings and other places where sounds might be disruptive.

As you can see in Figure 22.8, you can select to have Vista flash the active caption bar, the entire active window, or the whole desktop. That should get your attention!

Making It Easier to Focus on Tasks

The final choice in the Ease of Access Center list repeats most of the features we have just discussed. From this one screen you can enable or disable the Narrator, Sticky keys, Toggle keys, Filter keys, and visual alerts.

FIGURE 22.8

Vista will flash
to get your
attention.

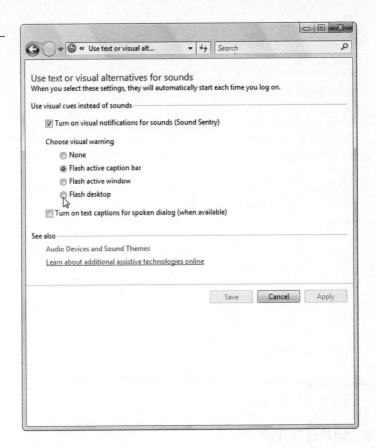

Using the Narrator

The Narrator reads onscreen events and typed characters. You can also have the Narrator move the mouse pointer to the active item. As another option, you can start the Narrator minimized so it doesn't take up space on your desktop.

When you start the Narrator it provides you with a dialog box similar to the one at the top of Figure 22.9. Check any of the desired options and click the Voice Settings button to see and change the language, voice, speed volume, and pitch of the reader. Click OK and Exit to save your selections.

FIGURE 22.9

Choose Narrator
options here.

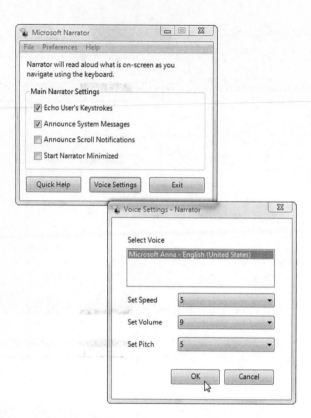

Using the Magnifier

The Magnifier zooms in on a portion of your screen so that you can see it better. The top part of the screen shows the location of the mouse pointer. The rest of the screen shows the "regular" view of the window. In Figure 22.10, for instance, you see a calendar. The magnification area shows the location of the mouse pointer and the area of the calendar around the pointer magnified for easier reading. You can use this tool to more easily see and select options.

Alternatively you can drag the magnification window around on your screen as you would a magnifying glass. Figure 22.11 shows an example of this. You can drag corners of the magnifier to change its size and shape if you like. Click the close box to quit the Magnifier.

> **tip**
>
> Another option for making your screen easier to read is to change the display size of text and other onscreen elements. You can do this in the Control Panel and with the View menus in many programs and explorers.

FIGURE 22.10
The top part of the screen shows a magnified version of the pointer and surrounding area.

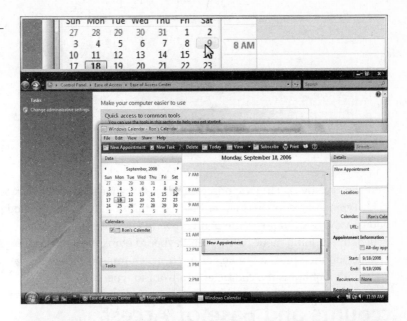

FIGURE 22.11
Drag the Magnifier around as you would a magnifying glass.

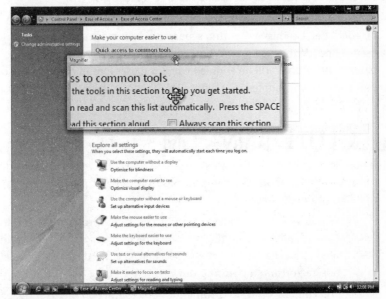

Using On-Screen Keyboard

You can use the On-Screen Keyboard, shown in Figure 22.12, to type. The keyboard should work with Vista on virtually any program you run on your computer. You can also use the onscreen version of keyboard navigation keys (Page Up, home, and so on).

FIGURE 22.12

You can use On-Screen Keyboard to type using your mouse or other pointing device.

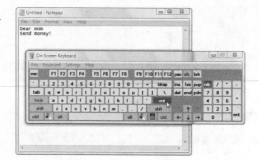

You can type by clicking the onscreen keys with your pointer, or click Settings and then Typing Mode to select either hover or scanning. In hovering mode, you use a mouse or joystick to hover the pointer over a key; the selected character is then typed. In scanning mode, On-Screen Keyboard scans the keyboard, highlighting letters; you then press a hot key or use a switch-input device whenever On-Screen Keyboard highlights the character you want to type.

User Accounts and Ease of Access

When people share a computer it's possible to set up different Ease of Access settings for each user. Do this by creating separate accounts for each user, or category of user—blind, deaf, and so on. When you save Access settings for specific users or groups of users the settings will be enabled when the user logs in. Learn more about setting up user accounts in Chapter 16, "Setting Up Windows Vista for Multiple Users."

THE ABSOLUTE MINIMUM

If you have special needs, and even if you don't, it's worth exploring the many features designed to make the computer as accessible as possible. You can use any of the following features:

- Windows Vista includes several accessibility programs including Magnifier (which enlarges the view of your screen), Narrator (which reads the contents of your screen aloud), and On-Screen Keyboard (which enables you to type onscreen using a pointing device).

- You can use Vista's recommendations to turn on a personalized set of features (such as enlarging the text size) based upon answers to a series of questions.

- You can also access accessibility options that control your hardware (sound, keyboard, mouse, and display) from the Control Panel. You can use these options to make these components more suited to your needs.

- If you share a computer it is possible to set up separate user accounts with different Ease of Access settings.

Index

B

Back button (Internet Explorer toolbar), 106

backgrounds (desktop), 211

Backup and Restore Center
opening, 268
restoring files, 271-272

backups, 266
Backup and Restore Center
opening, 268
restoring files, 271-272
complete system backups, 268
equipment, 266-267
programs, 267-268
restoring, 271-272
saving, 35-36
storing, 268

broadband Internet connections, 74-75
cable, 74
configuring, 80
DSL, 74
security, 74
sharing, 75
T1, 75
wireless, 75

browsers (web)
hijacking, 129
Internet Explorer, 79
Content Advisor, 135
default search engines, selecting, 113-114
email filters, 135
emailing web pages, 115
exiting, 105
Favorites Center, 119-122
file downloads, 117
history lists, 122-123
home pages, selecting, 118
navigating, 107
phishing filters, 136-137
pop-up blocking, 133
printing web pages, 115-116
privacy settings, 134
RSS feeds, 123-124
searching from home page, 111
starting, 104
text, 116-117
window, 105-107
selecting, 79

Brush tool (Paint), 330

bugs, 310

burning
CDs/DVDs, 57-58
music (Media Player), 176-177

C

cable Internet connections, 74

Calculator, 322, 337-338

Calendar, 332
events, 334
opening, 332
tasks, 335
views, selecting, 332

cameras (digital)
configuring, 185-187
drivers, 186
features, 184-185
memory cards, 184
pictures
importing with Photo Gallery, 188
previewing, 184
quality, 184
transferring to computer, 187-188

Cancel All Documents command, 42

canceling print jobs, 42

D

T

X-Y-Z

Safari®
BOOKS ONLINE
ENABLED

THIS BOOK IS SAFARI ENABLED

INCLUDES FREE 45-DAY ACCESS TO THE ONLINE EDITION

The Safari® Enabled icon on the cover of your favorite technology book means the book is available through Safari Bookshelf. When you buy this book, you get free access to the online edition for 45 days.

Safari Bookshelf is an electronic reference library that lets you easily search thousands of technical books, find code samples, download chapters, and access technical information whenever and wherever you need it.

TO GAIN 45-DAY SAFARI ENABLED ACCESS TO THIS BOOK:

- Go to **http://www.quepublishing.com/safarienabled**
- Complete the brief registration form
- Enter the coupon code found in the front of this book on the "Copyright" page

If you have difficulty registering on Safari Bookshelf or accessing the online edition, please e-mail customer-service@safaribooksonline.com.